Advances in
Digital Document
Processing and
Retrieval

T0350209

Statistical Science and Interdisciplinary Research

ISSN: 1793-6195

Series Editor: Sankar K. Pal *(Indian Statistical Institute)*

Description:
In conjunction with the Platinum Jubilee celebrations of the Indian Statistical Institute, a series of books will be produced to cover various topics, such as Statistics and Mathematics, Computer Science, Machine Intelligence, Econometrics, other Physical Sciences, and Social and Natural Sciences. This series of edited volumes in the mentioned disciplines culminate mostly out of significant events — conferences, workshops and lectures — held at the ten branches and centers of ISI to commemorate the long history of the institute.

Published*

*To view the complete list of the published volumes in the series, please visit:
http://www.worldscientific.com/series/ssir

Platinum Jubilee Series

Statistical Science and
Interdisciplinary Research — Vol. 13

Advances in Digital Document Processing and Retrieval

Editors

Bidyut Baran Chaudhuri
Swapan Kumar Parui

Indian Statistical Institute, India

Series Editor: **Sankar K. Pal**

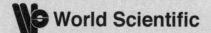

NEW JERSEY · LONDON · SINGAPORE · BEIJING · SHANGHAI · HONG KONG · TAIPEI · CHENNAI

Published by

World Scientific Publishing Co. Pte. Ltd.

5 Toh Tuck Link, Singapore 596224

USA office: 27 Warren Street, Suite 401-402, Hackensack, NJ 07601

UK office: 57 Shelton Street, Covent Garden, London WC2H 9HE

British Library Cataloguing-in-Publication Data
A catalogue record for this book is available from the British Library.

Statistical Science and Interdisciplinary Research — Vol. 13
ADVANCES IN DIGITAL DOCUMENT PROCESSING AND RETRIEVAL

Copyright © 2014 by World Scientific Publishing Co. Pte. Ltd.

ISBN 978-981-4368-70-4

In-house Editor: Chandra Nugraha

Printed in Singapore

Foreword

The Indian Statistical Institute (ISI) was established on 17th December, 1931 by a great visionary Prof. Prasanta Chandra Mahalanobis to promote research in the theory and applications of statistics as a new scientific discipline in India. In 1959, Pandit Jawaharlal Nehru, the then Prime Minister of India introduced the ISI Act in the parliament and designated it as an Institution of National Importance because of its remarkable achievements in statistical work as well as its contribution to economic planning.

Today, the Indian Statistical Institute occupies a prestigious position in the academic firmament. It has been a haven for bright and talented academics working in a number of disciplines. Its research faculty has done India proud in the arenas of Statistics, Mathematics, Economics, Computer Science, among others. Over seventy five years, it has grown into a massive banyan tree, like the institute emblem. The Institute now serves the nation as a unified and monolithic organization from different places, namely Kolkata, the Headquarters, Delhi, Bangalore, and Chennai, three centers, a network of five SQC-OR Units located at Mumbai, Pune, Baroda, Hyderabad and Coimbatore, and a branch (field station) at Giridih.

The platinum jubilee celebrations of ISI have been launched by Honorable Prime Minister Prof. Manmohan Singh on December 24, 2006, and the Govt. of India has declared 29th June as the "Statistics Day" to commemorate the birthday of Prof. Mahalanobis nationally.

Prof. Mahalanobis, was a great believer in interdisciplinary research, because he thought that this will promote the development of not only Statistics, but also the other natural and social sciences. To promote interdisciplinary research, major strides were made in the areas of computer science, statistical quality control, economics, biological and social sciences, physical and earth sciences.

The Institute's motto of 'unity in diversity' has been the guiding principle of all its activities since its inception. It highlights the unifying role of statistics in relation to various scientific activities.

In tune with this hallowed tradition, a comprehensive academic pro-gramme, involving Nobel Laureates, Fellows of the Royal Society, Abel prize winner and other dignitaries, has been implemented throughout the Platinum Jubilee year, highlighting the emerging areas of ongoing frontline research in its various scientific divisions, centers, and outlying units. It includes international and national-level seminars, symposia, conferences and workshops, as well as series of special lectures. As an outcome of these events, the Institute is bringing out a series of comprehensive volumes in different subjects under the title Statistical Science and Interdisciplinary Research, published by the World Scientific Press, Singapore.

The present volume titled "Advances in Digital Document Processing and Retrieval" is the thirteenth one in the series. The volume consists of twelve chapters, written by eminent scientists from different parts of the world. These chapters provide a current perspective of different areas of research and development, both from theoretical and application points of views, emphasizing the major challenging issues in document processing and retrieval. Several interesting application areas are covered together with the development of new methodologies and tools. I believe the state-of-the art studies presented in this book will be very useful to students, researchers as well as practitioners.

Thanks to the contributors for their excellent research contributions and to the volume editors Prof. B.B. Chaudhuri and Prof. S.K. Parui for their sincere effort in bringing out the volume nicely. Initial design of the cover by Mr. Indranil Dutta is acknowledged. Sincere efforts by Prof. Dilip Saha and Dr. Barun Mukhopadhyay for editorial assistance are appreciated. Thanks are also due to World Scientific for their initiative in publishing the series and being a part of the Platinum Jubilee endeavor of the Institute.

June 2010
Kolkata

Sankar K. Pal
Series Editor and Director

Preface

Digital document processing is still a charming topic for a large section of pattern recognition research community. While the older domains like printed text OCR, bar code readers, tabular form processors have taken back seats, newer ones like digital library, image and video text analysis, web document processing, document image mining, meta-data extraction and document retrieval have cropped up. Remarkable progress has been made both in online and in offline handwriting analysis. Document processing has special significance in a country like India that uses multiple languages/scripts and the Computer Vision and Pattern Recognition Unit of the Indian Statistical Institute is a forerunner in doing research on Indian multilingual multiscript documents. The current edited volume has come up partly from the extended versions of some selected papers presented at International Conference on Computing: Theory and Applications held in connection with the platinum jubilee celebration of the ISI and partly from the invited papers received from eminent researchers in the field.

The first chapter of this volume exposes the reader to the Markovian models that have been so successful in the processing and recognition of speech and script image signals. Here the authors employ the HMM (hidden Markov models) and CRF (Conditional Random Fields) to historical document analysis, another interesting and challenging application area. Historical document recognition has also been dealt with in Chapter 9 where several statistical models have been investigated in the context of this recognition task. The next chapter deals with a cutting-edge document synthesis technology with digital pen that allows maintenance of both paper and e-copy of the same document in the system. Retrieval of information can be more prompt and accurate by this approach, compared to the conventional multimedia systems. Chapter 3 presents an interesting work which explores the ability of the current document image analysis approaches to ensuring secure and accurate voting by the paper-based ballot system (being advocated after irregularities in some US elections).

The problem of information retrieval from document image database is addressed in Chapter 4. The authors propose here a document image retrieval method that searches images of documents on the basis of word shape coding without going through any OCR process. Several coding schemes for this purpose are proposed in the chapter. The fifth Chapter deals with indexing and retrieval from handwritten documents. The authors propose both template based and template free keyword spotting techniques for the purpose. The sixth Chapter deals with new components of the classical problem of bank check reading created due to the United States check 21 law that admits the image of a check as good as the check itself.

Two more theoretically oriented chapters, namely Chapter 7 and Chapter 8 deal respectively with statistical deformation model for handwritten character recognition and segmentation free OCR of old printed/typed documents like museum index cards by scanning n-tuple approach. The geometric layout, and more generally, appearance of the documents needs peer analysis to compress, rectify, interpret, categorize, index and even retrieve the documents. The statistical modeling of document appearance has been well surveyed in Chapter 10. The following chapter is concerned with recovery of physical and logical structure from electronic documents, especially in PDF format. The work is important since more and more e-documents are being generated for various applications. Finally, the last chapter deals with recognition of handwriting in an Indian script. Work on recognition of Indian script handwriting started much later than, say, that of Roman script handwriting and this is one of the earliest reports covering the topic.

We hope the readers of this edited book will get glimpses on the frontiers of digital document processing. The survey papers will provide the students and researchers necessary exposure to start work on the particular topic. Even for academicians of related disciplines, this book can be an interesting reading.

We express our indebtedness to the authors for their contributions as well as for their patience, as the volume took more time than usual to come out in print. We also thank the reviewers of the articles of the present volume. We also like to express our gratitude to the ISI Platinum Jubilee Core Committee and the Series Editor for giving us the opportunity to edit this volume. Finally, thanks are due to Mr. Bikash Shaw for preparing the camera-ready version of the volume.

B. B. Chaudhuri

S. K. Parui

Editors

Contents

Chapter 1

Document Image Analysis using Markovian Models: Application to Historical Documents

Stéphane Nicolas, Thierry Paquet, Laurent Heutte

Laboratoire LITIS, Universit de Rouen
UFR des Sciences, site du Madrillet, 76800 Saint Etienne du Rouvray,
France
stephane.nicolas@univ-rouen.fr

This chapter deals with the use of Markovian generative and discriminative models such as Hidden Markov Random Fields and Conditional Random Fields to proceed to the analysis of complex documents like literary manuscripts or historical documents. We propose to use such stochastic and contextual models in order to cope with local spatial variability, and to take into account some prior knowledge about the global structure of the document image. We first describe a hidden Markov random field model dedicated to document image labeling and we discuss the advantages and drawbacks of this model. Then we propose a more powerful discriminative model based on conditional random fields.

Contents

1.1. Introduction

In the last few years, improvements have been made in the field of handwriting recognition, especially in the context of commercial applications such as check reading, postal address recognition and form processing. These applications have mainly focused on word or phrase recognition.[1] Recently, the advances in digital technologies have motivated numerous institutions to move towards the use of digital document images rather than traditional paper copies of the original documents. This situation raises new requirements for indexing and accessing these digital sources.[2]

The valorization of our cultural heritage using digital technologies requires robust document image analysis methods to recognize the structure and to detect areas of interest facilitating the indexing of large corpora of ancient documents and the development of digital libraries. In a document image analysis process, segmentation is one important task because it is the process that allows to locate and to extract the entities to be recognized. While the use of the handwriting recognition approaches developed so far for commercial applications may provide interesting results on historical documents, proper segmentation of these documents prior to recognition is still a challenging task.

Many methods dedicated to machine printed document segmentation have been proposed,[3] but these methods cannot be directly applied to handwritten documents because of the spatial variability of handwriting. The few existing methods that have been developed for handwritten documents focus on a particular type of documents or a particular segmentation task (word or line extraction only). Furthermore these methods are based on a local analysis, and sometimes fail to find the correct solution. This is the reason why we propose to use a general formalism that could be adapted to different types of documents, and which takes into account some contextual information. Stochastic models have proved to be effective to cope with handwriting variability and ambiguities. For example, hidden Markov models are commonly used for sequential data segmentation and recognition. Similarly, in the case of image analysis, Markov Random Fields (MRF) have proven to be powerful stochastic models for 2-dimensional data. MRF models have been widely used during the last twenty years for various tasks of image analysis such as noise removal, restoration, binarization and segmentation. However, little work has been done on document image analysis, and as far as we know, this kind of model has never been used on handwritten documents. This is why we have explored the use of MRF models for the task of complex handwritten document image segmentation, such as literary drafts or historical documents.

In this chapter we present an application dedicated to the segmentation of some manuscripts of the French novelist Gustave Flaubert, into their elementary parts, namely: text lines, erasures, punctuation marks, interlinear annotations, and marginal annotations (just to mention the most important of them) or to detect areas of interest such as text body, header, margins, footer. In the Markov Random Field framework, segmentation is addressed as an image labelling problem. This problem can be solved using optimization techniques. In Section 1.2 we describe how Hidden Markov Random Field models can be used in the context of complex document image analysis. We describe the proposed model, and the procedures for parameter learning and image labelling using different decoding techniques. Then we illustrate the capabilities of our approach on different segmentation tasks of Flaubert's manuscripts. However, as Markov Random Fields are generative models, they have some drawbacks, especially when applied to discriminative tasks such as image labelling or classification. In Section 1.3 we therefore investigate the use of Discriminative Markov Models (known as Conditional Random Fields in the literature) to improve the segmentation performance. This section deals with the theoretical framework of these models and describes the proposed model. Then we compare the two theoretical frameworks on the same handwritten document image segmentation task.

1.2. Hidden Markov Random Field Models

Literary manuscripts can be considered to be produced by implicit layout rules used by the author. For example, in the case of Flaubert's manuscripts even if these rules cannot be formally justified, it is however experimentally verified by literary experts that Flaubert's manuscripts exhibit some typical layout rules characterized by an important text body occupying two thirds of the page and containing a lot of erasures; and a marginal area with some text annotations, as can be seen in Figure 1.1.

As the produced layout of the document is the result of the combination of these layout rules, Markov Random Fields (MRF) appear to be suited to model such layout using local dependencies. Furthermore, such stochastic models appear to be well suited to cope with the local spatial variability of placement of the layout elements.

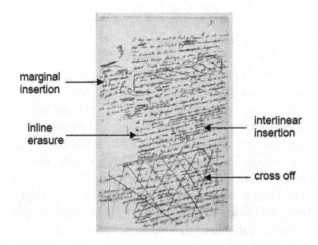

marginal
insertion

inline
erasure

interlinear
insertion

cross off

Fig. 1.1.   One example of Flaubert's manuscript layout.

1.2.1. *Theoretical foundations*

According to MRF formalism,[4] the image is associated with a rectangular grid G of size $n \times m$. Each site s on the grid is defined by its coordinates over G and is denoted by $s(i,j)$ $1 \leq i \leq n$ $i \leq j \leq m$. The set of sites is denoted by $S = \{s(i,j), 1 \leq i \leq n, 1 \leq j \leq m\}$. Following the stochastic framework of Hidden Markov Random Fields, the image gives access to a set of observations on each site of S denoted by $O = \{o(i,j), 1 \leq i \leq n, 1 \leq j \leq m\}$. Similarly, each site is associated with a random variable denoted X_s. The set of random variables over the whole grid defines the Hidden Markov Field X. Each random variable X_s takes its value in a discrete and finite set of q labels or states $L = l_i$ corresponding to a particular layout rule or class pattern. The problem of layout extraction in the image can then be formulated as the problem of finding the most probable state or label configuration among all the possible labelling E of the field X that can be associated with the image, i.e. finding the labelling which maximizes the posterior probability of X given the observations O :

According to the Bayes rule we have:

$$P(X/O)P(O) = P(O/X)P(X) = P(X,O)$$
$$P(X/O) = \frac{P(X,O)}{P(O)} = \frac{P(O/X)P(X)}{P(O)}$$

The prior $P(O)$ is a constant which is independent of the configuration

E of the label field X. So we can write

$$P(X/O) \propto P(X,O) = P(O/X)P(X)$$

Therefore, finding the most probable segmentation of the image is equivalent to finding the labelling which maximizes the joint probability:

$$\hat{X} = \arg\max_{X\epsilon E}(P(X,O)) = \arg\max_{X\epsilon E}(P(O/X)P(X))$$

which results in the following formula when applying Markovian hypothesis and independence assumption of observations:

$$\hat{X} = \arg\max_{X\epsilon E}[\prod_s P(o_s/x_s) \prod_s P(x_s/x_{s'}, s'\epsilon N_G(s))]$$

where $N_G(s)$ is the neighborhood of the site s.

While in this expression the term $P(o_s/x_s)$ can be computed using Gaussian mixtures to model the conditional probability densities of the observations, the calculation of the second term (i.e. $\prod_s P(x_s/x_{s'}, s'\epsilon N_G(s))$) which represents the contextual knowledge introduced by the model or prior model, appears to be intractable due to its non causal expression, i.e., interdependence between neighboring states. To overcome this difficulty, one generally uses simulation methods such as Gibbs sampling or Metropolis algorithm.[5] Another possibility is to restrict the expression to a causal neighboring system. In any case however, finding the optimal segmentation solution requires a huge exploration of the configuration set E. This consideration is especially important because handwritten document images are particularly large. This is related as MRF-MAP framework. According to the Hammersley-Clifford theorem, a MRF follows a Gibbs distribution.[4] So the prior model can be rewritten as follows:

$$P(X) = \frac{1}{z}\exp[-\sum_{c\epsilon C} V_c(X)]$$

where C is the set of all cliques over the image, defined according to the chosen neighboring system $N_G = \{N_G(s), s\epsilon S\}$. V_c is a potential function associated with the clique c and Z is a normalization constant called partition function in the MRF framework. Thanks to this theorem it is possible to compute the local probabilities on each site although the probability of the whole configuration is intractable. The local potential function can be derived from the joint local probabilities of the n-order cliques defined by the chosen neighborhood system. This allows introducing the joint energy $U(X,O)$ of a configuration of the field, by calculating the negative logarithm of the joint probability:

$$-\log(P(O|X)P(X)) = \sum_{s} -\log(P(O_s|x_s)) - \log(z) + \sum_{c\epsilon C} V_c(X)$$
$$-\log(P(O|X)P(X)) = U(X,O) - \log(z),$$
$$U(X,O) = \sum_{s} -\log(P(O_s|x_s)) + \sum_{c\epsilon C} V_c(X)$$

Thus, in the MRF-MAP framework, decoding (i.e. image labelling) involves maximizing the joint global probability $P(X, O)$ that is equivalent to minimizing the joint energy function, as Z is a constant:

$$\hat{x} = \arg\min_{x} U(X, O)$$

It is a non trivial combinatorial problem, because the energy function may not be convex and may exhibit many local minima. Different optimization techniques can be used to find the optimal configuration of the label field by minimizing the energy function. One can distinguish relaxation based approach and dynamic programming based approach. Some of these approaches are deterministic and some are stochastic. Another important criterion is the ability of these methods to find the global optimum of the energy function. Table 1.1 gives a classification of the main approaches in the literature on the basis of these criteria. In this table one can see the difference among Simulated Annealing (SA), Genetic Algorithms (GA), Ant Colony System (ACS), Iterated Conditional Modes (ICM), Highest Confidence First (HCF) and Region Merging method.

Table 1.1.   Classification of decoding methods.

	Relaxation methods deterministic	Relaxation methods stochastic	Dynamic programming
Optimal		SA[6], GA[13], ACS[14]	
Suboptimal	ICM[7], HCF[8]		Region merging method[9]

In the following subsections we describe the most commonly used techniques in practice.

1.2.1.1. *Simulated annealing*

This optimization method has been proposed by Kirkpatrick[6] in 1983 and has been introduced in computer vision by Geman and Geman[5] for image restoration using the MRF-MAP framework. It is a stochastic relaxation algorithm based on Metropolis sampling method, which can in theory find the global minimum of the energy function. This algorithm uses a so called "temperature" parameter which controls random label flipping, even if these label changes do not decrease the global energy. This process performs a random exploration of the search space and prevents convergence to local minima. The higher the temperature, the higher the probability of a label change. On the contrary, if the temperature is low, only label changes that decrease the energy are allowed. During the relaxation process the temperature parameter is gradually decreased starting from a high value, according to a predefined cooling function. In order to ensure convergence to a global optimum one has to set the initial value of the temperature high enough, and has to use an adaptive temperature decreasing function that is slow enough. In theory a logarithmic cooling function is recommended. For each temperature value, several relaxation iterations are done on the entire image site set. Sites are visited randomly or according to a predefined strategy. The number of iterations has to be high enough too. In the simulated annealing method only the temperature and the number of iterations must be predefined. The optimality of the final solution and the computational cost depend closely on the setting of these parameters. The main problem is that there is no theoretical rule for determining the correct values of these parameters. In practice they are determined empirically. Another main drawback of this algorithm is its prohibitive computational cost. In fact, this algorithm explores the search space "blindly" and therefore requires many updates of the label configuration before convergence. The main advantage of this algorithm however is that it does not require any particular initialisation of the label field, the exploration of the search space can start from any configuration.

1.2.1.2. *Iterated Conditional Modes (ICM)*

The Iterated Conditional Mode (ICM) algorithm has been proposed by Besag[7] in 1986. It is an iterative and deterministic relaxation algorithm based on a gradient descent strategy which converges quickly to a local minimum of the energy function. The ICM algorithm can be considered as a special case of the simulated annealing method with zero temperature. For each image site, the label which gives the largest local energy decrease is chosen (deterministic choice). The principle of the algorithm is the following. Starting from an initial configuration of the label field, all the image sites are visited according to a predefined strategy and a site label is updated by a label that gives the largest local energy decrease, thus causing a decrease

Table 1.2. Classification of decoding methods.

Choose an initial temperature $T = T_0$
Choose any initial configuration $x(0)$ of the label field X
repeat
    $i = 0$
   repeat
          Choose a site s (according to any visit strategy or randomly)
          and randomly change its label x into z .
          Compute
          if $\Delta U > 0$ replace x by z
          else replace x by z only if $p < \exp(\Delta U/T) p \epsilon [0, 1]$
          (uniform distribution)
          $i + +$
    until $i = N_{\text{iter}}$
$T = f(T) = a.T$ where $0 < a < 1$
until $T < e$ (freezing)

of the global energy of the label field. As the modification of a site label may modify the local energy of the neighbouring sites, the process is repeated until the convergence to a local minimum of the global energy of the label field is reached, or until a predefined stop condition is satisfied. This stop condition may be based for example on the number of labels modified during one iteration or the number of iterations performed. This method is very fast but the final quality of the segmentation depends strongly on the initial configuration of the label field, since only a local minimum of the energy function can be reached. This algorithm is recommended with an efficient initialization process which is able to produce an initial configuration near the global minimum of the energy function.

Table 1.3. ICM algorithm.

Label field initialization $x(O)$
Computation of the new label field configuration $x(n + 1)$
from previous configuration

   1. sites s are visited according to a predefined visit strategy

      $x_s(n + 1) = \arg \min_{l \epsilon L} U_s(X_s(n) = l, Y_s = y_s)$

      with $L = \{l_i\} 0 < i < q$

      n=n+1

   2. Back to step 1. Until stop criterion is reached.

1.2.1.3. *Highest Confidence First (HCF) algorithm*

The Highest Confidence First (HCF) algorithm introduced by Chou and Brown,[8] is a variant of the ICM algorithm, and is therefore a deterministic relaxation algorithm too.

Considering the fact that the visit order of the sites influences the convergence of the relaxation process, instead of examining all the sites systematically without any prior knowledge to lead the process, the main idea of this algorithm is to use a particular strategy.

The site labels are updated successively according to a stability criterion, starting from least stable sites. With this strategy, only unstable sites are considered. The stability measure is calculated as the difference between the current local energy of a site, and the possible lowest local energy for this site.

The least stable site is always processed first, because it is the most likely to change its label and a label change may have some incidence on the labelling of neighbouring sites. A heap is used to control the visit order. In this heap sites are ordered according to their stability measure. The site at the top of the heap is the least stable. The algorithm stops when all sites are stable.

Table 1.4.   HCF Optimization method.

All sites are marked as "uncommitted"
Compute the stability G of all sites and create a heap P according to stability measure, where the least stable site is placed at the top.
 	
Take the first s at the top of the heap P.
 	
if $G_s >= 0$, where G_s is the stability measure of site s **end**
else
    if s is an uncommitted site, commit it and associate label l
    which gives the lowest local energy
    else change its label l to the label l_{min} which
    gives the largest local energy decrease
    end if
 	
Update stability measure of site s and of its neighbours
 	
Put the site s in heap again.
Adjust heap P according to stability measures.
end if

1.2.1.4. *2D Dynamic Programming*

In 2003 Geoffrois proposed to adapt the Dynamic Programming principle which is one-dimensional in nature, to two-dimensional or n-dimensional spaces in general.[9] Prior to this work Dynamic Programming had already been applied by Derin[10] for MRF-based image segmentation in computer vision. This principle of 2D Dynamic Programming has been applied by Geoffrois[11] in the context of MRF-MAP framework to energy minimization, for handwritten digit recognition. This algorithm solves the problem efficiently by exploiting the grid structure of random fields. The main idea is to divide the image recursively into sub regions. The n best configurations of a region are determined among the $n \times n$ configurations obtained by merging the two sub regions it contains. This merging process is repeated iteratively starting from unitary sub regions corresponding to exactly one site, for which initialization is simple (Maximum Likelihood of the data term of the energy function), until a region covering the entire image is obtained. This method uses the "divide and conquer" principle of dynamic programming.

Assume that two neighboring rectangular regions O_1 and O_2 are associated with their respective state configurations $X_1(i,j)$ and $X_2(i,j)$. Then, the joint probability of the region $O = O_1 \cup O_2$ and its associated state configuration $X(u,v)$ defined by:

$$X(u,v) = \begin{cases} X_1(i,j), \text{ if } (u,v) = (i,j); \\ X_2(k,l), \text{ if } (u,v) = (k,l). \end{cases} \tag{1.1}$$

can be derived as follows:

$$P(X,O) = P(X_1,O_1)P(X_2,O_2)I(X_1,X_2)$$

where the expression

$$I(X_1,X_2) = \prod_{g \in G_1, h \in G_2, h \in N(g)} P(x_g, x_h)$$

denotes the interactions between the two state configurations. As

$$P(x_g, x_h) = P(x_g) \times P(x_g) \times I(x_g, x_h)$$

The term

$$I(x_g, x_h)_{g \in G_1, h \in G_2, h \in N(g)} = \frac{P(x_g, x_h)}{P(x_g) \times P(x_g)}$$

is thus the interaction term between two sites at the boundaries of the two regions to be merged. If we take into account the contextual local dependence between sites in Markov Random Fields, it appears that there are only interactions between sites belonging to the boundaries of the regions during the merging process. As a consequence it is not necessary to determine all the possible configurations of entire regions, but simply all the configurations of region boundaries, and for each of them the best configuration of the inside. This leads to reduction of the number of configurations to memorize during the merging process. However, in practice the number of configurations to memorize is high, especially if the image is large. This is the reason why in practice a pruning strategy is applied to reduce the number of configurations to store. Only the best configurations with minimum energy are stored. This parameter is the pruning threshold. This is the only parameter of this method, though it is very hard to determine. Indeed, if this threshold is too low, the optimality of the final solution is not guaranteed, and on the contrary if it is too high the number of intermediate configurations to store and the combinatorial complexity become intractable. Due to this pruning, this method is suboptimal and the quality of the result depends on the merging order. We may consider different merging orders, as for example line horizontal merging, column vertical merging, or alternative merging (Figure. 1.2). Many other merging strategies can be used.

Other optimization techniques have been proposed in the literature for image labelling using MRF-MAP framework, such as Mean Field Annealing,[12] Genetic Algorithms,[13] or Ant Colony System.[14] We do not describe these methods here.

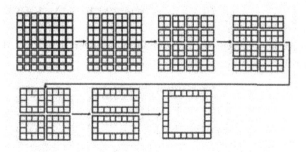

Fig. 1.2.   Alternative merging strategy.

1.2.2. *Application of MRF labelling to handwritten document segmentation*

When using MRF-MAP labelling framework to segment images, one has to simply make some choices concerning the modeling of the probability density function of observation emission, the clique potential function and the optimization method used to minimize the energy function. In this work we are interested in segmenting handwritten documents, such as drafts or literary manuscripts, into their elementary parts using a prior MRF model. We describe here our implementation choices to solve this task.

1.2.2.1. *Probability densities*

The probability densities are modeled by Gaussian mixtures. The parameters of the mixtures are learned using manually labelled images, using the Expectation Maximization (EM) algorithm. The number of Gaussians is determined automatically using the Rissanen criterion. We use Bouman's CLUSTER software to learn the number of Gaussian components and mixture parameters.

1.2.2.2. *Clique potential functions*

The joint energy on the image is given by:

$$U(X, O) = -\sum_s \log(P(o_s/x_s)) + \sum_c V_c(X)$$

where V_c are the potentials (or the energy) associated with the cliques of the graph.

$$U(X) = -\log P(X) = \sum_c -\log P_c(X) = \sum_c V_c(X)$$

If we consider the second order cliques associated with a 4-connected neighborhood:

$$c = C_1 \cup C_2 \cup C_3 \tag{1.2}$$

$$C_1 = \{(i,j), 1 \le i \le n\} \tag{1.3}$$

$$C_2 = \{(i,j), (i+1,j), 1 \le i \le n, 1 \le j \le m\} \tag{1.4}$$

$$C_3 = \{(i,j), (i,j+1), 1 \le i \le n, 1 \le j \le m\} \tag{1.5}$$

then we have:

$$V_c(X) = \sum_{c=\{g,h\}, h \epsilon N(g), g \epsilon N(h)} -\log P(x_g, x_h) \tag{1.6}$$

The joint probability $P(x_g, x_h)$ can be expressed in the following way:

$$P(x_g, x_h) = P(x_g)I(x_g, x_h)P(x_h) \qquad (1.7)$$

where $I(x_g, x_h)$ is the interaction term between adjacent labels. Then the prior energy $U(X)$ is defined by:

$$U(X) = \sum_{c \in C} V_c(X) = -\sum_{s \in S} \log(P(x_s)) - \sum \log(I(x_g, x_h)) \qquad (1.8)$$

The interaction terms are defined as mutual information terms taking into account only the horizontal and vertical directions (4-connectivity) as follows:

As for the Gaussian mixture parameters, these probabilities are learned using some labelled examples, by counting the frequency of each possible transition. If a rule transition does not appear in the learning examples, its probability is not set to zero but to a very low value, making it not impossible but very unlikely. Finally, the clique potential functions are defined as follows:

In a similar way, according to these definitions, the use of 2-order cliques with a 8-connected neighboring is very simple. One has only to take into account diagonal interactions too. The different n-order cliques associated to 4-connected and 8-connected neighborings are illustrated in Figure 1.3.

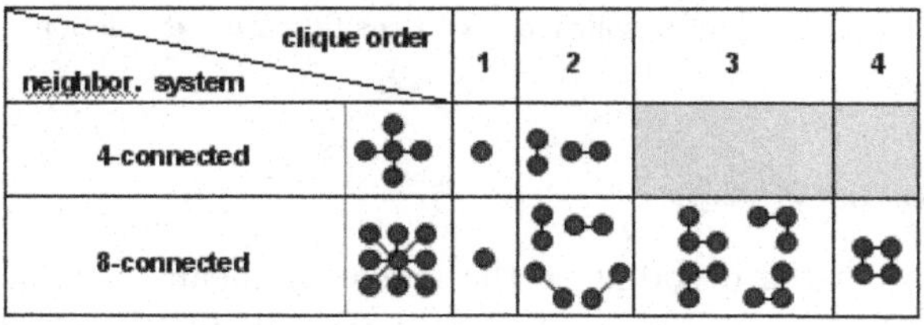

neighbor. system \ clique order	1	2	3	4
4-connected				
8-connected				

Fig. 1.3.   Neighboring systems of order 1 and 2 with their corresponding cliques.

1.2.2.3. *Observations*

Observations are features extracted from each site at position on the grid overlaid on the image. As we work on binary images, we have chosen to extract from each site a bi-scale feature vector based on pixel density measurement. This vector contains 18 features. The first 9 features are the densities of black pixels in cell g(i,j) and in its 8-connected neighbours at the first scale level. Based on the same principle, the remaining 9 features are the densities of black pixels extracted at the second coarser scale level (see Figure 1.4). Each cell at this scale corresponds to a 3×3 window at the previous scale. Note that the size of the cell on the grid must be adapted to the size of the smallest objects or layout elements we want to extract in the image. The choice of this size is necessarily the result of a compromise between the segmentation quality and the computational cost. The smaller the cells, the finer is the labelling. But if there are too many sites, the energy minimization process will be more complicated. Depending on the segmentation task, we can use different sizes of a cell.

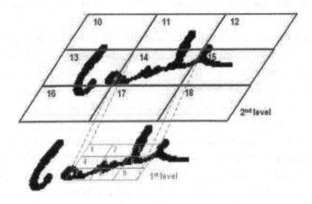

Fig. 1.4. Multiresolution pixel density feature extraction.

1.2.2.4. *Decoding strategy*

To proceed with the decoding of the image by means of minimization of the energy function, we have implemented several of the methods described in the literature, mainly ICM, HCF, and 2D dynamic programming. We have tested and compared these methods. The results are provided in the next section. We have implemented simulated annealing too, but we have tested this algorithm only on very small image fragments, not on an entire manuscript image, because of the very high computational complexity of this algorithm. Therefore, we will not provide experimental results obtained by this algorithm.

1.2.3. *Results*

The analysis of the results of a document image segmentation algorithm is a difficult and not always a well defined task, since there are very few protocols and image databases for performance evaluation.[15] The few existing ones are only designed for machine printed documents for which the proposed methodologies and metrics used to compare the algorithms are meant for well defined classes of methods or documents (newspaper, mail, form, postal address). To the best of our knowledge, there is no such methodology and metric in the field of handwritten documents or historical documents.

As our approach is able to produce labelling at different analysis levels using different grid sizes, we present here the results obtained from two different segmentation tasks working at two different scales. The first task consists in labelling large areas of interest in manuscript images, such as text body, margins or text blocks, working at a coarse resolution. For this task we provide quantitative results in term of labelling rates and processing time, for several decoding methods. The results obtained are also illustrated visually and discussed. For the second task which consists in text line labelling, we show the ability of this approach to perform at a finer level, in order to extract and separate small entities such as words or parts of words and erasures. For several reasons explained below, we provide for this task qualitative results only obtained from a few images of full page of handwriting and parts of pages taken from a database of Flaubert's handwritten manuscripts.

1.2.3.1. *Zone labelling*

In order to evaluate precisely the performance of our approach and to compare the decoding methods with respect to the labelling rate and processing time, we have first considered a segmentation task where a simple coarser labelling is possible. In this case, it is easy and fast to label a database of Flaubert manuscript images manually for model learning and ground truthing. The task we consider consists in labelling the main regions of the manuscripts such as text body, margins, header, footer, page number, and marginal annotations (see Figure 1.5.a). The model contains 6 labels. The database contains 69 manuscript images at 300 dpi resolution. The average dimension of the images is 2400×3700. All the images of the database have been segmented and manually labelled according to the 6 defined labels.

The database of 69 pages has been divided into 3 equal parts: one for the learning of the model parameters (parameters of the Gaussian mixtures, clique potential functions), another for model setting, and the last one for testing. We use a regular grid where the dimension of each cell is 50×50 pixels. We compare the results obtained by a Mixture Model using Maxi-

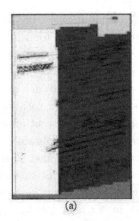 

(a)   (b)

Fig. 1.5.   Zone labelling at a coarser scale: (a) ground truth (b) result with Markovian labelling using the following color/label convention: red = page number, green = header, blue = text body, pink = footer, cyan = text block, yellow = margin (color online).

mum Likelihood criterion and the results obtained by ICM, HCF and 2D Dynamic Programming (2D DP) decoding with the ground truth labelling manually produced (Figure 1.5). For each decoding method we evaluate the global labelling rate (GLR) by counting the number of well-labelled sites and the normalized labelling rate (NLR) by counting the average number of well-labelled sites for each label class.

$$\text{GLR} = \frac{\text{True Positive} + \text{True Negative}}{\text{True Positive} + \text{False Positive} + \text{True Negative} + \text{False Negative}}$$

$$\text{NLR} = \frac{\sum_{i=0}^{q-1} \left[\frac{\text{True Positive}}{\text{True Positive} + \text{False Negative}} \right]_{l_i}}{q}$$

where q is the number of label classes and l_i is the i-th label.

For each decoding method we also give the average processing time in seconds for one page decoding. This time is only related to the decoding process while probability distribution estimation is not taken into account. Results are provided in Table 1.5.

These results show that the use of an MRF model increases the normalized labelling rate and that the HCF algorithm outperforms the other decoding methods. Furthermore, HCF algorithm is faster than 2D dynamic

Table 1.5. Average labelling rates obtained with different implementations of our CRF model and using ICM inference.

	Gaussian mixture	Local MLP	MRF	CRF
GLR (%)	88.00	86.60	90.30	84.60
NLR (%)	83.70	87.50	88.20	87.40
Time (s)	-	0.21	0.29	0.61

programming method. The difference between GLR and NLR is due to non homogeneous class repartition in the dataset (see Figure 1.6).

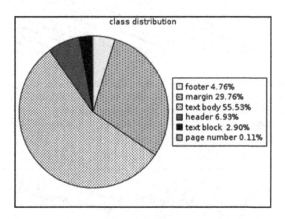

Fig. 1.6. Class distribution in the dataset.

1.2.3.2. *Text line labelling*

Let us recall that Flaubert's manuscripts contain a lot of deletions and crossed out words or lines (see Figure 1.1). Therefore, in this second experiment, we have tried to evaluate the capabilities of our method to work at a finer analysis level, on a specific task which consists in separating words (or parts of words) and deletions, and to extract text lines using a prior model which integrates several states. For this purpose we have first defined a model made up of 4 states: "pseudo-word", "deletion", "diacritic" and "background". We work at the pixel level using a regular grid of 1×1 cells and we use the 2D Dynamic Programming method of Geoffrois et al for decoding.[11] For this task we provide only qualitative results because it is very hard to manually label images at the pixel level for ground truthing. Figure 1.7.a presents the results obtained with this model on a page fragment. Figure 1.8.a shows a zoom on a deletion area where words and deletion strokes are completely connected. One can see here that the deletion lines are well separated from the strokes below. This result highlights the superiority of this method among the approaches working at the connected component level since it is able to segment different objects which are connected together. Figure 1.8.b shows similar results on a fragment containing a word and an erasure connected by a descending loop. Both components are well separated.

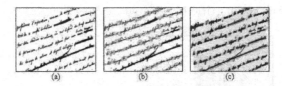

Fig. 1.7.   Segmentation results obtained on a page fragment: (a) using a 4-state model; (b) using a 5-state model; (c) using a 6-state model, with the following color/label convention: white = background, green = textual component, blue = erasure, pink = diacritic, cyan = inter-word spacing, yellow = inter-line spacing (color online).

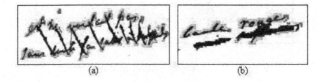

Fig. 1.8.   Segmentation results obtained on some complex page fragments using the 4-state model.

This model is able to extract word fragments and erasures, but does not model text lines. So we have refined this model by introducing an additional "inter pseudo-word space" state. The addition of this state makes it possible thereafter to extract the text lines because one can define a text line as a sequence of "pseudo-words" separated by "inter-word spaces". Thus, from the results returned by the method, it is possible to extract text lines or other objects of higher level (such as text blocks), by applying label merging rules. Globally the results are promising, the inter-word spaces are well segmented (see Figure 1.7.b). Finally, in the same way, we have defined a third model with 6 states by adding an "inter-line" state to the previous model, in order to model the inter-line spacing also. The knowledge of inter-line spaces helps to segment text lines and to detect text blocks in a better way. The result obtained with this model on the same fragment of a page is shown in Figure 1.7.c and the result obtained on a full page is shown in Figure 1.9.

Fig. 1.9.   Segmentation results obtained on a complete Flaubert manuscript page using a 6-state model with the following color/label convention: white = background, green = textual component, blue = erasure, pink = diacritic, cyan = interwords spacing, yellow = interline (color online).

For these three models the results are globally satisfactory. However, if we look locally at the results, we can see that some pixels are misclassified. One has to keep in mind that the 2D dynamic programming algorithm with pruning procedure is a sub-optimal decoding algorithm. It means that the final segmentation obtained is not the optimal one. Some configurations of the label field can be locally less probable and can thus be pruned during the merging procedure, though they could be globally the optimal ones. If the size of the image is large and if there are a lot of states in the model, the number of possible configurations of the label field is very large. In this case, it is not possible to store all possible intermediate solutions, and hence the pruning threshold should not be too high. On the other hand, if this threshold is too low, the final configuration retained may be one of the least probable ones (because of involving not probable transitions during the region merging). The choice of the merging strategy is thus important for the final segmentation result. However, the choice of features extracted from the observations is also important. In summary, these experiments on two different labelling tasks show the ability of the approach to work at different levels of analysis and to extract areas of interest in complex documents such as literary manuscripts. The system could benefit from user interactions and multiscale approach in order to improve the labelling results.

1.2.3.3. *Conclusion*

As pointed by He et al,[16] Markov Random Fields have two main drawbacks. First, they rely on strong hypotheses about the independence of observations, for inference tractability reasons. These hypotheses are too strong for image labelling. For these reasons only local relationships between neighbouring nodes are incorporated into the model. The second one is their generative nature. Markov Random Fields attempt to model the joint distribution of the observed image and the corresponding label field. So an important effort is made to model the observation distribution. However, during decoding, the problem is to estimate the conditional distribution of the label field according to the observed image. So there is no need to try to model the joint distribution which may be very complex. It is better to model the conditional distribution of the label field given the observations. Consequently, less training data are needed. This is the reason why discriminative models, such as Conditional Random Fields, have recently been proposed to directly model the conditional distribution.

1.3. Conditional Random Field Models

CRF models were initially introduced in the field of information extraction by Lafferty[17] for part-of-speech tagging and syntactical analysis. Till now they have mainly been used for sequential data modeling. A few works involving 2D CRF models for image analysis have been proposed recently.[16,18] But to the best of our knowledge, except the work of Szummer[19] on diagram recognition and the work of Feng[20] on handwritten word recognition, CRF models have not so far been applied to document image analysis. The superiority of CRF models compared to MRF models has been generally reported for sequence modeling. Contrary to MRF and other generative models that define a joint probability over observation and label configurations, which requires in theory the enumeration of all possible observation configurations for the calculation of the normalization constant, discriminative models like CRF directly model the conditional probabilities of label configurations given the observations. Furthermore, CRF models do not require any independence hypothesis about the observations and are particularly efficient for discriminative tasks like segmentation, labelling or recognition.

1.3.1. *Proposed model*

Whereas the MRF model gives access to the posterior probability indirectly using the Bayes rule decomposition $P(X/O) \propto P(O/X)P(X)$, a CRF model does not use this decomposition and therefore provides a direct formulation of the discriminative task i.e. discrimination between the labels. Such a model aims at defining a probability distribution on the possible label configurations given an observation. The general form of a CRF model is given by the following formula:

$$P(X = x/O = o) = \frac{1}{Z} \prod_{s \epsilon S} \exp[\sum_k \lambda_k f_k(x, o, s)] \qquad (1.9)$$

A CRF model is thus defined as the product, on a set of sites, of the exponential of a linear combination of k functions called feature functions, depending on the observation o, the label configuration x and the current site s. Z is a normalization factor traditionally called the partition function. By considering the negative logarithm we can introduce the global conditional energy:

$$U(X = x/O = o) = -\log(P(X = x/O = o)) \qquad (1.10)$$

$$= -[\sum_{s \epsilon S} U_s(X_s = x_s/X^s = x^s, O = o)] - \log Z \qquad (1.11)$$

where X^s is the configuration on the remainder of the label field X except in s, and $U_s(X_s = x_s/X^s = x^s, O = o)$ is the local conditional energy of the label x_s at the site s given the label configuration on the remainder of the label field, and the observation. This local energy (or local potential) U_s is defined as a linear combination of feature functions:

$U_s(X_s = x_s/X^s = x^s, O = o) = \sum_k \lambda_k f_k(x, o, s)$ The main advantage of CRF models over MRF models is that they do not decompose the posterior probability into a data model and a prior model. In the context of MRF models these two sub-models are known to be difficult to estimate. Furthermore, generative models such as Gaussian mixtures are known to be limited to using low dimensional observation vectors. CRF models do not suffer from these drawbacks. The modeling and the solving of problems using conditional random fields require to define the feature functions and to choose a parameter learning method and an inference method. We now explain our proposed model and our choices for these issues.

1.3.1.1. *Feature functions*

The feature functions are real valued functions. These functions allow integrating into the model the prior knowledge about the domain under consideration. In the CRF model of Lafferty, the observations are discrete, so the feature functions are binary functions which return a one value if a given phenomenon is observed and zero otherwise. But here we have continuous observations. So like Kumar et al,[18] and more recently He et al,[16] we have chosen to model the feature functions by using discriminative classifiers. We use Multilayer Perceptron (MLP) for this task because they are fast and provide good generalization properties even in high dimensional spaces. However, we could consider other classifiers such as SVM or logistic classifiers. Our CRF model can be seen as a network of interconnected classifiers taking their decision using image features as well as contextual information by incorporating the decisions of the neighboring classifiers. The local conditional energy is defined according to the following relation:

$$U_s(X_s = x_s/X^s = x^s, O = o) = \sum_{k=1}^{K} \lambda_k f_k(x, o, s)$$

where K stands for the number of discriminative components taken into account in the model, λ_k is the weight associated with the kth component and $f_k(x, o, s)$ is the score provided by the kth discriminative classifier of the combination. As we use MLP classifiers we can consider that theses scores are some estimates of the local conditional probability $P(x_s/x, 0, s)$ of attributing the label x_s to the site s given a feature set on the label configuration and the observations in the vicinity of s.

1.3.1.2. *Model inference*

The techniques used for conditional random field model inference are similar to those proposed for Markov random field inference. In the 2D case, the model has a general graph structure. As a consequence, there is no exact inference method for such a structure, and the search for only a sub-optimal labelling solution is possible. The most popular techniques for inexact inference on random field models are the Belief Propagation algorithm and the sampling techniques such as Gibbs or Metropolis sampler. Stochastic relaxation methods such as simulated annealing or ICM algorithm can also be used. These algorithms find an approximate solution of the optimal field labelling using MAP criterion, i.e., by maximizing the global posterior probability of the label configuration given the observation:

$$\hat{x} = \arg\max_x P(X = x/O = 0) \qquad (1.12)$$

It is equivalent to minimize the global posterior energy:

$$\hat{x} = \arg\min_x U(X = x/O = 0) \qquad (1.13)$$

The global posterior energy is defined as:

$$U(X = x/O = o) = -[\sum_{s \epsilon S} U_s(X_s = x_s/X^s = x^s, O = o)] - \log Z \qquad (1.14)$$

In this formula Z is a constant. So minimizing the global energy is equivalent to maximizing the local posterior energy $U_s(X_s = x_s/X^s = x^s, O = o)$ at each site. As there are interactions between sites, the problem is non-causal and we have to use iterative optimization procedures once again. So, for MRF models, we have chosen to use ICM (Iterated Conditional Modes) and HCF (Highest Confidence First) algorithms for inference because they are known to be fast and efficient. The principle of the inference is the following. We proceed to a first labeling using only the local classifier and the intrinsic image features. During this first labeling process, the contextual information about the labeling on the neighboring sites is not taken into account. This process initializes the label field and computes at each site the values of the local feature function. These features are then used as inputs for the contextual classifier. For the next iterations the contextual feature function is also taken into account to evaluate the local potential function (log of the conditional probability) at each site of the image. The inference then involves visiting all the sites and evaluating for each of them the score of the potential function for each possible label l_i of the set L, by combining the outputs of the classifiers. This score can be seen as the energy for assigning the label l_i to the site s given the observations and the energies of the possible label configurations in the vicinity of the site s. The label providing the highest score is assigned to the current site, but all the other conditional energies are memorized. These energies are iteratively updated during the inference of the label field. This updating process is repeated until convergence of the label configuration.

1.3.1.3. *Parameter learning*

Learning the parameters of the model consists of training the MLPs and determining the weights λ of the linear combination. As we have manually labeled data, we can use a supervised approach. For each image of the training database, we dispose of the corresponding ground-truth labeling. In this study, the labeling has been entered manually using a simple image editor and using a particular lookup table so as to associate a particular label to each color. All MLPs are trained using the back-propagation algorithm. The weights of the linear combination are determined simply using a gradient descent method in order to minimize the labeling error at each site.

1.3.2. *A two level CRF model*

In the first experiment we have considered only two levels of analysis ($k = 2$) and we have defined two feature functions: an observation feature function f_O and a label feature function f_L. The observation feature function accounts for the contribution of the label of site s of the observation field while the label feature function f_L accounts for the contribution of the neighboring labels to the label of site s. The f_O feature function takes into account only the features extracted from the observation O on a local window of analysis. The f_L feature function takes into account the contextual information, i.e., the label energies over a neighborhood defined by a window of analysis. The local conditional energy function $U_s(X_s/X^s, O) = \lambda_O f_O$ at each site s is defined by a linear combination (Figure 1.10) of the two feature functions f_O and f_L:

$$U_s(X_s/X^s, O) = \lambda_O f_O + \lambda_L f_L \qquad (1.15)$$

We use MLP classifiers to model these feature functions. The scores provided by such classifiers can be considered as estimates of posterior probabilities. Then we can express the local energy as follows:

$$U_s(X_s/X^s, O) = \lambda_O P_O(X_s/O) + \lambda_L f_L(X_s/X^s) \qquad (1.16)$$

This formulation combines a local discriminative model and a contextual discriminative model that allow capturing the information obtained from the observation field and the information obtained from the label field X in a limited neighborhood. This model allows catching a rich context and thus a good regularization and homogenization of the label field X while taking into account the observed information. Furthermore, by considering a discriminative framework, it is possible to relax the conditional independence hypothesis of the observations. This takes into account correlated features on a wide neighborhood.

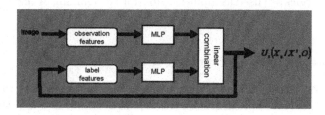

Fig. 1.10. Linear combination of the local and global information.

1.3.2.1. *Observation features*

The observation feature function only takes into account features extracted from the image, at a given site (local image features). This function models the data association that is the relation between the label associated with a given site s and the local observation at this site. We take into account the same feature sets as those we used in the MRF model (see Section 1.2), namely, the multi-resolution pixel density features and the site relative position. These features are extracted from each site and form a feature vector that is the input to the MLP which models the local feature function. The scores returned by the MLP are the values of the feature function for the different possible labels $l_i \in L = \{l_1, ..., l_q\}$ that can be associated with the current site s.

1.3.2.2. *Label features*

The label feature function only takes into account the local conditional energies $U_s(X_s = l_i, i = 1, ..., q/X_N, O)$ on the label field X in a neighborhood N around the current site. This neighborhood is determined by defining a sliding window the size of which depends on the quantity of contextual information we wish to integrate. For example, using a window of size 3×3

and considering a label set of size $q = 3$ we can define 27 conditional posterior probabilities, that is, a vector of 27 contextual features as input to the contextual MLP.

1.3.2.3. *Learning*

The observation MLP is first trained only on the features extracted from the image. The output of the MLP is used to estimate the data association conditional energies $U(X_s/O)$ at each site s of the image. Then these conditional energies are used as input features for the training of the contextual MLP.

1.3.3. *Integrating more contextual information*

We have first considered only two analysis levels, and we present the results obtained from this implementation (impl.1) in Section 1.3.4. But the global formulation of our model allows integrating easily more information sources in the decision. So a second model is also proposed by integrating a third feature function called global feature function.

1.3.3.1. *Global feature function*

An analysis of the label field X at a more global level is taken into account by a third feature function called global feature function. This global analysis is carried out using a third MLP. This classifier estimates the posterior probabilities $P(X_s = l_i, \forall l_i \epsilon L / F_G(X))$ of associating the label l_i to the current site s given a set F_G of global statistical features extracted from the global label configuration over a larger neighborhood than that considered by the contextual feature function. The global classifier is also a contextual classifier that takes into account the label configuration at a coarse resolution. At this resolution, the label field is divided into several zones by superposing a grid H larger than the initial grid. Each cell of this grid gives access to a set of sites. Statistical parameters are computed on these cells. We construct the co-occurrence matrix of the labels on each cell for different orientations. More precisely, four co-occurrence matrices are calculated for the orientations of $0°, 45°, 90°$ and $135°$. From these four co-occurrence matrices, five Haralick parameters are computed.[21] Here the originality of our approach is that we determine these features not directly from the image, but from the label configuration.

1.3.3.2. *Combination of the information sources*

This second model integrates three information sources operating at three different levels of analysis. Each of them is modeled by an MLP. At each image site and for each of these three information sources, the MLP classifier takes a decision according to the source taken into account. The local conditional energy $U(X_s/X^s, O)$ in each site s, given the observations O and the remainder of the field X, is now defined by $U(X_s/X^s, O) = h(f_O, f_L, f_G)$ where h is a combination function of the three information sources: observation source, label source and global source. In practice, there are several ways to implement this combination function. We propose two combination solutions.

1.3.3.3. *Linear combination of the information sources (impl.2)*

The simplest way to integrate the global feature function with our CRF model is to combine it with the output of the previous model. In this case the model integrates in a sequential manner two combination levels. The output is then a non-linear combination (Figure 1.11). The training of the weights of these two combinations is performed in two steps. First the weights λ_O and λ_L of the first combination are trained on the training set in order to maximize the average labelling rate without taking into account the global information. These weights being optimized, those of the second combination $\lambda_O - L$ and λ_G are determined using the same procedure but taking the global information into account. This type of combination allows controlling easily the quantity of information given by the global feature function compared to the information given by the local model. The first combination summarizes local information whereas the second one integrates global information.

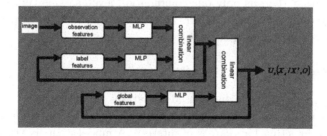

Fig. 1.11. Cascading combination of the three analysis levels.

1.3.3.4. *Combination of the information sources using an MLP (impl.3)*

We have also investigated the use of a Multilayer Perceptron as a combination function of the different information sources (Figure 1.12). Indeed, the theoretical and mathematical definition of an MLP is rather close to that of a conditional random field since it acts as a non-linear combination of features. The values of the output of the three feature functions for the different possible labels, feed the input of one single MLP. If the label set contains q labels, the dimension of the feature vector applied at the input of the combining MLP will be $3q$. Using this type of combination the three information sources are combined in parallel.

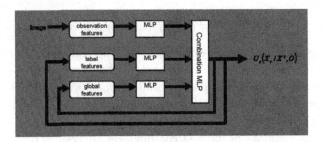

Fig. 1.12.   Combination of the three analysis levels using an MLP.

The quantity of information provided by each component depends on the weights of the MLP, but cannot be known explicitly, as that is the case when one uses a linear combination. The learning of this model consists of training the three MLP modeling the three feature functions, on the training dataset, hence of training the combining MLP. The training of all the MLPs is performed using the backpropagation algorithm. The advantage of this solution is that there is only one combination level, so it is very simple to combine several information sources. Its main drawback is the prohibitive time required for training the MLP.

1.3.4. *Experiments and results*

For the experiments we have used a dataset of 69 images of Gustave Flaubert's manuscripts. We consider a labelling task at a block level which consists of detecting large areas of interest. A model with six states is defined for this task, and the parameters are learned on manually labelled images. The states are "text body", "text blocks", "page numbers", "margins", "headers" and "footers". The size of the grid is fixed empirically to obtain a good compromise between complexity reduction and quality of the labelling for the task under consideration. We choose a size of 50 × 50 pixels which corresponds roughly to the width of the inter-word spaces and to the height of the ascending or descending letters. Table 1.6 shows the labelling rates obtained at the pixel level with the three implementations of our CRF model. Comparison with the results obtained using a local classifier applied at each site using different sizes of context (the set 1 corresponds to a 3 × 3 contextual window and the set 2 to a 5 × 5 window) is also given. The results show that by increasing the number of levels of analysis (impl.3 versus impl.1) we obtain better results than when using a single local classifier. Among the different implementations, the MLP combination (impl.3) seems to be the best.

Table 1.6. Average labelling rates obtained with different implementations of our CRF model and using ICM inference.

	Local MLP	Impl.1	Impl.2	Impl.3
Set 1	90.56	92.55	93.90	94.04
Set 2	90.56	93.91	93.93	94.16

Table 1.7 compares the average pixel labelling rate (ALR) provided by our CRF model with the average labelling rate obtained using our previous MRF model described in Section 1.2. In comparison, the labelling rates obtained with a local classification approach based on a generative model (Gaussian mixtures) or based on a discriminative classifier (MLP), without context integration, are also provided. These results show that discriminative CRF models outperform the traditional generative MRF models in terms of a general image labelling task. Figure 1.13 shows an example of labelling results.

Table 1.7. Comparison of labelling rates obtained with different models.

	Gaussian mixture	Local MLP	MRF	CRF
ALR (%)	83.70	87.50	90.56	93.91

1.4. Conclusions and Outlook

We have proposed and presented two Markovian models for 2D data labelling, particularly for document image segmentation : a Hidden Markov

Fig. 1.13.　Example of labelling results on a manuscript of Flaubert.

Random Field model and a Conditional Random Field model. The first one is a generative model which can be separated into a data model (local likelihood modelled by gaussian mixtures assuming independence of the observations) and a contextual prior model defined on the 2-order cliques of the label field. Our Conditional Random Field model is based on a combination of discriminative classifiers such as Multilayer Perceptron Neural Networks taking into account features on the image observations and features on the possible label configurations at different levels of analysis. Simple combination solutions such as linear combinations are used. But potentially much more efficient solutions, such as information fusion using belief functions, will be considered in the future. Our first aim is to show that even simple combination solutions of different information sources operating at different levels of analysis, are interesting and efficient. One of the main advantages of both models (MRF and CRF) is that they can be learned automatically using machine learning procedures, with only a few simple parameters to be set manually. These parameters are mainly related to the definition of the sites, the neighboring system, the labels and the features appropriate for the problem under consideration. It would be quite simple for the user to define these parameters using a graphical user interface or by providing a few manually labeled examples using any drawing software. By using learning procedures, our approaches do not require any complex intervention of the user. This allows an easy adaptation to different types of documents and different analysis tasks. The results we have obtained on Flaubert's manuscripts show that the CRF model provides better results than MRF generative models. These results are similar to those presented in other recent works on conditional random fields.[16,18] Indeed, by directly modeling the posterior probability of the label configuration given observations (or posterior energy), which takes into account discriminative and dependent features and uses discriminative classifiers, the CRF models are much more efficient than the MRF models which rely on simplification hypothesis and generative models such as Gaussian mixtures, that are less efficient for segmentation or classification tasks. Future work may involve integration of more intrinsic and contextual features in the model, the replacement of MLP by logistic classifiers which are faster to train, the study of more efficient combination solutions, the definition of hierarchical CRF models for document image analysis, and the application of our models to other image analysis problems.

Acknowledgments

The authors would like to acknowledge Jim Mason (president of Kappa Image LLC) for his valuable suggestions.

References

1. H. Bunke, "Recognition of Cursive Roman Handwriting, Past, Present and Future", Proceeding of the seventh International Conference on Document Analysis and Recognition (ICDAR'03), pp. 448-459, Edinburgh, Scotland, 2003.
2. H. Baird, "Digital Libraries and Document Image Analysis", Proceeding of the seventh International Conference on Document Analysis and Recognition (ICDAR'03), pp. 2-14, Edinburgh, Scotland, 2003.

3. Nagy, G, "Twenty years of document image analysis in pami", IEEE Trans. on Pattern Analysis and Machine Intelligence, Vol. 22, n1, pp. 38-62, 2000.
4. Chellappa, R. and Jain, A., editors (1993). Markov Random Fields - Theory and application, Academic Press.
5. S. Geman, D. Geman, "Stochastic relaxation, Gibbs distributions and the Bayesian restoration of images". IEEE Trans. on Pattern Analysis and Machine Intelligence, Vol. 6, pp. 721-741, 1984.
6. S. Kirkpatrick, C. D. Gellatt and M. P. Vecchi, "Optimization by Simulated Annealing", Science (1983), no. 220, pp. 671-680, 1983.
7. J. E. Besag, "On the statistical analysis of dirty pictures", Journal of the Royal Statistical Society B, vol. 48, no. 3, pp. 259-302, 1986.
8. P. Chou, C. Brown, "The theory and practice of Bayesian image labeling", International Journal of Computer Vision, 4, pp.185-210, 1990.
9. E. Geoffrois, "Multi-dimensional Dynamic Programming for statistical image segmentation and recognition", International Conference on Image and Signal Processing, pp. 397-403, Agadir, Morocco, 2003.
10. H. Derin, H. Elliott, "Modeling and segmentation of noisy and textured images using Gibbs random fields", IEEE Trans. on Pattern Analysis and Machine Intelligence, Vol. 9, n1, pp. 39-55, 1987.
11. E. Geoffrois, S. Chevalier, F. Prteux, "Programmation dynamique 2D pour la reconnaissance de caractres manuscrits par champs de Markov", proceedings of RFIA, Reconnaissance de Formes et Intelligence Artificielle, pp. 1143-1152, Toulouse, France, Janvier 2004.
12. S.Z. Li, Markov Random Field Modeling in Computer Vision, Springer, Tokyo, 1995.
13. E.Y. Kim, S.H. Park, H.J. Kim, "A genetic algorithm-based segmentation of Markov Random Field modeled images", IEEE Signal processing letters 11(7): 301-303, 2000.
14. S. Ouadfel, M. Batouche, "MRF-based image segmentation using Ant Colony System", in Electronic Letters on Computer Vision and Image Analysis (LCVIA), vol. 2, n1, pp. 12-24, August 2003.
15. "Performance Evaluation: Theory, Practice, and Impact", T. Kanungo, H. S. Baird, R.M. Haralick, Guest Editors, special issue of International Journal on Document Analysis and Recognition, vol. 4, n3, march 2002.
16. X. He, R.S. Zemel, M. A. Carreira-Perpinan, "Multiscale Conditional Random Fields for Image Labeling", IEEE Computer Society Conference on Computer Vision and Pattern Recognition (CVPR'04), pp. 695-702, Washington DC, USA, 2004.
17. J. Lafferty, A. McCallum, F. Pereira, "Conditional Random Fields: Probabilistic Models for Segmenting and Labeling Sequence Data", 18th International Conference on Machine Learning, pp 282-289, Williamstown, USA, 2001.
18. S. Kumar and M. Hebert, "Discriminative random fields: A discriminative framework for contextual interaction in classification", in proceedings of the 9th IEEE International Conference on Computer Vision (ICCV'03), volume 2, pages 1150-1159, 2003.

19. M. Szummer and Y. Qi, "Contextual Recognition of Hand-drawn Diagrams with Conditional Random Fields", In 9th International Workshop on Frontiers in Handwriting Recognition (IWFHR'04), pages 32-37, Tokyo, Japon, 2004.

20. S. Feng, R. Manmatha and A. McCallum, "Exploring the Use of Conditional Random Field Models and HMMs for Historical Handwritten Document Recognition", Proceedings of the 2nd International Conference on Document Image Analysis for Libraries (DIAL'06), pages 30-37, Lyon, France, 2006.

21. R. Haralick, K. Shanmugan and I. Dinstein, "Textural features for image classification", IEEE Trans. On SMC, vol. 3, n6, pp. 610-621, 1973.

Chapter 2

Information Just-in-Time: Going Beyond the Myth of Paperlessness

Hiromichi Fujisawa, Hisashi Ikeda, Naohiro Furukawa, Kosuke Konishi

Central Research Laboratory, Hitachi, Ltd.
1-280 Higashi-koigakubo, Kokubunji, Tokyo, Japan.

Shoichi Nakagami

Government & Public Corporation Information Systems Division,
Hitachi, Ltd.
hiromichi.fujisawa.sb@hitachi.com

Information Just-in-Time or *iJIT* is a concept that signifies the idealistic state of information to be ready for use when it is necessary. Because of the great successes of search engines being used for World-Wide Web, we are apt to think that the issues of information availability have been almost solved. In reality, however, they have not. We still have problems around information access to paper documents, for example. This paper presents a possibility of turning physical paper into 'incarnation' of the information that exists in computers, contrary to the current view. The system we propose here keeps two versions of the same information, one in paper and the other in computers, equivalent even when the paper version is given handwritten annotations. The system uses a digital pen technology to enable this. The result being pursued is that users may take best part of both paper and electronic documents, and the paper version may be discarded anytime without any loss of information.

Contents

2.1. Introduction

How well are we doing in office today? This is a question we would like to pose regarding the information activities of knowledge workers. It is true that, thanks to today's IT advances, we are far better off than decades ago. For example, we may look for unknown information by using web search from among millions of millions of web documents with results of candidates in a second. We may use Internet to exchange information with colleagues at remote sites or share it with any person in the world. Documents are created and circulated in an electronic form, which increases our productivity. We may draw more exciting examples.

However, the answer to the previous question doesn't seem to be hundred percent positive. We still have problems for better knowledge work. It is clear when we look at our desktop and cabinets, which are flooded with and surrounded by paper documents. We often search paper documents, with frustration, for information that we have seen some time earlier. The search is necessary for clarification and/or confirmation. Then the next question is why we are still depending on physical paper. The reasons are well analyzed by Sellen and Harper in their book[1] "The Myth of the Paperless Office." It seems that there are indeed knowledge activities that need paper for better efficiency.

To illustrate to which direction we would like to go, we introduce in this paper a concept of *Information Just-in-Time*[2] , or *iJIT* in short, and give one more close look at the knowledge activities which consist of acquisition of information, reading, thinking and writing. We find room for improved intelligence amplification especially in reading and writing processes. These processes require more brain involvement for thinking and remembering, so the physical pen and paper are more natural and require less cognitive load. We consider that this is a real reason for our sticking to paper documents. But clearly, the use of paper in these processes forbids us from receiving the same benefits of electronic documents.

We propose in this paper a system by which we keep two versions of the same information, one in physical paper and the other in electronic documents, consistent with each other all the time. Documents created and circulated are usually electronic these days, and they are printed for use, i.e., for reading, understanding and commenting. The solution we propose relies on a digital pen technology from *Anoto®*.[3] A so-called on-demand printing system developed by us can print the contents of any documents together with unique *Anoto* dots. Therefore, these printed documents may receive marks and annotations, which can be captured by digital pens and then transmitted to the system. Because the dot pattern is sheet specific, the system can keep track of each page of printed documents and the corresponding annotations. In other words, the pages and annotations are synchronized. The system will be described in some more detail including a researcher's collaboration system, which is in a pilot test use at our laboratories.

This paper is made from an invited talk given at ICCTA2007 held at Indian Statistical Institute, Kolkata, India, for its celebration of the Platinum Jubilee.

2.2. Information Just-in-Time

2.2.1. *Personal Information Environment*

To realize *Information Just-in-Time, iJIT*, we first have to analyze human knowledge activities once again. They comprise acquisition of information, reading and interpretation, thinking, and writing. Actually the process is not straightforward. It is rather complex as shown in Fig. 2.1. For instance, reading, interpretation, thinking and writing require further information for clarification, comparison, confirmation, and so on. Reading and interpretation often accompany marking, annotating and writing, because we know we might come back to this information at a later stage even when our memory would be vague. In a sense, this kind of information collection in terms of paper documents with marks and annotations is "half cooked ingredients for the final plates of foods." It is stored locally near the worker's desktop.

The point we would like to stress in this paper is that knowledge workers rely heavily on this kind of local information. Of course, global search on Internet, social networks and collaboration networks are indispensable to reach global information in a short time. This means that we need still better *personal information environment* that supports the total process of information acquisition, reading, thinking and writing. And one way to

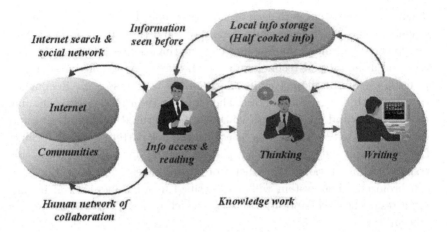

Fig. 2.1. Human knowledge work process. Each stage of reading, thinking and writing requires more information for clarification, comparison, confirmation, and so on. Among such information, the information that has been seen or read once before is often sought for. Personal Information Environment that supports easy access to such information is being developed.

attack this problem is to cast light on the problems around paper documents still in heavy use, and solve those problems.

2.2.2. Hot/Warm/Cold Documents

Classes of documents as named *hot/warm/cold documents* by Sellen and Harper[1] reflect the situation well. Hot documents are those to which we so often access for reference. The computer screen is now large enough to show multiple pages of documents simultaneously, but they are still not sufficient. Navigation on paper is quicker and more flexible. Cross-reference is easier because of spatial flexibility. Adding jotting and notes is also easier. The human sense of space plays an important role in dealing with many items simultaneously. A computer screen, which serves as a window to peep into the *digital world*, is still small in this sense. As a result, our desktops are flooded with paper documents (Fig. 2.2).

Warm documents are those that have been once hot but are not being accessed so frequently now (Fig. 2.3). They possibly carry marks and annotations inside, which help easy re-reading and also remind a reader of his/her ideas evoked in the past reading (Fig. 2.4). Marks and annotations are indexes to our brain memory. In addition, the warm documents may have corrections to the text, numbers, etc., made in terms of handwritten

Fig. 2.2. Hot documents under use and hot documents waiting for access.

Fig. 2.3. Warm documents (left) and cold documents (right).

annotations. This happens often actually. This fact cannot be overlooked especially when the paper version of such documents is the latest version, i.e., the situation where the original documents are not updated. So those documents cannot be disposed.

Cold documents have the same attributes as the warm documents but to a less degree. The probability of access is smaller but we keep them just in case. Again, they are not disposed of because of the cost of scanning them into computer. An additional observation to be noted here is that warm/cold documents have usually a file structure. Namely, they are bound in physical folders manifesting their strong mutual relevance. So if we are going to keep or put those documents in an electronic form, we have to extract such mutual relevance information and try not to lose such information.

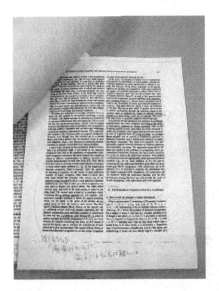

Fig. 2.4. Annotated documents. Marks and annotations are reminiscent of thorough reading and the reader's understanding process. Sometimes they show reader's critiques and his/her own ideas. It can be considered that they are virtually the indexes (or links) to the memories of his/her brain.

2.2.3. *Proposed Approach*

The approach proposed in this paper is to turn paper documents into 'incarnation' of digital originals. If this is possible in reality, we may dispose paper documents without any loss of information. That is, we take advantages of paper when the documents are hot, and we rely on digital counterparts with paper versions disposed of, when the documents become warm or cold. We consider this a big conceptual leap, because we are going to reverse the physical and virtual relationship. Under this new concept, the physical entities are going to be digital documents, and the virtual entities the printed hardcopy.

The questions are then how to deal with marks and annotations given to paper documents, and how to keep the mutual relevance information. In answering these questions, we use a digital pen technology to capture handwritten annotations and other related information digitally, and we are developing a 'hybrid document' management system (HDMS) to synchronize documents and added annotations. The roles of HDMS are to store digital documents, to print hardcopies, to acquire annotation stroke data together with pen attributes, to find the correspondence between stroke data and unique page identity, and to keep such information in a database. Extraction and use of mutual relevance information has not been well considered in the current framework. The next section will describe this solution.

2.3. Digital Pen Solution

As one of the business partners of *Anoto*, we have been developing digital pen solutions which use digital pen and paper with *Anoto* functionality.[3-5] The technology and exemplar applications[6,7] from us are described in this section. Other related works may be found somewhere else.[8-11]

2.3.1. *Anoto Functionality*

The *Anoto*'s basic idea is in the dot pattern preprinted on a sheet of paper and in the pen with a small camera inside (Fig. 2.5). The camera continuously captures images of small areas that include 6 by 6 dots. Dots are on the grid points macroscopically, but each of them is actually slightly displaced from the exact grid point microscopically. Because there are four ways of displacement for each dot, i.e., left, right, up and down, there are mathematically 436 different patterns in such 6 by 6 dot arrangements.

Their proprietary technique is in this mathematical arrangement of dots, whose pattern is unique throughout the space of 60 million km^2 , equivalent to 97 trillion A4-sized pages. In this way, an image of a 6 by 6 dot area gives after some computation an x-y coordinate in that huge space (and a coordinate in the sheet of paper) and a unique page address. The huge space is hierarchically divided into *segment, shelf, book and page*, in their terminology. Therefore, the page address has the form of 10.50.5.12 for example. Portions of the space are licensed to users through one of the several different business models. One model is that a printing company buys an area of such dot pattern from *Anoto*, and sells printed paper forms to end users. Another is that a system integrator or an IT solution provider obtains a license from *Anoto* to sell areas of dot patterns to a system operator.

The features of this technology that are indispensable in our applications are, in addition to capturing pen movements (stroke data), the capabilities of identifying a unique page address and providing date/time stamps and a pen ID. The uniqueness of a dot pattern is important to identify a unique sheet of paper or a unique page of similar notebooks. For example, when ten copies are made from a document, annotation data of one of the copies

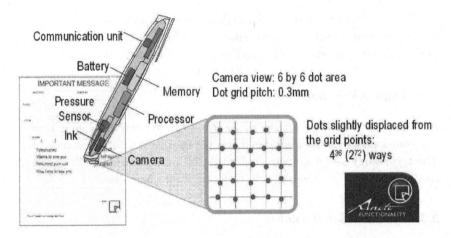

Fig. 2.5. Digital pen and paper. Paper forms are preprinted with specially arranged dots. A ballpoint pen with camera and electronics is used just as usual to write anything on the paper. While writing, the camera captures images of dots, which are then analyzed to locate the positions of the pen. The x-y coordinate data is stored in the internal memory and sent to computers through Bluetooth wireless communication or a USB cable. Other information such as pressure, pen posture, time and pen ID is also recorded and sent to computers.

can identify when and to which copy it has been written, and who wrote it. Identification of time and writer is an important feature to realize such applications where traceability and authenticity of documents is critical.

2.3.2. Data Entry Applications

We have developed application systems in e-Government related areas and others including the postal office, the police, and hospitals. In hospitals, for instance, there are still forms and documents to be handwritten for some reasons. Medical records are one of those, which are made by medical technicians and nurses. They check and monitor their patients in an examination room and at bedside, writing down the observations on paper forms. Since hospital information systems already take the place of information management, such handwritten forms have to be scanned every day, which is time consuming. A hospital which introduced Hitachi's digital pen solution (Fig. 2.6), could eliminate the human data entry task by making such information available and shareable by other doctors and nurses almost in real time.

Another digital pen solution example other than that of e-Government is a fish market application (Fig. 2.7) which has reduced the data entry cost

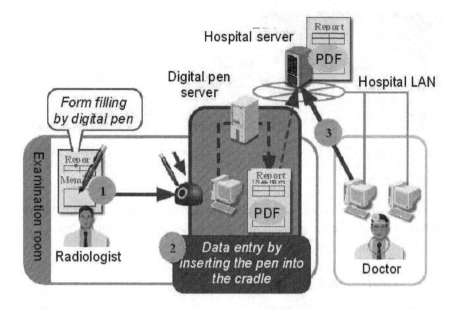

Fig. 2.6. Hospital application. By using a digital pen, handwritten contents of medical records are now digitized while being written and sent to a computer automatically. Face-to-face communication between nurses and patients has a higher priority than human-computer interaction.

to one tenth without changing the existing task flow of fish landing from fish boats. On the average about 2000 paper forms of the landed fishes were filled out every day, and in busiest days, 4000 forms had to be filled out. It took about 6 hours for three workers to key in the data. Handwriting on the paper forms was kept by adopting the digital pen solution. Captured handwritten data is now sent to a computer and automatically recognized by handwritten character recognition software. Including the verification task for character recognition, it now takes only 30 minutes or so to make the data available for further processes. The data is now used for bidding and for neatly printed statements delivered to the buyers.

2.4. iJIT Collaboration Platform

We have developed a pilot system, *iJIT Collaboration Platform*, by which we attempt to solve the problems analyzed in Section 2.2 based on the digital pen approach. The system comprises client software running of user PCs, and server software for on-demand printing and hybrid document

Fig. 2.7.   Fish market application. Form filling is done on the scene while sellers inspect and evaluate landed fishes visually. Handwriting is a most natural and easiest way to record the evaluation results.

management. The client software collects digital pen data, sends it to the server, requests the server to make hardcopies, retrieves annotated documents from the server, and displays them on PCs.

2.4.1. *On-Demand Printing*

A data entry solution of a digital pen normally uses batches of paper forms, which are preprinted by a printing company for instance. However, office applications for knowledge workers require a different approach. As discussed in Section 2.2, documents that are the target of our consideration are those created by commercial office application software of PC, those received from others, and those uploaded from web sites. And then, the 'data' we want to capture is marks and annotations made on those documents, which include underscores, circles enclosing words, handwritten text added to page margins, and any other handwritten strokes. Therefore, users should be able to print any documents with a unique dot pattern for their own. On-demand printing is an answer to this demand by using laser-beam printers found in offices.

One technical problem however is that the dots need to be seen by the pen camera even when the dots are in the midst of a black area such as a thick character stroke or pictures. Laser-beam printers from some of the manufactures solve this problem by using carbon black ink for the dots and mixture of other color inks for black color. Because the pen camera is sensitive to near-infrared light, it can see only the carbon black but not color inks, i.e., the black color made from the mixture of other color inks is transparent to the camera. We are using OKI printers which are certified by *Anoto*.

The digital pen solution provides software for the on-demand printing functionality, which runs on a server to which users make requests of printing. The server software actually has another important functionality of managing digital documents and of synchronizing annotations, where documents with synchronized annotations are called hybrid documents (HD).

2.4.2. Hybrid Document Management System

Hybrid Document Management System (HDMS) is server software receiving requests from client PCs. It stores and keeps track of original documents, printed PDF versions of documents, their printing conditions, annotations captured by digital pens, and meta data including annotation writer (or pen ID) and date/time. Any PC application software can create original documents. Then, the user may print them by requesting it to an on-demand print server (ODPS). When a document is printed, ODPS always keeps a PDF file in HDMS. It means that HDMS keeps a PDF file corresponding to the hardcopy. Hardcopies, i.e., hot documents, are then given marks and annotations, which are first sent to a client PC through Bluetooth wireless communication or a USB cable, and then sent to HDMS from the PC (Fig. 2.8).

As described in Section 2.3, annotation data consists of sets of stroke data (pen coordinates), pen ID and time stamp. Then, by calling *Anoto* functionality, stroke data can identify a page address of the annotation, equivalently the corresponding PDF file and then the original digital document. In this way, HDMS can synchronize digital documents, their PDF files, stroke data, writer identity and date/time. This means that the user can search for documents, original or PDF version, by specifying date/time of annotation or printing, printed person, writer of annotation, and/or document file name. It is to be noted here that the same document can be given annotations by multiple users using different pens.

Now the *iJIT* Collaboration Platform is installed and in pilot use in our laboratory which has five remote sites connected by Intranet. So far, about 250 digital pens have been delivered to the volunteering researchers, and 25 on-demand printers have printed over 23,000 pages since October 2006.

2.4.3. Research Notebook Application – iJITNote

On top of the *iJIT* Collaboration Platform created an application for research notebooks, *iJITNote*. Notebooks with uniquely identifiable *Anoto* dots have been delivered to researchers for daily research work. So far about 200 *iJITNote* notebooks are in use. Research departments that conduct a lot of experiments using test equipment for instance had been sharing their

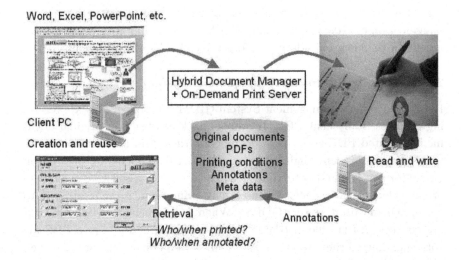

Fig. 2.8.   iJIT collaboration platform.

data by copying and/or faxing pages of their notebooks. Today, they can almost instantaneously share pages of their notebooks. For research teams that have separate remote offices sharing experiments, such data sharing is mandatory.

Another value of the research notebooks with digital pens is anti-counterfeit control. It has been recognized as important to keep authenticity of notebooks, experimental results and other kinds of records. The digital pen solution is a good one answering to such demands thanks to its time stamps and pen ID information. Actually, the digital pens have security measures such as encryption of the contents of internal memory. As for anti-counterfeit, an application program can check the time sequence of different strokes made by multiple writers, by relying on the data on handwriting date/time kept in HDMS. For example, it can be checked whether a signature given by a supervisor at the bottom of a notebook page is followed in time by some other writings. If there were any writings later on, such additional writings could be a counterfeit. This kind of function can be applied to other documents as well.

Research notebooks often require pasting other paper clips such as pictures, tables, and graphs. *iJITNote* enables such activities. Fig. 2.9 shows pasting of a graph made by a spreadsheet program. Of course, the graph is printed by using the on-demand print function. It is clipped from a page by scissors and pasted onto a page of a research notebook. Then, he/she draws

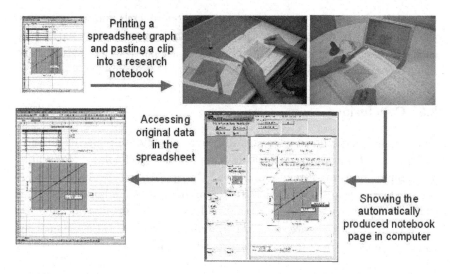

Fig. 2.9. Research notebook application iJITNote running on iJIT Collaboration Platform.

small diagonal lines on each corner of the pasted graph by using a digital pen. Each of the lines should start with a point on the notebook page, go onto the pasted corner and then go out to the notebook page again. The application program can analyze these lines to determine the location of the pasted clip on the page, which came from a spreadsheet in this case. And then, it identifies the hardcopy clip to be a spreadsheet graph, so it can regenerate virtually the pasted notebook page inside the computer as shown in Fig. 2.9 What is good about it is that he/she can click the *iJIT-Note* browser on PC to show the original spreadsheet carrying the original data. As the records of experiments are stored digitally in computers these days, it is beneficial for researchers to be able to keep track of every piece of data. Again, the time stamp information may detect a counterfeit if there is any.

2.4.4. *Future Directions*

We are still accumulating the experiences of the test users (researchers) of our system. They have already expressed merits and weak points that should be improved in future. One of such future demands is a more sophisticated search function such as annotation search. A research is underway so that handwritten character recognition can be used to realize such queries. Another issue for the system is the use of mutual relevance relationships among the documents. Documents written, referenced, and annotated in the same time frame can be considered mutually relevant. By extracting such relevance information from the history of use patterns, the system may make recommendations to the user when one of the documents is revisited.

2.5. Conclusions

This paper has discussed why we still heavily depend on paper documents and proposed an approach of using a digital pen technology. Presented are a pilot platform system and some of the applications we have built on top of it, which are now applied to researchers at our laboratories. The system supports on-demand printing and hybrid document management. More than 200 people are using the system and we are still accumulating the experiences targeting a more improved system.

Acknowledgments

The authors are grateful to the volunteering researchers using digital pens and notebooks for their giving us evaluation of the system including productive criticisms and ideas for improvements. One of them is Makoto Iwamoto at our laboratory who participated in thorough discussions in developing the concept of *iJIT* system.

References

1. A. J. Sellen and R. H. R. Harper, The Myth of the Paperless Office, *MIT Press* (2001).
2. H. Fujisawa and L. Kerschberg, Workshop on Information Just-in-Time (WI-JIT2005): Seeking a New Knowledge Management Paradigm, Wissensmanagement (LNCS Volume), 676-678 (2005).
3. Anoto, http://www.anoto.com
4. Anoto, Anoto SDK for PC Applications, Version 3.3 (2006).
5. Anoto, Paper Interface Guidelines - Anoto Components, (2006).
6. H. Ikeda, K. Konishi and N. Furukawa, *iJITinOffice*: Desktop Environment Enabling Integration of Paper and Electronic Documents, *UIST2006* (2006).
7. H. Ikeda, N. Furukawa and K. Konishi, *iJITinLab*: Information Handling Environment Enabling Integration of Paper and Electronic Documents, *Co-PADD2006* (2006)
8. F. Guimbretire, Paper Augmented Digital Documents, *UIST2003* (2003).
9. C. Liao and F. Guimbretire, PapierCraft: A Command System for Interactive Paper, *UIST2005* (2005)

10. R. Yeh, C. Liao, S. Klemmer, F. Guimbretire, B. Lee, B. Kakaradov, J. Stamberger and A. Paepcke, ButterflyNet: A Mobile Capture and Access System for Field Biology Research, *CHI2006*, 571-580 (2006).

11. M. C. Norrie, B. Signer and B. N. Weibel, Print-n-Link: Weaving the Paper Web, *DocEng2006* (2006).

Chapter 3

The Role of Document Image Analysis in Trustworthy Elections

George Nagy* and Daniel Lopresti[†]

*ECSE DocLab, Rensselaer Polytechnic Institute, Troy, NY, USA
[†] CSE Department, Lehigh University, Bethlehem, PA, USA

Reports of irregularities in recent US elections have resulted in a groundswell for paper-based voting systems, either in the form of paper ballots recorded by Optical Mark Reading (op-scan) or Voter Verifiable Paper Audit Trails printed within the voting booth by the digital vote recording system. Issues of interest to the Document Image Analysis community include accurate and unbiased human and machine recognition of both the marks denoting valid votes and the printed audit trail, either during the immediate tally of the vote by the ballot reader and the verification of the VVPAT by the voter, or during subsequent tally, recount, or audit after the vote is closed. These issues are intertwined with ballot and paper trail design and production. Scanning synthetic ballots that exhibit a range of degradations provides a means of evaluating commercial vote readers, and of associating mark recognition accuracy with voter behavior. Although currently OMR and OCR readers recognize each mark or character independently, Voter Intent (the legal criterion for a valid vote) may be more readily taken into account by evaluating all the marks on the same ballot together. Bias can be removed from human auditing by blind recording and by homogeneous class display (which also accelerates audits). Usability issues are raised by the wide range of voter skills, abilities, and education, and the short, intensive duty cycle of voting machines operated by non-technical personnel. DIA research on some of these topics may also benefit other critical financial and educational applications.

Contents

3.1. Introduction

This chapter is a survey of opportunities for the application of document image analysis (DIA) to interpreting and verifying paper records, including voter ballots, used in political elections. Current techniques in DIA are the result of fifty years of evolution. Nevertheless, we believe that a thorough examination of the role of paper in casting and verifying votes can bring new emphases and challenges to DIA while at the same time yielding machinery for conducting elections that is measurably better – more secure, accessible, and trustworthy – than what is currently in use, a topic of much current interest in many countries today.

No system of voting is without controversy. It is safe to say that perfect accuracy, transparency, security, and privacy in voting are desirable but unachievable goals. It seems somewhat paradoxical that the transition to electronic voting has proceeded in a straightforward fashion in some counties, while at the same time inciting great controversy in others. We begin by briefly summarizing electronic voting as it has been implemented in India, an example of the former case, and then proceed to a more detailed discussion of the issues that have arisen in the United States as well as the role that DIA may play in addressing these problems.

In India, electronic voting machines are seen as being more secure (from physical capture) than traditional ballot boxes. The potential for voter fraud is reduced by marking the voter's left index finger with an indelible ink immediately after the vote has been cast, a process that has been in place since the early 1960's. The voting machines themselves are stored under heavy security until the votes are counted and a winner declared.[1]

Electronic voting machines used in India are manufactured by one of several domestic companies, but employ a microchip made in Japan and sealed to prevent tampering. Unlike voting machines used elsewhere, these are not general-purpose computers running an off-the-shelf operating system, but rather dedicated hardware with a fixed, simple design. There are two units in the system, connected by a cable: a Control Unit which is under the control of an elections official, and a Balloting Unit which is located in the voting booth. The official in charge of the election must activate the Balloting Unit via the Control Unit before the voter is allowed to vote. Voters are presented with a button for each choice to be made in the election. The hardware is battery-operated so that it may be used reliably in locations where electricity is unavailable.[2]

The simplicity and uniformity of the systems used for electronic voting in India may be seen as inspiring confidence in the electoral process. In the United States, on the other hand, what was once seen as an expensive but straightforward transition to electronic voting is now viewed with increasing suspicion as a situation rife with potential risks and vulnerabilities. Poor software engineering practices, supposedly secure passwords widely publicized on the Internet, flimsy locks that can be picked in a few seconds (or opened with ubiquitous minibar keys), and machines that are reprogrammable with only a minute or two of access are just a few examples of the problems that have been uncovered. Computer security experts have stated unequivocally and with near unanimity that paper can play a fundamental role in guaranteeing safe and secure elections, either in the form of hand- or machine-marked ballots, or as a Voter Verified Paper Audit Trail (VVPAT). However, the processing of such records during the initial counting of votes or in the conduct of recounts has raised its own set of problems which span technical and social boundaries. The main topic of this chapter, then, is how DIA research may be brought to bear to facilitate the incorporation of paper records in the voting process.

3.2. History

The earliest applications of DIA targeted the conversion of typewritten documents into text files through Optical Character Recognition (OCR). Many of these documents had a very simple format because they were copied from original sources by human typists specifically for input to OCR, a process that was less expensive than keypunching them. Others were preprinted turn- around forms such as invoices where the location and typeface (e.g., OCR-A) of preprinted critical information (a customer name and address, for example) could be tightly controlled at the source of the document.

Applications to specialized large-volume applications like postal addresses, bank checks, and postal money orders followed in time, improving over the decades in accuracy and throughput. More recently, full-fledged forms-processing for medical claims, income taxes, and purchase orders became viable through contextual post-processing. A significant fraction of such forms – usually filled out by hand – still requires operator intervention. The development of low-volume "personal" OCR systems was spurred by the advent of (1) microprocessors fast enough to perform feature extraction and classification without additional hardware and (2) low-cost scanners for the large facsimile market. However, the recognition of typeset print turned out to be more difficult than expected. Only within the last ten years have we seen volume conversion of archival books and journals for digital libraries. Without human correction, the quality of OCR output still leaves much to be desired.

Mark-sense readers preceded OCR by several decades: the IBM 805 Test Scoring Machine was introduced in 1937. Because punch card technology was already well developed, it was easy to add sensors to detect conductive marks made by "electrographic" pencils. Optical Mark Recognition (OMR), introduced in the 1950s, measured reflectivity instead of resistance, allowing use of a much wider range of writing instruments for multiple choice examinations. For a standard examination, the questions were printed next to the "bubbles." For low volume tests, general-purpose answer sheets, with numbered rows and columns of bubbles, were used in conjunction with an instruction sheet.

The bubbles were lined up in columns, with one photodetector for each column. Two additional photosensors scanned fiducial marks, aligned with each row of bubbles, at the edges of the sheet. The row and column sensors were ANDed to avoid triggering false positives by stray marks between rows. The bubbles were relatively large and the marks had to fill most of the bubble in order to be surely sensed. This technology was eventually adapted to election ballots (Figure 3.1) modeled on the classic Australian secret ballots which had been in use since 1858 (when they were, of course, counted by hand).

The development of reliable, low-cost facsimile scanners had an impact on OMR as on OCR. The sensors now swept the entire page, and even small marks were covered several times by several sensors as the paper transport slid the page under the sensor bar (Figure 3.2). Image processing techniques could now be applied to discriminate marks according to shape and color rather than only total reflectance. This lead to new designs for more space-efficient and more easily applicable marks, such as horizontal or vertical line segments in a diamond, or filling a gap in a broken arrow. Further, 1-D or 2-D barcode reading for unique ballot identification could be added at little cost.

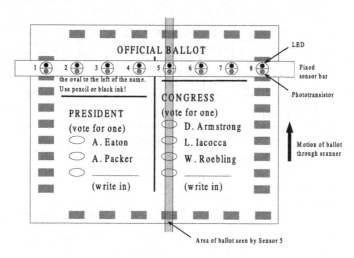

Fig. 3.1.   OMR scanner with a single discrete photosensor for each column of bubbles. (adapted from Counting Mark-Sense Ballots, Voting and Elections web pages by Douglas W. Jones, Department of Computer Science, The University of Iowa, 2002).

OMR is only one of many current voting technologies. Typical examples of three other popular types of ballot casting machines are illustrated in Figure 3.3. Lever-actuated voting machines with mechanical gear counters were widely used in the United States until recently, but are now being abandoned because of the prohibitive cost of replacement parts and because they appear to violate the accessibility for disabled voters requirements of the Help America Vote Act (HAVA). In many election districts, votes are registered by punching out selected chips on a card with a stylus. Punched card readers are, however, vulnerable to partially removed chips ("hanging chads" in Florida made headlines in the Year 2000 US Presidential Election), and may also violate HAVA.

The most common current technology is Direct Recording Electronic (DRE) voting machines that tally votes entered on a touch-sensitive screen to internal memory in the machine. Often, votes are recorded redundantly across several memory modules, some volatile, some non- volatile. Recently these machines have come under criticism for a variety of reasons, including the possibility they can be "hacked" to steal an election. Consequently, opinion in the US has seen a swing towards a desire for paper-based technologies that reduce the risk of accidental or deliberate falsification of election results. In particular, legislative bodies are increasingly mandating either paper ballots or a Voter Verifiable Paper Audit Trail (VVPAT).

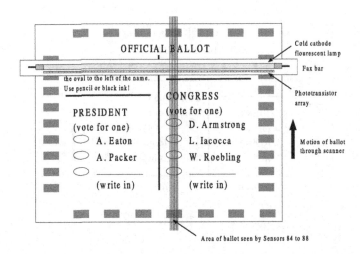

Fig. 3.2. OMR scanner with a fax bar photosensor assembly. (adapted from from Counting Mark-Sense Ballots, Voting and Elections web pages by Douglas W. Jones, Department of Computer Science, The University of Iowa).

Fig. 3.3. Alternative voting technologies: lever machine, punched card, DRE.

While it is obvious that paper ballots provide a direct hardcopy record that can be later recounted by hand or by machine, VVPAT also allows immediate comparison of a cast vote with a permanent human-readable record on paper by attaching a small printer to the electronic voting machine. In either case, the paper record is routed without further access by the voter to a secure container that is sealed after the close of voting and retained for a possible recount or audit. While VVPAT has been touted as a cost-effective way to upgrade existing DRE machines, whether voters can be expected to pay close attention to a paper record printed after-the-fact is a serious concern that has been raised and may make VVPAT less desirable than a return to hand- or machine-marked paper ballots.

Indication of possible problems in ballot reading include unexpectedly large over or under counts. An overcount occurs when the number of votes cast exceeds the number of voters. Undercounts typically occur because voters vote for only some of the offices or propositions appearing on the ballot. It is important to note that overvoting detected on a particular ballot (for example, voting for two candidates for the same office when only one choice is allowed) typically invalidates the ballot in question. Under such circumstances, the ballot is usually flagged for manual examination, so mistakes will likely be caught. Hence, it is higher than normal rates of undervoting, which is legal, that is more likely to raise concerns of undetected errors in a system.

As it stands today, paper is often treated as a simple "add-on" to all-electronic systems when it should be an integral component in trustworthy voting technology. A good deal of attention is already being paid to other parts of election systems; but there has been little effort to elucidate the substantial benefits that accrue when paper artifacts are accorded the attention they deserve. Election records can be seen as a new DIA application where the DIA and OCR communities can bring improvements to current practices.

The remainder of this chapter is organized as follows. The causes and manifestations of the current interest in paper-based voting technologies are discussed in Section 3.3. Some possible directions for research on problems specifically associated with voting systems are proposed in Section 3.4. Leads to past and ongoing research on various aspects of election machinery are presented in Section 3.5. Brief conclusions are given in Section 3.6.

3.3. Problems with Current Voting Technologies

As we have already noted, our purview is limited to elections in the United States, although similar concerns have been raised in other countries. Florida's infamous "butterfly ballot" and resulting recount efforts during the 2000 Presidential Election, leading directly to the Help America Vote

Act, have initiated dramatic changes in the way America votes. Not long
after the subsequent introduction of electronic voting equipment, computer
security experts and concerned citizens began raising serious questions regarding the reliability and trustworthiness of such systems when collecting,
storing, and tabulating votes.[3-8] Direct Record Electronic Voting (DRE)
systems, once seen as a straightforward albeit expensive solution, are increasingly regarded as an unacceptable compromise.

In its recent draft report on Voluntary Voting Systems Guidelines for
2007,[9] the Security and Transparency Subcommittee for the Technical
Guidelines Development Committee of the National Institute of Standards
and Technology (NIST) wrote:

> "One conclusion drawn by NIST is that the lack of
> an independent audit capability in DRE voting systems is
> one of the main reasons behind continued questions about
> voting system security and diminished public confidence
> in elections. NIST does not know how to write testable
> requirements to make DREs secure, and NIST's recom-
> mendation to the STS is that the DRE in practical terms
> cannot be made secure. Consequently, NIST and the STS
> recommend that VVSG 2007 should require voting systems
> to be of the SI [software independent] "class," whose read-
> ily available (albeit not always optimal) examples include
> op scan and DRE-VVPAT [Direct Record Electronic with
> Voter Verifiable Paper Audit Trail]."

Here the term *independent* is taken to mean a record of the vote that is
maintained physically beyond the scope of malicious software to modify it,
e.g., a paper record. The NIST report continues on to observe that the use
of paper to provide independent auditing capabilities in elections is entirely
practical, but that there are undeniably open technical issues that can and
should be addressed:

> "The widespread adoption of voting systems incorpo-
> rating paper did not seem to cause any widespread prob-
> lems in the November 2006 elections. But, the use of paper
> in elections places more stress on (1) the capabilities of vot-
> ing system technology, (2) of voters to verify their accuracy,
> and (3) of election workers to securely handle the ballots
> and accurately count them. Clearly, the needs of voters

and election officials need to be addressed with improved
and new technology. The STS believes that current paper-
based approaches can be improved to be significantly more
usable to voters and election officials ..."

Introducing (or, rather, re-introducing) paper into the election process
is not above criticism, some of which is certainly valid. It is essential
to eliminate or mitigate the current drawbacks associated with hardcopy
form. There are also a myriad of other, non-technical concerns that have
been voiced, ranging from a feeling that paper is "old fashioned," to worries
about increased "litter," and the added cost of the required consumables
(paper, ink/toner for printers, etc.). A recent article in the New York
Times[10] hits on a number of the key points:

> "New federal guidelines, along with legislation given a
> strong chance to pass in Congress next year, will proba-
> bly combine to make the paperless voting machines obso-
> lete, the officials say. States and counties that bought the
> machines will have to modify them to hook up printers,
> at federal expense, while others are planning to scrap the
> machines and buy new ones ...
>
> Advocates for the disabled say they will resist his bill,
> because the touch-screen machines are the easiest for blind
> people to use ...
>
> Paul S. DeGregorio, the chairman of the federal
> Election Assistance Commission, which was created by
> Congress in 2002 to set voting standards, also cautioned
> against rushing to make changes, especially since some
> counties also ran into problems with printers in this year's
> elections ...
>
> Beverly Kaufman, the county clerk [in Harris County,
> TX], said she and other election officials elsewhere disliked
> the paper requirement ... 'Every time you introduce some-
> thing perishable like paper, you inject some uncertainty
> into the system,' Ms. Kaufman said."

Touch-screen systems do indeed offer the option of providing audio output (text-to-speech) for blind voters, as well as feedback for positioning
one's finger to cast a vote. This goal does not necessitate the use of DRE
systems that record votes electronically, however. Ballot-marking devices

provide the same touch-screen interface for voting without tallying the votes themselves; rather, they produce a printed paper ballot which the voter can then place into a scanner, much as if the voter marked on a regular ballot with a standard pen or pencil.

The evidence that major hurdles lie ahead is growing rapidly, at least with respect to VVPAT. In another recent article, the Atlanta Journal-Constitution[11] reports:

> "An examination of the much discussed e-voting paper-trail audit system used in several Georgia districts revealed that the process is far from a silver bullet. The paper-trail solution gained popularity in the wake of many warnings from computer scientists that e- voting machines were vulnerable to tampering. Cobb County, Ga. head of elections Sharon Dunn recently testified in front of state officials, who are considering making paper-trails mandatory in all of the state's voting districts, regarding the effort needed to manually count the 976 printouts generated in the district: Twenty-eight people took part in the five-day task of counting the votes from 42 races, and teams often had to restart their counts as numbers did not match up. Dunn testified, 'It looks easy until you have to do it.' ... MIT political science professor specializing in elections Charles Stewart said, 'Audits ask humans to do something that computers are generally better at doing.' "

There are undeniably problems that must be addressed. For example, paper jams can wreak havoc when DRE (Direct Recording Electronic) systems are equipped with printers to produce a paper audit trail. Cuyahoga County, Ohio, found that a manual count did not match the computer-tallied results because 10 percent of ballots were either smeared, torn, crumpled, or blank.[12] In Chester County, PA, a close election that would determine the majority party in the PA House of Representatives was disputed when one party insisted that a recount be conducted by running the optical scan ballots through a different brand of scanner hardware, noting that the tallies can vary depending on the system in use.[13]

The certification examinations for electronic voting systems in Pennsylvania are a matter of public record[14] and are videotaped. During the recent certification of one optical scanning system,[15] the final vote tallies for nearly all of the candidates of one political party were wrong, while the votes for the candidates of the other party were all right. There is no reason to suspect the scanner was functioning incorrectly – the system provided no indication that anything was amiss. In the end, a decision was reached that the problem was due to some unspecified hardware/software flaw. Nevertheless, the system was certified for use. A group at the University of Connecticut has shown how easy it is to reprogram the Diebold AV-OS ballot scanner into misreading ballots.[16] The presence of such failure modes in paper- based electronic voting systems, completely undetectable during normal operation, is one of the urgent issues that need to be addressed.

Trustworthy elections are a function of the experience and attitudes of the citizens who use the system (or decide not to) as well as of the hardware and software used to collect, tabulate, and audit votes. E-voting protocols shown to be mathematically "sound" through a rigorous theoretical analysis might still fail to win public acceptance if the voting process is regarded as incomprehensible, the threats are not well understand by average citizens, or the procedures for auditing elections and conducting recounts do not inspire confidence.

In a professional telephone survey conducted in the fall of 2006,[17] 523 Pennsylvania voters expressed moderate levels of confidence in the new e-voting systems, but they also expressed overwhelmingly support for machines that show voters paper verification of the votes they cast, with 81% stating they believe such verification is important. In comparing the public's trust in electronic voting with their trust in other widely-used technologies, voting machines came out somewhere in the middle. Overall, respondents trust electronic voting machines much less than automated teller machines (ATMs), but more than financial transactions on the Internet or even airport security systems.

DIA issues are presented by all three alternative uses of hardcopy in electoral systems:

(1) VVPAT output by DRE systems,
(2) human-marked ballots counted by hand or via image processing techniques, and
(3) machine-marked ballots which likewise can be counted either way.

While many computer security experts argue strongly in favor of options (2) and (3), option (1) may be popular with municipalities that have already invested heavily in current DRE e-voting systems. Some believe it may be possible to upgrade such systems with the addition of a printer in a way that mitigates certain of the shortcomings in the current products.

Option (2) requires the development of more efficient and effective methods of counting and auditing paper ballots, both at the voting location and at election headquarters. However, the most promising and interesting possibilities may lie with option (3), which spans both the reading and interpreting of ballots from current screen-based ballot-marking devices (essentially computer-controlled printers) to the development of new direct-action electro-optical marking devices, as exemplified by the use of "smart pens" to record votes both electronically and on paper simultaneously in a recent small-scale Scottish election.[18] Alternatively, op-scan forms could be marked while overlaid on a graphic tablet, with a pen that can be sensed electronically yet leaves a mark on the form. However, many of the DIA issues that relate specifically to the accurate and robust interpretation of marks on paper are shared by the three options.

3.4. Experimental Approaches to Reliable Processing of Voting Records

We have cited above a range of problems that are inherent in the hardware and software design of current optical scanning systems. In this section, we propose developing experimental techniques for collecting data that will allow characterizing existing voting systems or lead to new designs. We discuss

(1) the statistical distribution of mark sense errors as a function of ballot quality;
(2) blind recording for unbiased visual auditing based on ballot images;
(3) homogeneous class displays (HCD) for speeding up manual recounts;
(4) RFID and digital watermarking for securing paper ballots;
(5) impact on error behavior when VVPAT is used with DRE systems;
(6) test procedures for paper handling under operational constraints;
(7) access for handicapped voters.

3.4.1. *Statistical distribution of mark sense errors*

Some examples of valid and invalid markings, extracted from the official State of Michigan voting guide for election officials[19] are shown in Figures 3.4 and 3.5. Although the ballots may give explicit directions for filling in ovals or connecting the heads and tails of arrows, ballots cannot be disqualified merely because a voter fails to obey the directions. The law mandates that the vote should be interpreted according to the voter's intention.

The sensitivity of an OMR vote tabulating machine to deviations from ideal marks and absence of marks can be tested through synthetically generated marks that straddle the dividing line between valid and invalid marks. An experimental protocol could be printing marks that span the range from clearly valid to clearly invalid with respect to sensitivity to five characteristics: (1) position, (2) size, (3) contrast, (4) color, (5) shape.

Ballots with series of synthetic marks, with both single and combined distortions, could be run through selected OMR scanners. For automated data collection it would be essential to identify each test ballot with a bar code. Classification statistics should be aggregated per mark, per ballot, and per machine. These distributions would allow informed inferences about the effects of misalignment, reflectance calibration, writing instruments. It would be desirable to also estimate joint error probability distributions, which would be necessary for an op-scan system that makes appropriate use of style information instead of making an independent decision on each mark. Recent research on recognizing fields of same-source characters could help exploit the consistency of marks for different offices by the same voter.[20]

We omit detailed calculations of the required sample size, but believe that a reasonable experimental design calls for repeated scanning of ballots in three layouts (tight, medium, loose) and five characteristics as listed above. If one thousand ballot specimens (with a total of about 100,000 marks) of each of the 15 designs were printed and run 10 times through an OMR ballot reader at 1 second per ballot, then testing a single reader would require $15 \times 10 \times 1,000 = 150,000$ seconds or approximately 40 hours. The number of runs can be reduced without loss of statistical significance by a more sophisticated experimental design with intermixed characteristics. Figure 3.6 shows a synthetic ballot with a range of variation in the marks.

The mark sense technology used today was developed decades ago and is largely based on binary image processing. With current scanner technology, there is little cost, speed, or storage benefit associated with binary scans. We should therefore investigate the intrinsic trade-off between depth (number of gray levels) and spatial sampling rate (pixels per unit area) for ballot scanners, as well as improvements for gray-scan binarization, based on existing algorithms. As a byproduct of the above experiments, data can be gathered on the throughput (peak and average, per machine), failure rate, and failure mode of each machine, keeping track of fixed and operating cost and physical scanner characteristics (size, weight, and vulnerability to tampering).

Estimating the positive response rate of an OMR system as a function of various distortions does not by itself allow estimating its expected error rate in an actual election. Further analysis, based on image processing and pattern recognition, is required to determine the population statistics of the characteristics of ballot marks. This can be done only with access to actual ballots. Fortunately, US law requires preservation of ballots for a two month period after each election. Such research would ideally take into account demographics such as age, gender, education and income, but that is far afield of DIA.

3.4.2. Unbiased context-free visual auditing based on ballot images

Recounts and audits can be triggered by very close elections, by specific complaints possibly due to a disagreement between exit polls and reported results, or by a number of overvotes or undervotes over a legally set threshold. However, corrupt vote counters could add spurious marks to ballots, thereby invalidating them (because of conflicting marks) in subsequent recounts. If instead votes are counted on displays of digital ballot images, this avenue for compromising election results is rendered unworkable.

Auditing elections through electronic images of the paper trail offers certain additional benefits over auditing the paper trail itself. The main advantage is that image-based auditing can be carried out simultaneously by physically separated election inspectors in parallel. Furthermore, it is infinitely repeatable because the electronic image is preserved intact. There is, however, an added cost for a limited amount of write-once storage for each scanner. Whether such auditing would prove acceptable to voters is a key question that requires social science expertise. There is still, however, the possibility of voluntary or involuntary bias in counting. Blind Recording is a simple way of avoiding such bias.

Human vote counts using context versus human counts without using context (oddly called *blind recording*) can be compared experimentally. Context is present when enough of the ballot is visible to the human counter to identify the party, candidate, or proposition for which a vote was cast. We note that context removal requires more than simply masking the preprinted information, because in any single election the position of the

Valid markings: Each of the examples provided below is a <u>valid vote</u> as there is a mark within the "predefined area" for casting a vote.

Invalid markings: Each of the examples provided below is an <u>invalid vote</u> as a mark does <u>not</u> appear within the "predefined area" for casting a vote.

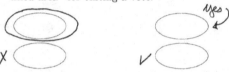

Corrections: A correction that causes a "false" tabulator read does not count as a valid vote. (Counts for top position only.)

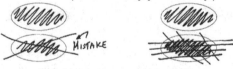

Stray marks: "A stray mark made within a predefined area is not a valid vote. In determining whether a mark within a predefined area is a stray mark, the board of canvassers or election official shall compare the mark with other marks appearing on the ballot." (Counts for top two positions only.)

Candidate A

Candidate B

Candidate C

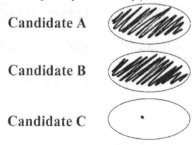

Fig. 3.4. Examples of valid and invalid marks for oval OMR targets.[19]

Valid markings: Each of the examples provided below is a <u>valid vote</u> as there is a mark within the "predefined area" for casting a vote.

Invalid markings: Each of the examples provided below is an <u>invalid vote</u> as a mark does <u>not</u> appear within the "predefined area" for casting a vote.

Corrections: A correction that causes a "false" tabulator read does not count as a valid vote. (Counts for top position only.)

Stray marks: "A stray mark made within a predefined area is not a valid vote. In determining whether a mark within a predefined area is a stray mark, the board of canvassers or election official shall compare the mark with other marks appearing on the ballot." (Counts for top two positions only.)

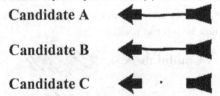

Fig. 3.5. Examples of valid and invalid marks for arrow OMR targets.[19]

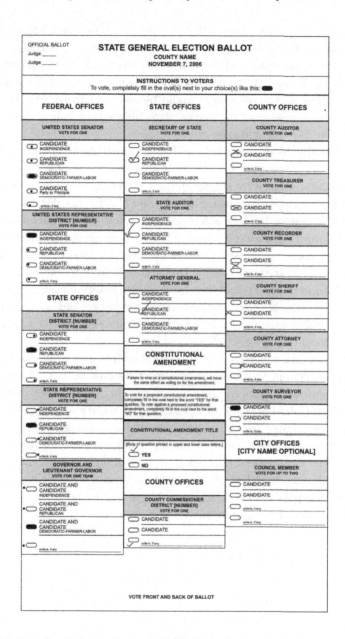

Fig. 3.6.   Synthetic marks for testing OMR sensitivity to position and size.

targets is fixed and can be readily memorized. The mark areas of each ballot must be displayed in pseudo-randomly scrambled positions. This is illustrated in Figures 3.7 and 3.8, where the former shows the original ballot as voted (left) and the shuffled ballot (right), while the latter shows the blinded version of the ballot as it would be audited. To help judge "voter intent" by commonality of the marks' style, all the targets in a given ballot should be displayed simultaneously.

It is desirable to scan synthetic ballots at much higher spatial sampling rate than is necessary for mark-sensing in order to be able to construct lower-resolution images by sub-sampling. Lowering image resolution can result in less expensive and faster devices and also further decrease storage cost, but this cannot be done safely without quantitative understanding of the resolution/error trade-off. Since some research groups advocate injecting artificial noise for stress-testing of election machinery, one could find out whether, contrary to our earlier conclusions,[21] artificial noise provides a viable test procedure. Typical document image quality measures are based on the distribution of the shape and size of the foreground components. A measure of ballot quality can be based on earlier research on statistically detectable local distortions.[22-28]

Semi-automating election recounts could address one of the most pressing issues in moving to paper support for electronic voting. An example of a successful semiautomatic recognition system is the Remote Encoding System of the United States Postal Service. When the automated OCR system fails to recognize an address (as indicated by a disagreement between street address, city, state, country and zip code), an image of the envelope is routed over a high-speed network to a bank of human data entry operators. While human encoding of postal address images has been an economic success for the postal service, additional legal and social constraints must be taken into account for election systems.

3.4.3. *Homogenous class display*

A second means of verifying automated mark sense counts is inspired by a long-established methods of OCR verification, Homogenous Class Display (HCD). Here the isolated images where a mark was registered are grouped for display. The images where a mark was not registered are similarly grouped. The positive marks are displayed simultaneously , and the human operator is asked to enter any discrepancies. The negative (i.e., blank) instances are displayed in similar groupings, and again the operator notates any perceived discrepancies. This is demonstrated in Figure 3.9.

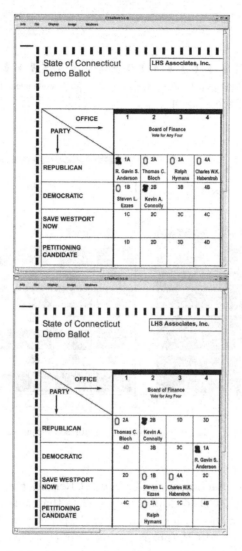

Fig. 3.7.   Original (upper) and shuffled (lower) ballot images.

Spurious marks can be introduced to assess human error rate. (In some OCR service bureaus, the operators are notified of the presence of artificial errors in order to keep them alert.) HCD is, in principle, a very fast and convenient method of verifying automated counts, but it can never be accepted without experimental evidence of its accuracy.

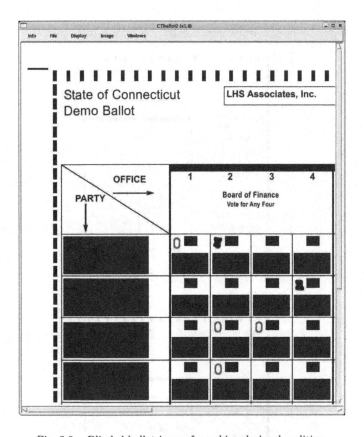

Fig. 3.8.   Blinded ballot image for unbiased visual auditing.

Following the practice of the US Postal Remote Encoding System,[29] one could modify HCD to display only bullets that were not classified as marked or blank with very high confidence. Experience with high-accuracy financial OCR and MICR (magnetic ink character recognition) suggests that reject/error ratios of the order of 100:1 or even 1,000:1 are necessary to achieve acceptable levels of undetected errors at the election precinct level. Since errors within a ballot are likely to be correlated, a more sophisticated reject strategy can be based on the confidence level of multiple marks on the same ballot.

To avoid tedious ground-truthing, the database described in Section 3.4.1 could be used in conjunction with a database of the values of the various degradation parameters for each target. Human accuracy on

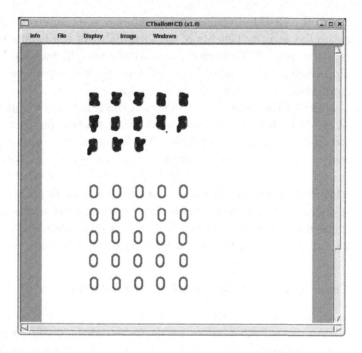

Fig. 3.9. Homogeneous Class Display (HCD).

the paper ballots themselves can be compared with human accuracy on their images as a function of ballot characteristics, scan resolution, inspection speed, display size, and display quality. The resulting information should be valuable for both election planning and commercial development of improved voting machinery.

Experimental protocols can be designed to find out whether the proposed procedures can guarantee the absence of systematic bias, and to determine how many duplicate audits are required to reduce the expected number of random errors to some acceptable level.

3.4.4. *Unique identification of ballots*

Several classical voting scams are based on ballot switching which can take place on the way to the voting station, when the ballots are collected, or during a recount. Although in recent years physical security measures and custody-chain policies appear to have largely eliminated en- masse ballot substitution, embedding radio frequency identification (RFID) in ballots,[30] or watermarking or 2-D bar-coding could guarantee voter anonymity without giving up the security benefits of the identifiably of the ballots themselves. Some current RFID devices, such as the Hitachi mu-chip,[31] are already thin enough to be embedded in medium- weight paper, and their cost is approaching that of a single sheet of paper.

The simplest RFID system would suffice. A single unique 12-digit number is associated with each ballot prepared for an election precinct. It is recorded at the time the ballot is printed. The list of numbers is separately transmitted to the district election officials, who can verify that they correspond to the collected ballots. If the blank ballots are handled by the voters rather than automatically fed to a remote-control mark printer, then it may be desirable to introduce a further read station in the local scanner. However, the possibility of concealed external RFID readers, that would allow associating a ballot with a voter, presents a threat to voter privacy.

3.4.5. *Error characteristics of DRE with VVPAT*

As mentioned in Section 3.3, DRE with VVPAT provides the voter an opportunity to verify that the touch-screen device recorded the vote correctly. This is done by inspecting a printed output generated by a separate device attached to the touch screen, much like the verification of a charge-card transaction through a printed receipt. The record could be designed for OMR or OCR, but in either case before casting the vote, the voter must be able to ascertain by visual inspection that it corresponds to his or her intention. The voter cannot obtain a copy of the printed record of the vote, because this may allow payment for a prespecified vote ("vote selling"), but the record is preserved for audits and recounts.

A major drawback of the roll-paper record provided by some e-voting vendors is that it preserves not only each vote, but also the voting sequence. This could be compared to the observed arrival of voters and imperil voter anonymity. Most such systems therefore print only enough information (at the beginning and the end of a voting session) to support a limited form of tallying from the paper record, recording the full audit trail on a write-once medium. Many questions regarding the adequacy of such audits remain to be resolved, however. Assuming that cut-paper printers with full vote records (a la the "Mercuri Method"[32]) are substituted for roll-paper printers, then such a device bears a superficial resemblence to a machine ballot marking system. The major difference is that here the vote is still recorded electronically, and the paper record may never be scanned.

Since such systems may be adopted by some election districts, it is important to assess the error rate of the OCR system necessary to process the human-readable record.[33] Research is required to determine the most effective means of reaching the required accuracy. Possible candidates include (1) an appropriate OCR font, (2) adequate vertical and horizontal spacing,[34] (3) self-inking paper or carbon-film ribbon, (4) coded input, and (5) maintenance-free sealed printer design.

We note that markings created by a human must be minimal in order to save time. No voter (or test-taking student) would want to darken three bubbles instead of one in order to record a single bit of information! This same constraint does not, however, apply to either machine-generated marks or to machine-generated alphanumeric symbols. It takes only a very short code to represent a single bit of data extremely reliably: even a simple five-bit majority code lowers the error rate by three orders of magnitude. It should therefore be possible devise appropriate means of encoding votes intended for OMR (optical mark recognition) or OCR. Note, however, that the coded representation must be fully interpretable by voters, otherwise malicious software could produce two different records and exploit the lack of readability of the machine record to bias the election results.

3.4.6. *Development of testing procedures for voting systems*

Reviews of the procedures for certifying e-voting systems suggest that test protocols that already fall short of providing the necessary assurances will break down completely for the systems that process paper voting records at ultra-low error rates. New estimation techniques will be required, as will operational procedures for differentiating voter error from machine error, determination of optimal "reject" rates for mark sense systems, sampling methods for comparing the results of electronic and paper tallies, statistical methods for uncovering suspicious runs of votes that may indicate a latent hardware or software malfunction, and the insertion of predetermined test votes into the voting stream to catch errors as early as possible. Although some of these issues are outside the purview of DIA, current practices in bank check and postal address reading may suggest several quality control measures appropriate for election systems.

For the DIA community, the major user interface issues are those that pertain to e-voting systems that produce hardcopy records, including the positioning and rendering of candidate names (choice of font, font size, colors, layout of the ballot/audit trail), feedback to confirm votes, mechanisms for correcting mistakes as well as for confirming or cancelling ballots, and implications for access by the disabled (Section 3.4.7). The critical variables include voting time, voter confidence, required training, voter and device error rates, and system cost, durability, and robustness.

The impact of "wear and tear" on voting systems is different than in financial, postal, and standardized test-grading applications because of the preponderance of minimally trained poll workers and local officials. In contrast to research and commercial settings, voting machines are often kept locked in dusty, humid storerooms most of the year.

Beyond inhospitable storage environments, software bugs, and malicious attempts to compromise the system, there is no doubt that human error is responsible for a great many problems. While voter error rates have been studied fairly extensively (e.g., in the reports on voter error rates by the Caltech/MIT Voting Technology Project), the impact of errors made by poll workers and local election officials have received less attention. How can poorly-trained and perhaps technology-hostile workers inadvertently mess things up? Can better design mitigate such problems?

3.4.7. *Affordances for voters with disabilities*

Providing voting systems accessible to citizens with disabilities was one of the driving forces behind the Help America Vote Act that allocated over two billion dollars for voting equipment. Touch screen systems provide several obvious affordances in this regard, including the ability to increase the font size and contrast ratio for voters suffering from visual impairments, the option of incorporating text-to-speech synthesis (TTS) to "read" ballots to voters who are blind, multilingual display options that are set to the voter's preferred language when he/she first approaches the machine, and sufficient portability/flexibility to allow voters in wheelchairs to make use of the system.

We note, however, that the careless incorporation of paper records in the election process can "break" many of these affordances. A VVPAT cannot be verified by someone who cannot see; current systems often print such records on narrow, low-contrast, cheap devices designed for printing retail sales receipts in small and poorly distinguishable characters.[35]

An informative study conducted by researchers at Georgia Tech[36] produced the following conclusions:

- Voters with disabilities were 7% to 20% less likely to report satisfaction with the equipment than voters without disabilities.

- Of the complaints that voters expressed, 20% concerned the display characteristics of on- screen text, 31% were regarding the placement or design of controls, and 48% were due to the quality of the audio/sound output.
- More voters with disabilities reported problems (60%) than voters without disabilities (39%).
- Finally, 16% of voters said that lack of privacy was a key concern in using e-voting machines.

Hence, while HAVA was intended to address the question of accessibility, it is clear that many issues still remain. Methods must be developed to evaluate the readability (content) and legibility (appearance) of the short, low-entropy messages involved in voting. The primary concern is how the use of paper records in an election setting, either as ballots or as a VVPAT, impacts voters with disabilities. Paper should not be seen as adverse to accessible elections.

3.5. Some Related Efforts

An excellent survey on all aspects of counting mark-sense ballots is the already mentioned.[37] A recent ACM-sponsored USENIX workshop was dedicated specifically to voting systems.[38] Some of the papers presented at that venue are relevant to our topic.

Aslam and Rivest offer a simple formula for computing the size of an audit, should one be necessary. The formula can be computed with a hand calculator: perhaps if one cannot trust computers to count votes, then using a computer to calculate how much of an audit is needed for an election would also be a mistake. The formula yields a guaranteed bound on the significance of the results and provides a basis for cost-benefit analysis of improved audit procedures.[39]

Calandrino et al. point out that ballot-by-ballot auditing is far more efficient than precinct auditing. They present a scheme for choosing which ballots to audit. The ballot must be scanned and then given unique identifying numbers, presumably after the election so that the ID's can't be used to link back to the original voter. It is assumed that the ballots can be scanned and read by machine with no errors. These results are then correlated with the manual audit.[40]

Researchers at Rice show that human auditors have trouble counting VVPAT ballots by hand. They find it very tiresome and make many mistakes, supporting the need for automating the tally of the paper trail.[41]

An intriguing idea drawn from Game Theory is offered in.[42] It is suggested that many basic problems with running elections will diappear if the voter is given the option of deciding, at the last minute, not to cast a particular (encrypted) ballot, but rather demand that the system decrypt it to prove that it has been recorded correctly and not tampered with. The voter is then given a chance to encrypt and cast another ballot, of course. The claim is that if the voter can be permitted to act unpredictably, so that the system never knows if a given ballot will be cast or challenged, many options for tampering with the election are eliminated.

Another potentially valuable suggestion is the use of "prerendered" ballots that consist essentially of bitmaps of ballot images with semantics unintelligible to a computer system. The voting machine has an interface that the human can deal with, but that the machine can't understand sufficiently to know what the human is trying to do (hence making it hard for someone to hack the machine to steal votes). This also makes the internal software of the voting machine simpler, and therefore easier to verify, since all it has to do is display a prerendered- interface, not actually render it in real time.[43] The experimental protocols suggested in Section 3.4.1 are, in fact, based on prerendered ballots.

The DIA research opportunities described in Section 3.4 are complementary to existing efforts examining various aspects of electronic voting. Below we list some of the better-known activities, noting that there are also many researchers working individually.

ACCURATE (Center for Correct, Usable, Reliable, Auditable, and Transparent Elections) is a multi-institution voting research center funded by the National Science Foundation (NSF) under its CyberTrust program. In a broad sense, the goals of the center – to research ways in which technology can be used to improve voting, to educate the public about voting-related issues, and to serve as a resource to a variety of constituencies. A perusal of the research interests and publications of ACCURATE participants shows work on user interfaces, privacy, testability of voting systems, and new data structures for more secure auditing. The usability of traditional (hand-marked) paper ballots was examined in a study involving human subjects.[44] Not reflected in the center's activities is the sort of work we have described on characterizing the machine processing of paper voting records, developing methods that result in ultra-low error rates, exploring new ways of using paper to facilitate trustworthy elections, and measuring public trust and acceptance of these various alternatives.

The Center for Information Technology Policy at Princeton University addresses societal issues that go beyond electronic voting, such as privacy and security, that have a connection to advances in computer technology. Their publication of a detailed analysis of the flaws in a touch screen e-voting system produced by a major vendor just before the 2006 midterm election raised public awareness of these issues.[8]

Created in the wake of the 2000 presidential election, the MIT-CALTECH Voting Technology Project performs large-scale longitudinal studies of elections for residual votes, comparing the original results and recounts sorted by technology.

The UConn Voting Technology Research Center takes as its mission advising state agencies in the use of voting technologies and developing procedures for safely using such equipment in elections. As with the Princeton Center for Information Technology Policy, they performed a detailed analysis of an existing e-voting system (in this case, an optical ballot scanner) identifying numerous security flaws.[45]

3.6. Concluding Remarks

It is difficult to conceive of anything with broader impact than the development of reliable and trustworthy voting technology. Because elections in many countries, including the United States, are governed by laws and procedural rules promulgated at multiple levels of government, the preparations required by the sheer size of many elections, and the cost of change in terms of equipment purchase, voter education, and the training of election officials, voting technologies tend to evolve slowly. Even before Robert Putnam published *Bowling Alone*,[46] which documents how the erosion of social connections in the United States has diminished public trust, scholars and political observers alike have worried about declining rates of voting and public apathy toward politics. We are now at a cross-roads, with several radically different voting technologies competing for acceptance. It is therefore timely to examine the human and cybernetic dimensions of the major contenders, with a focus on the role to be played by paper records.

Known image processing methods can be used to minimize undetected failure. We can devise tests for detectable failures, develop real-time diagnostics, warn the poll workers and election judges about such failures, and provide guidelines for ballot layouts that ensure random or systematic errors do not disadvantage one candidate over another. We can help accelerate the drawn-out transition from binary to grey-scale and color scanning for text and mark images, and perhaps transfer some results to more secure terminals for electronic transactions.

Research on this topic can also engender more efficient human involvement in OCR and OMR in similar ultra-low error-rate applications like educational testing, where interaction will remain indispensable for decades. The importance of unbiased human intervention and improved error- estimation will increase as data entry tasks are being passed down to the end user in financial, marketing, medical, and census applications. It is a topic where the DIA community, which has traditionally concentrated on wholly automated systems, must assume a pro-active role.

References

1. Wikipedia. Elections in India (November, 2007).
   http://en.wikipedia.org/wiki/Elections_in_India.
2. Wikipedia. Indian voting machines (November, 2007).
   http://en.wikipedia.org/wiki/Indian_voting_machines.
3. T. Kohno, A. Stubblefield, A. D. Rubin, and D. S. Wallach. Analysis of an electronic voting system. In *Proceedings of the IEEE Symposium on Security and Privacy* (May, 2004).
4. M. A. Wertheimer. Trusted agent report: Diebold AccuVote-TS voting system. Technical report, RABA Innovative Solution Cell (January 20, 2004).
5. H. Hursti. The Black Box Report: Critical security issues with Diebold optical scan design. Technical report, Black Box Voting Project (July 4, 2005).
6. The machinery of democracy: Protecting elections in an electronic world. Technical report, The Brennan Center Task Force on Voting System Security (June 27, 2006). http://www.brennancenter.org/ programs/downloads/-Full%20Report.pdf.
7. H. Hursti. Diebold TSx evaluation: Critical security issues with Diebold TSx. Technical report, Black Box Voting Project (May 11, 2006).
8. A. J. Feldman, J. A. Halderman, and E. W. Felten. Security analysis of the Diebold AccuVote-TS voting machine. Technical report, Princeton Center for Information Technology (September 13, 2006).
9. W. Burr, J. Kelsey, R. Peralta, and J. Wack. Requiring software independence in VVSG 2007: STS recommendations for the TGDC. Technical report, National Institute of Standards and Technology (November, 2006). http://vote.nist.gov/DraftWhitePaperOnSIinVVSG2007-20061120.pdf.
10. I. Urbina and C. Drew. Changes are expected in voting by 2008 election. The New York Times (December 8, 2006).
11. C. Campos. Voter paper trail not an easy path. Atlanta Journal-Constitution (December 22, 2006).
12. S. Manning. Paper jams a problem for electronic voting. The Washington Post (Associated Press) (December 21, 2006).

13. Associated Press. Parties outline recount proposals with house control at stake (December 12, 2006). www.whptv.com.
14. Examination reports issued by the Secretary of the Commonwealth. http://www.hava.state.pa.us/hava/cwp/view.asp?a=1283&Q=445840.
15. Commonwealth of Pennsylvania: Certification videotape for Diebold Optiscan e-voting system (November 22, 2005). Michael Shamos, examiner.
16. A. Kiayias, L. Michel, A. Russell, N. Sashidar, A. See, and A. Shvartsman. An authentication and ballot layout attack against an optical scan voting terminal. In *Proceedings of the USENIX/ACCURATE Electronic Voting Technology Workshop* (August, 2007). http://www.usenix.org/events/evt07/tech/.
17. C. Borick, D. Lopresti, and Z. Munson. 2006 survey of public attitudes toward electronic voting in Pennsylvania. Technical Report Department of Computer Science and Engineering LU-CSE-06-35, Lehigh University/Muhlenberg College Institute of Public Opinion (October 3, 2006).
18. Electronic voting "world first". BBC News Online (September 27, 2006). http://news.bbc.co.uk/2/hi/uk_news/scotland/tayside_and_central/5385086.stm.
19. *Determining the Validity of Optical Scan Ballot Markings.* State of Michigan, Department of State (July, 2006).
20. S. Veeramachaneni and G. Nagy, Analytical results on style-constrained bayesian classification of pattern fields, *IEEE Transactions on Pattern Analysis and Machine Intelligence.* **29**(7), 1280–1285 (July, 2007).
21. Y. Li, D. Lopresti, G. Nagy, and A. Tomkins, Validation of image defect models for Optical Character Recognition, *IEEE Transactions on Pattern Analysis and Machine Intelligence.* **18**(2), 99–108 (February, 1996).
22. E. H. B. Smith, Characterization of image degradation caused by scanning, *Pattern Recognition Letters.* **19**(13), 1191=1197, (1998).
23. E. H. B. Smith. Scanner parameter estimation using bilevel scans of star charts. In *Proceedings of the International Conference on Document Analysis and Recognition*, pp. 1164–1168, Seattle, WA (September, 2001).
24. E. H. B. Smith. Bilevel image degradations: Effects and estimation. In *Proceedings of the Symposium on Document Image Understanding Technology*, pp. 49–55, Columbia, MD (April, 2001).
25. E. H. B. Smith. Estimating scanning characteristics from corners in bilevel images. In *Proceedings of SPIE Electronic Imaging, Document Recognition and Retrieval VIII*, vol. 4307, pp. 21–26, San Jose, CA (January, 2001).
26. E. H. B. Smith and X. Qiu. Relating statistical image differences and degradation features. In eds. D. Lopresti, J. Hu, and R. Kashi, *Document Analysis Systems V*, vol. 2423, *Lecture Notes in Computer Science*, pp. 1–12. Springer-Verlag, Berlin, Germany, (2002).
27. E. H. B. Smith and X. Qiu, Statistical image differences, degradation features and character distance metrics, *International Journal of Document Analysis and Recognition.* **6**(3), 146–153, (2004).
28. E. H. B. Smith and T. Andersen. Text degradations and ocr training. In *Proceedings of the International Conference on Document Analysis and Recognition*, pp. 834–838, Seoul, Korea (August-September, 2005).

29. D. Amato, E. J. Kuebert, and A. Lawson. Results from a performance evaluation of handwritten addrecognition system for the United States Postal Service. In *Proceedings of the Seventh International Workshop on Frontiers in Handwriting Recognition*, Amsterdam, The Netherlands (September, 2000).

30. D. Lopresti and G. Nagy. Chipless RFID for paper documents. In *Proceedings of SPIE Electronic Imaging, Document Recognition and Retrieval XII*, vol. 5676, pp. 208–215, San Jose, CA (January, 2005).

31. M. Usami, A. Sato, K. Sameshima, K. Watanabe, H. Yoshigi, and R. Imura. Powder lsi: An ultra small rf identification chip for individual recognition applications. In *IEEE International Solid-State Circuits Conference*, (2003). Paper 22.7.

32. R. Mercuri. Eletronic voting. http://www.notablesoftware.com/evote.htm.

33. P. Garrison, D. Davis, T. Andersen, and E. H. B. Smith. Study of style effects on OCR errors in the MEDLINE database. In *Proceedings of SPIE Electronic Imaging, Document Recognition and Retrieval XII*, vol. 5676, pp. 28–36, San Jose, CA (January, 2005).

34. E. H. B. Smith. PSF estimation by gradient descent fit to the ESF. In *Proceedings of SPIE Electronic Imaging, Image Quality and System Performance III*, vol. 6059, pp. 28–36, San Jose, CA (January, 2006).

35. S. Rice, G. Nagy, and T. Nartker, *Optical Character Recognition: An Illustrated Guide to the Frontier*. (Kluwer Academic Publishers, Boston/Dordrecht/London, 1999).

36. P. M. A. Baker, R. G. B. Roy, N. W. Moon, and M. Willaims. Disabilities, (e) voting and access: A survey of voter satisfaction, (2005). http://www.cacp.gatech.edu/Presentations/CSUN_2006/Paul/CSUN_2006_e-vote.pdf.

37. D. W. Jones. Counting mark-sense ballots (February, 2002). http://www.cs.uiowa.edu/ jones/voting/optical/.

38. USENIX/ACCURATE Electronic Voting Technology Workshop (August, 2007). http://www.usenix.org/events/evt07/tech/.

39. J. Aslam, R. Popa, and R. Rivest. On estimating the size and confidence of a statistical audit. In *Proceedings of the USENIX/ACCURATE Electronic Voting Technology Workshop* (August, 2007). http://www.usenix.org/events/evt07/tech/.

40. J. Calandrino, J. A. Halderman, and E. Felten. Machine-assisted election auditing. In *Proceedings of the USENIX/ACCURATE Electronic Voting Technology Workshop* (August, 2007). http://www.usenix.org/events/evt07/tech/.

41. S. Goggin and M. Byrne. An examination of the auditability of Voter Verified Paper Audit Trail (VVPAT) ballots. In *Proceedings of the USENIX/ACCURATE Electronic Voting Technology Workshop* (August, 2007). http://www.usenix.org/events/evt07/tech/.

42. R. Rivest. Three voting protocols: ThreeBallot, VAV, and Twin. In *Proceedings of the USENIX/ACCURATE Electronic Voting Technology Workshop* (August, 2007). http://www.usenix.org/events/evt07/tech/.

43. K.-P. Yee. Extending prerendered-interface voting software to support accessibility and other ballot features. In *Proceedings of the USENIX/ACCURATE Electronic Voting Technology Workshop* (August, 2007). http://www.usenix.org/events/evt07/tech/.

44. S. P. Everett, M. D. Byrne, and K. K. Greene. Measuring the usability of paper ballots: Efficiency, effectiveness, and satisfaction. In *Proceedings of the Human Factors and Ergonomics Society 50th Annual Meeting*, Santa Monica, CA, (2006).

45. A. Kiayias, L. Michel, A. Russell, and A. A. Shvartsman. Security assessment of the diebold optical scan voting terminal. Technical report, UConn Voting Technology Research Center (October 30, 2006).

46. R. B. Putnam, *Bowling Alone: The Collapse and Revival of American Community.* (Simon & Schuster, 2000).

Chapter 4

Information Retrieval from Document Image Databases

Shijian Lu and Chew Lim Tan

*Institute for Infocomm Research, A*STAR, Fusionopolis,
Singapore, 119613*
slu@i2r.a-star.edu.sg.

*Department of Computer Science, School of Computing, National
University of Singapore, Singapore, 117543*
tancl@comp.nus.edu.sg

With the proliferation of digital libraries, an increasing number of document images of different characteristics are being produced. Information retrieval accordingly becomes an urgent problem for the access of the text information within these archived document images. This chapter presents a word shape coding approach that retrieves document images without OCR (optical character recognition). Several word shape coding schemes are presented, which convert a word image in a word shape code by using a few topological word shape features such as character boundary extrema, character holes, and character water reservoirs. A document image can then be converted into a document vector that encodes the occurrence frequency of the contained word images. Document images can thus be retrieved based on the similarity between the converted document vectors. Experiments show that the word shape coding approach is fast, robust, and capable of retrieving document images efficiently without OCR.

Contents

4.1. Introduction

With the proliferation of digital libraries and the promise of paper-less office, an increasing number of document images of different characteristics are being digitized and archived. To access these digitized text information,[1] archived document images need to be first converted to ASCII text through OCR (optical character recognition) under the traditional scenario. However, for a huge amount of document images archived in digital libraries, the OCR of all of them for the retrieval purpose is wasteful and has been proven prohibitively expensive, particularly considering the arduous post-OCR correction process. Under such circumstances, a fast and efficient document image retrieval technique will greatly facilitate the access of the desired text information through the Internet, or at least significantly narrow the archived document images to those interested.

This chapter presents a word shape coding approach that retrieves document images without OCR. Three word shape coding schemes are described, namely (1) scheme I which uses character boundary extrema,[2,3] (2) scheme II which is based on the character stroke categorization,[4] and (3) scheme III which uses character holes and character water reservoirs.[5] The proposed word shape coding approach has a few advantages. First, it is fast, efficient, and can be used to retrieve document images without OCR. Second, the collision rate of the three word shape coding schemes is very low. This point guarantees that text contents of document images can be properly captured if word images are correctly encoded. Third, the three word shape coding schemes are tolerant to the variations in text fonts and text styles. This point is required as well becasue document text of different fonts and styles should be encoded uniformly. Last and most importantly, the three word shape coding schemes are tolerant to the character segmentation error resulting from various types of document degradation.

The rest of this chapter is organized as follows. Section 4.2 first reviews some reported document image retrieval work. Section 4.3 then presents the three word shape coding schemes. After that, Section 4.4 describes the document image retrieval technique including the document vector construction and the document similarity measurement. Some related issues such as the coding ambiguity and coding robustness are then discussed in Section 4.5. Finally, some concluding remarks are drawn in Section 4.6.

4.2. Related Work

A number of document image retrieval techniques[6] have been reported. Some works[7–11] retrieve document images through word image matching. For example, the earlier work by Hull[10] proposes to measure the similarity between imaged documents according to a set of numeric "descriptors". Later, he proposes to measure document similarity by using the pass codes of fax images.[11] In the work by Chen *et al.*,[9] a hidden Markov model is utilized for keyword spotting where input is constructed by using word contours and the autocorrelation of column of pixels. In another two works by Chen *et al.*,[7,8] the contents of imaged documents are summarized by grouping word images into equivalence classes.

Some character shape coding schemes have also been reported for the document image retrieval, which convert a character image into a predefined code. A word image can then be translated into a word shape token by grouping the converted character shape codes. Document images can accordingly be retrieved by using the resultant word shape tokens. For example, Nakayama converts character images by seven codes and then uses the converted character shape tokens for content word detection[12] and document image categorization.[13] Similarly, Spitz *et al.* take a character shape coding approach for language identification,[14] word spotting,[15] and document image retrieval.[16] We also propose a character shape coding scheme that converts character images by capturing the vertical cut information.[17]

The word image matching approach described above depends heavily on the text fonts and styles. Word images of different fonts and styles are frequently quite different and so cannot be matched properly. By capturing some font and style tolerant character shape features (such as character ascenders and descenders), the above character shape coding approach is much more tolerant to the variation in text fonts and styles. However, the character shape coding approach is very sensitive to the text segmentation error. In particular, for document images of low quality, the accuracy of the converted character shape codes will drop dramatically by the character segmentation error resulting from various types of document degradation.

4.3. Word Shape Coding

This section describes three word shape coding schemes. In particular, the coding scheme I encodes word images through the categorization of character strokes. The scheme II instead encodes word images by using character boundary extrema and the number of horizontal word cuts. The coding schemes I and II are fast and the resultant word shape codes are efficient for the document image retrieval. However, the coding scheme I is quite sensitive to the document skew. The coding scheme III encodes word images by using character holes and character water reservoirs. It is much more tolerant to the document skew, though the corresponding coding process is a little slower compared to that of the coding schemes I and II.

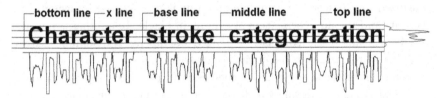

Fig. 4.1.   The detection of words and text lines through the projection profile analysis and the illustration of the top line, bottom line, x line, base line, and middle line of text.

4.3.1. *Word Shape Coding by Character Stroke Categorization*

This section presents the coding scheme that encodes word images through the character stroke categorization.[4] To categorize character strokes properly, word and text line images need to be detected first. We locate word and text line images through the analysis of the horizontal and vertical projection profiles. As Fig. 4.1 shows, for Roman document images, the horizontal projection profile normally shows two peaks at the x line and base line positions. Besides, there normally exist a number of zero-height sections in the vertical projection profile of text lines due to the inter-word blanks. Words and text lines can therefore be located based on the peaks and the zero-height sections of the horizontal and vertical projection profiles. The middle line of text lying in the middle of the x and base line can also be located based on the detected x lines and base lines illustrated in Fig. 4.1.

We classify character strokes into eight categories for the word shape coding. The desired character strokes are first detected through scanning each located text line at the middle line position from left to right. If the horizontal scan line intersects a text pixel, all text pixels within the same column between the top line and bottom line labeled in Fig. 4.1 are determined as part of the desired character stroke. Consequently, a desired character stroke pertains to all text pixels within a rectangle specified by a black run scanned by the middle line of text in horizontal direction and the top line and bottom line in vertical direction. For the three word images in Fig. 4.1, the black pixels in Fig. 4.2 show the detected desired character strokes.

We classify the desired character strokes illustrated in Fig. 4.2 into eight categories as follows for word shape coding:

1): Curved/skewed strokes having text pixels lying below the base line (curved/skewed strokes of "y", "g", $\cdots$).

2): Curved/skewed strokes lying between the x line and base line (curved/skewed strokes of "o", "c", $\cdots$).

3): Curved/skewed strokes having text pixels lying above the x line (curved/skewed strokes of "X", "Z", $\cdots$).

4): Vertical straight strokes stretching below the base line (vertical straight strokes of "p", "q", $\cdots$).

5): Vertical straight strokes lying between the x line and base line (vertical straight strokes of "r", "n", $\cdots$).

6): Vertical straight strokes stretching above the x line (vertical straight strokes of "b", "h", $\cdots$).

7): Vertical straight strokes lying between the x line and base line and having text pixels lying above the x line (vertical straight strokes of "i", "ü", $\cdots$).

8): Vertical straight strokes stretching below the base line and having text pixels lying above the x line (vertical straight strokes of "j").

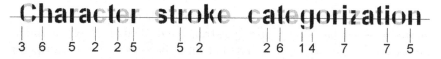

Fig. 4.2. The desired character strokes highlighted by pixels of the black color and the corresponding character stroke codes.

The vertical straight strokes in categories 4, 6, and 8 can be easily differentiated from those curved/skewed ones in categories 1, 2, and 3 because they contain at least one column of solid text pixels stretching above the x line or below the base line. The differentiation between the vertical straight strokes in 5 and 7 and those curved/skewed ones lying between the x line and base line in 2 is based on the compactness of the desired character strokes evaluated as follows:

$$T = \frac{N_t}{W * H} \qquad (4.1)$$

where W and H refer to the stroke width (width of a black run) and the x height. N_t gives the number of text pixels within the rectangle specified by the W and H. For vertical straight strokes in categories 5 and 7, text pixels almost fill up the rectangle specified by the black run and the x height. But for curved/skewed strokes, there normally exist a large proportion of background pixels within that rectangle. The two characters "r" and "o" within the word image "stroke" in Fig. 4.2 illustrate the two types of character strokes.

We denote the desired character strokes by the category labels described in the last subsection. Fig. 4.2 shows the codes of some desired character strokes of the three word images. Each character can thus be converted into a digit sequence through the concatenation of the codes of its desired character strokes. Similarly, a word image can be converted into a digit sequence through the concatenation of the codes of the characters it contains from left to right. For the three word images in Fig. 4.2, the corresponding word shape codes can be represented by three digit sequences "*3365255252625*", "*26522622*", and "*2256214225722567225*, respectively. Table 4.1 shows the codes of 52 Roman letters and numbers from 0 to 9. It should be noted that character "g" may be encoded by either "11" in Roman font or "14" in Arial font. However, other character or characters seldom generate the "11" and "14" in general case. Therefore, "11" and "14" can be treated as equivalent during the word shape coding.

4.3.2. *Word Shape Coding by Character Boundary Extrema*

This section presents the word shape coding scheme that encodes word image by using character boundary extrema and the number of horizontal word cuts[2,3] illustrated in Fig. 4.3. For Latin-based text, the upward and downward text boundary normally forms an arbitrary curve. Character boundary extrema are defined as the local extrema of those upward and

Table 4.1. Shape codes of 52 Roman letters and numbers 0-9 under the first word shape coding scheme.[4]

Characters	Shape codes	Characters	Shape codes
a	25	bk	62
cexszY	2	d	26
fltEFIJLPT14	6	g	11/14
h	65	i	7
j	8	m	555
nu	55	ovAVÄ	22
p	42	q	24
r	5	w	222
y	12	BDKR	63
Z23579	3	CSGOQUXôÔ068	33
HÜ	66	M	6226
N	626	W	2222
âä	37	üûñ	77

downward boundary curves. In particular, upward character extrema can be detected from six boundary patterns illustrated in Fig. 4.4. The downward text boundary also takes six patterns, which are actually 180 degree rotation of the six upward patterns. For example, the upward boundary of characters "e" and "i" in the word "retrieval" in Fig. 4.3 correspond to the two patterns shown in Fig. 4.4 c and d, respectively. For the sample word image "retrieval", the black pixels in the word images on the left of Fig. 4.3 illustrate the extracted upward and downward text boundaries. The black dots in the word images on the right show the detected character extrema.

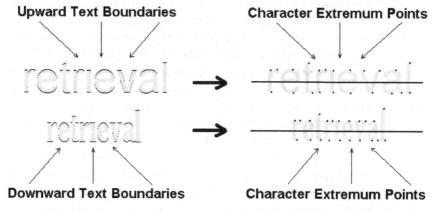

Fig. 4.3. The figure on the left gives upward and downward text boundaries, while the one on the right shows the character boundary extrema and the number of horizontal word cuts. Both features are tolerant to the font variation and text segmentation errors.

Character extrema are tolerant to the variation in text fonts and the text segmentation errors due to low image quality. These two properties are illustrated by the sample word "retrieval" in Fig. 4.3, which is typed in "Arial" and "Gloucester MT Extra Condensed", respectively. As we can see, the characters "a" and "l" within the word on the bottom row are erroneously connected. With traditional character shape coding techniques,[12,13,15,16] these two characters will be treated as one connected component and the resulting word shape code will be totally different from the real one. But character extrema are able to capture word shapes properly even if characters are not correctly segmented. Similarly, the number of horizontal word cuts, which is equal to the number of intersections between character strokes within a word image and the middle line of text, is tolerant to the variation in text fonts and text segmentation errors as well. For the word image "retrieval", 11 horizontal word cuts can be detected correctly in the presence of font variation and text segmentation error.

We encode word images by using extracted character boundary extrema and the number of horizontal word cuts. In particular, the extracted character extrema are first classified into three categories based on their positions relative to the x line and base line of text. The first category pertains to the extrema that lie far above the x lines, which normally lies along character ascenders. The second category pertains to those lying between the x lines and base lines. The third category pertains to those lying far below the base line, which normally lie along character descenders. We denote the character extrema within the above three categories as *3*, *2*, and *1*, respectively. A word image can thus be converted into a digit sequence through the combination with the number of horizontal word cuts.

The boundary extrema of a connected component are encoded as follows. Given a connected component, two digit sequences are first constructed by converting the corresponding upward and downward boundary extrema from left to right. The longer sequence is then set as the initial sequence and the shorter one is checked for the digit "1" or "3". If one of them is found, the digit at the same position of the initial sequence is replaced by the "1" or "3" because "1" or "3" are more distinguishable than "2". If the two sequences have the same length, any of the two can be set as the initial sequence, which is then updated in the similar way based on the other sequence. Take the character "h" as an example. Its upward and downward sequences correspond to "32" and "22". Therefore, any of the two sequences can be set as the initial sequence. However, the final sequence ("32") can be determined properly by the rule above no matter which one is chosen as the initial sequence. Table 4.2 lists the codes of 52 Roman letters where the digits converted from character boundary extrema and the number of horizontal cuts are separated by the symbol "|". It should be noted that the number of horizontal cuts in Table 4.2 is counted based on each individual character.

Table 4.2. Shape codes of 52 Latin letters and numbers 0-9 under the second word shape coding scheme.[2,3]

Characters	Shape codes	Characters	Shape codes
a, n, u, v	22|2	r, x	22|1
b, h, k, A, R	32|2	k	32|1
c, e, i, s, z	2|1	o	2|2
d	23|2	B, D, G, O, Q	3|2
f l, t, C, E-F, I-J, L, P, S-T, Z	3|1	w	222|4
g, y, p	12|2	N	33|3
j	1|1	Y	33|1
m	222|3	M	332|4
q	21|2	W	333|4
H, K, U, V, X	33|2		

Each word image can thus be converted into a word shape code that is composed of two parts including the digits converted from character boundary extrema and the number of horizontal word cuts. Take the word

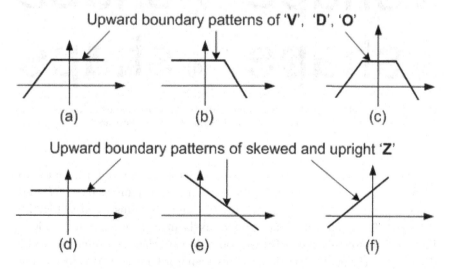

Fig. 4.4. Six upward character boundary extremum patterns.

image "retrieval" in Fig. 4.3 as an example. The corresponding word shape code can be represented by a digit sequence 2223222222223|11 where the two subsequences 2223222222223 and 11 separated by a symbol "|" are encoded based on character boundary extrema and the number of horizontal word cuts, respectively. For the digit sequence 2223222222223, the digits 22, 2, 3, 22, 2, 2, 22, 22, and 3 are converted from the boundary extrema of characters "r", "e", "t", "r", "i", "e", "v", "a", and "l", respectively.

4.3.3. Word Shape Coding by Character Holes and Reservoirs

This section presents the word shape coding scheme that encodes word images by using character ascenders and descenders, character holes, and character water reservoirs illustrated in Fig. 4.5. Based on the observation that character ascenders and descenders normally lie above the x line and below the base line, character ascenders and descenders can be simply located based on the x line and base line of the text described above. Character holes and character reservoirs can then be detected through the analysis of character white runs as described below.

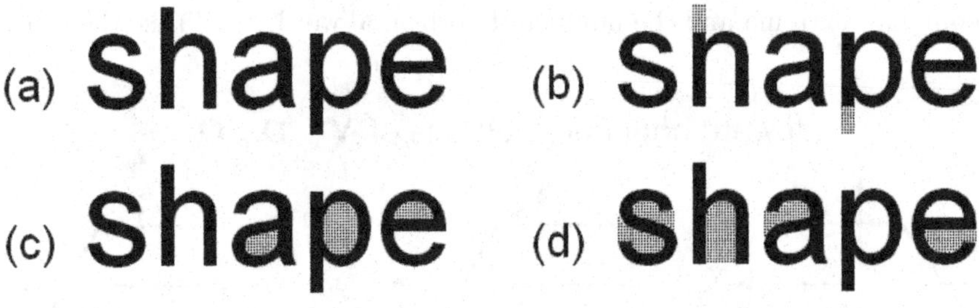

(a) shape (b) shape (c) shape (d) shape

Fig. 4.5. Utilized topological word shape features including character ascenders and descenders in (b), character holes in (c), and character water reservoirs in (d).

Scanning vertically (or horizontally) from top to bottom (or from left to right), a character white run can be located by a beginning pixel BP and an ending pixel EP corresponding to "01" and "10" illustrated in Fig. 4.6 ("1" and "0" denote white background pixels and gray foreground pixels in Fig. 4.6). As we only need leftward and rightward character reservoirs to be discussed in the next subsection, we just scan word images vertically column by column from left to right. Clearly, two vertical white runs from the two adjacent scanning columns are connected if they satisfy the following constraint:

$$BP_c < EP_a \ \& \ EP_c > BP_a \qquad (4.2)$$

where $[BP_c \ EP_c]$ and $[BP_a \ EP_a]$ refer to the BP and EP of the white runs detected in the current and adjacent scanning columns. Consequently, a set of connected vertical white runs form a white run component whose centroid can be estimated as follows:

$$\begin{cases} C_x = \dfrac{\sum_{i=1}^{N_r}(EP_{i,y}-BP_{i,y})BP_{i,x}}{\sum_{i=1}^{N_r} EP_{i,y}-BP_{i,y}} \\[4mm] C_y = \dfrac{\sum_{i=1}^{N_r}(EP_{i,y}-BP_{i,y})(EP_{i,y}+BP_{i,y}+1)/2}{\sum_{i=1}^{N_r}(EP_{i,y}-BP_{i,y})} \end{cases} \qquad (4.3)$$

where the denominator gives the number of pixels (component size) within the white run component under study. The numerators instead give the sums of the x and y coordinates of pixels within the white run component. Parameter N_r refers to the number of white runs within the white run component under study.

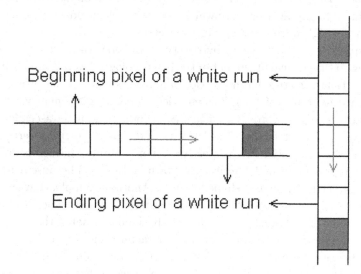

Fig. 4.6. The illustration of the beginning pixel and ending pixel of a horizontal and a vertical white runs.

Character holes and character water reservoirs can thus be detected based on the openness and closeness of the detected white run components illustrated in Fig. 4.5 c and d. Generally, a white run component is determined as closed if all neighboring pixels on the left of the first and on the right of the last constituent white run correspond to text pixels. On the contrary, a white run component is determined as open if some neighboring pixels on the left of the first or on the right of the last constituent white run lie within the background (corresponding to non-text pixels). Therefore, a leftwards and rightwards closed white run component results in a character hole (such as the hole of character "o"). At the same time, a leftwards (or rightwards) open and rightwards (or leftwards) closed white run component results in a leftwards (or rightwards) character water reservoir (such as the leftward reservoir of character "a").

Each word image can thus be represented by a word shape code through the coding of the three types of word shape features. To deal with the character segmentation error, we particularly convert word images by using character ascenders and descenders, character holes, and leftward and rightward character reservoirs. We do not use upward and downward reservoirs (such as those with "u" and "n") based on two observations. Firstly, most character segmentation errors are due to the touching of two or more adjacent characters within a word image at the x line or base line position. Secondly, a typical character touching at the x line or base line position introduces an upward or downward reservoir, which does not affect the leftward or rightward reservoirs in most cases.

We represent word images by two types of codes that are designed according to the vertical alignment of the five topological word shape features. If a word shape feature has no vertical alignments (such as the leftward and rightward reservoirs of "x"), it is encoded alone. In particular, we encode the five topological word shape features including character ascenders and descenders, character holes, and leftward and right character reservoirs by "l", "n", "o", "u", and "c", respectively. For example, characters "o" and "c" are represented by themselves as shown in Table 4.3 because neither of them has vertically aligned shape features. Another example, character "b" can be simply represented by "lo", indicating a character hole (o) directly on the right of a character ascender (l). It should be noted that we represent character descenders and leftward character reservoirs by "n" and "u" above because both characters ("n" and "u") have no utilized word shape features and so will not be encoded under this word shape coding scheme.

On the other hand, if a word shape feature has vertical alignments (has word shape features vertically aligned with it such as character "e" whose hole lies right above its rightward reservoir), the word shape feature together with its vertical alignments normally determines a Roman letter uniquely. Under such circumstances, we represent the pattern of the word

Table 4.3.　Shape codes of 52 Roman letters and numbers 0-9 (character marked by "*" will be discussed below) under the third word shape coding scheme.[5]

Characters	Shape codes	Characters	Shape codes
a	a	b	lo
cC	c	d	ol
e	e	f	f
g	g^*	hlIJLT17	l
i	i	j	j
ktK	lc	o	o
p	no	q	on
s	s	xX	uc
y	y	z	z
A	A	B8	B
CG	C	DO04	O
E	E	F	F
HMNUVWY	ll	P	P
Q	Q	R	R
S	S	Z	Z
2	2	3	3
5	5	6	6
9	9		

shape feature together with its vertical alignments by that uniquely determined Roman letter. For example, character "a" can be encoded by itself because a leftward reservoir right above a hole uniquely indicates an entity of character "a". Character "s" can be encoded by itself as well because a rightward reservoir right above a leftward one (both lying between the x line and base line of the text) uniquely indicates an entity of character "s".

Table 4.3 shows the word shape coding scheme III where 52 Roman letters and digits 0-9 are represented by 35 codes. In particular, the most frequent 26 lowercase Roman letters are represented by 18 codes. A word image can thus be converted to a word shape code in the similar way as described above. For example, the word image "shape" in Fig. 4.5 a can be represented by a code "slanoe" where "s", "l", "a", "no", and "e" are converted from the five spelling characters, respectively. It should be noted that the feature position helps to improve the coding performance as well. For example, though "s" and "S" both have a rightward reservoir above a leftward one, their reservoir positions are different with one's (s) rightward reservoir lying between the x line and base line and the other's (S) lying above the x line of the text.

4.4. Document Image Retrieval

Based on the three word shape coding schemes described in the last Section, a document image can be converted into a document vector that encodes the occurrence frequency of the contained word images. Document images can then be retrieved based on the similarity between the converted document vectors.

4.4.1. *Document Vector Construction*

Given a scanned document image, the corresponding document vector can be constructed through the coding of the contained word images one by one. Under the proposed document image retrieval framework, each document vector element is composed of two components including a unique word shape code (WSC) and a word occurrence number (WON), giving the frequency of the corresponding word image within the document image under study as follows.

$$\text{WSV} = \left[(\text{WSC}_1 : \text{WON}_1), \cdots , (\text{WSC}_{N_w} : \text{WON}_{N_w}) \right] \qquad (4.4)$$

where N_w refers to the number of unique word shape code within the studied document image. Therefore, the document vector constructed here is quite similar to the document vector constructed by using the ASCII text.[1] In particular, the word shape component corresponds to the term and the word frequency component gives the corresponding term frequency.

The document vector construction process can be summarized as follows. Given a word shape code converted from a word image within the document under study, the corresponding document vector is searched for the element with the same word shape code. If such element exists, the word frequency component of that document vector element is increased by one. Otherwise, a new document vector element is created and the corresponding word shape and word frequency components are initialized with the converted word shape code and one, respectively. The document vector construction process terminates until all word images within the document image under study have been converted and examined as described above. To cancel the document length effect, the word frequency component of the constructed document vector must be normalized as follows before they can be used for document similarity measurement:

$$\overline{\text{WON}}_i = \frac{\text{WON}_i}{\sum_{i=1}^{N} \text{WON}_i} \qquad (4.5)$$

where WON_i gives the occurrence number of the ith word shape code. N refers to the number of the unique word shape codes within the studied document vector. Therefore, the denominator term gives the sum of word occurrence numbers within the studied document vector.

4.4.2. *Document Similarity Measurement*

The similarity between two document images can thus be evaluated based on the similarity between their document vectors. In particular, the similarity between the two document vectors DV_1 and DV_2 can be evaluated according to their frequency components by using the cosine measure as follows:

$$\text{sim}(DV_1, DV_2) = \frac{\sum_{i=1}^{V} DVF_{1,i} \cdot DVF_{2,i}}{\sqrt{\sum_{i=1}^{V}(DVF_{1,i})^2 \cdot \sum_{i=1}^{V}(DVF_{2,i})^2}} \qquad (4.6)$$

where V defines the vocabulary size, which is equal to the number of unique word shape codes within the DV_1 and DV_2. $DVF_{1,i}$ and $DVF_{2,i}$ specify the word frequency information. In particular, if the word shape code under study finds a match within DV_1 and DV_2, $DVF_{1,i}$ and $DVF_{2,i}$ are determined as the corresponding word frequency components. Otherwise, both are simply set at zero.

It should be noted that Latin documents normally contain a large number of high-frequency stop words. These high-frequency stop words must be removed from the converted document vectors before the document similarity evaluation because they frequently dominate the direction of the converted document vectors. We simply utilize the stop words provided by the Cross-Language Evaluation Forum (CLEF).[18] In particular, all stop words listed by CLEF are first transliterated into a stop word template according to any of the three word coding schemes described above. The converted document vectors are then updated by removing elements that share the word shape component with the constructed stop word template.

4.5. Discussions

This section evaluates the three word shape coding schemes described above as well as their performance on the document image retrieval. In particular, the three word shape coding schemes are first evaluated in term of the coding ambiguity and their tolerance to the document degradation. Based on

Table 4.4.   Collision rates of the three word shape coding schemes.

Collision word no	Scheme I[4]	Scheme II[2,3]	Scheme III[5]
0	0.2317	0.3769	0.7221
1	0.0991	0.1368	0.1381
2	0.0587	0.0714	0.0479
3	0.0472	0.0518	0.0266
4	0.0335	0.0406	0.0171
5	0.0295	0.0305	0.0102
6	0.0262	0.0278	0.0077
7	0.0241	0.0224	0.0061
≥ 8	0.4495	0.2414	0.0230

the fact that document images can be retrieved successfully if the similarity among them can be measured properly, the performance of the document image retrieval is then tested by the document similarity evaluated based on the document vectors constructed by one of three word shape coding schemes described above.

4.5.1. *Coding Ambiguity*

The performance of the three word shape coding schemes is first evaluated. To retrieve document images properly, the converted word shape codes must be distinguishable enough so that words of different spellings have different word shape codes. We test the coding ambiguity based on the collision rate, which is defined by the number of words sharing the same word shape code. A dictionary composed of 57000 English words is used for the coding ambiguity evaluation. In particular, the 57000 English words are first transliterated into word shape codes according to the three word shape coding schemes described above. The coding collision rates are then calculated based on the converted word shape codes.

Table 4.4 shows the collision rates of the three word shape coding schemes. As Table 4.4 shows, the collision rate of the coding scheme III[5] is obviously lower than that of the coding scheme I.[4] Such results can be explained by the fact that the coding scheme III represent 52 Roman letter and digits 0-9 by using 35 codes, while the coding scheme I represents them by using 24 codes only. In addition, the collision rate of the coding scheme I is also lower than that of the coding scheme II.[2,3] This is due to the fact that the coding scheme II encodes word imageS just using three different codes (i.e. 1, 2, and 3). Consequently, more coding ambiguity is introduced due to this limit though Roman letters and digits 0-9 are represented by 19 different codes under the coding scheme II.

Table 4.5.   Accuracy of the three word shape coding schemes.

Document types	Scheme I[4]	Scheme II[2,3]	Scheme III[5]
Synthetic	0.9446	0.9446	0.9489
With impulse	0.7016	0.6445	0.9373
With Gaussian	0.6999	0.6245	0.9211
Scanned at 600 dpi	0.8539	0.8502	0.9286
Scanned at 300 dpi	0.8459	0.8347	0.8542

4.5.2. *Coding Robustness*

Besides the coding ambiguity, the coding robustness is also essential for the success of the document image retrieval. Basically, the coding scheme needs to be tolerant to the variations in text fonts and styles. At the same time, it should be tolerant to noise and various types of document degradation so that text contents of document images of different characteristics can be captured properly.

The coding robustness is tested by 80 text documents selected from the Reuters-21578[19] where every 20 deal with one specific topic. For each text document, a computer generated document image is first created by using Photoshop. After that, two document images are further created by adding impulse noise (noise level = 0.05) and Gaussian noise ($\sigma = 0.08$) to the computer generated document image. At the same time, for each of the 80 text documents, two document images are also physically scanned at 600 dpi (dots per inch) and 300 dpi, respectively, by using a generic document scanner. As a result, five sets of document images are created where each set is composed of 80 document images dealing with four topics. Lastly, words within the five sets of document images are converted into word shape codes by using the three word image shape coding schemes.

Table 4.5 shows the coding accuracy under various types of document degradation. As Table 4.5 shows, for synthetic document images, the three coding schemes achieve around the same coding accuracies. However, the accuracy of the coding schemes I and II becomes worse for document images with impulse noise or Gaussian noise, while the code scheme III is just slightly affected. Such experimental results can be explained by the character holes and reservoirs, which are much more tolerant to the noise than the character strokes and character boundary extrema used in the coding schemes I and II. Furthermore, compared with the character shape coding, the three word shape coding schemes are all tolerant to the character segmentation error resulting from the document degradation such as the low image resolution. For example, when document images are scanned at 300 dpi, the character segmentation error rate may reach up to 40%, especially for those printed in serif font. Under such circumstance, the accuracy of the character shape coding approach[13,15,17] will drop dramatically. However, the three word shape coding schemes are still capable of achieving over 80% coding accuracy.

4.5.3. Document Similarity Measurements

We evaluate the document image retrieval based on the document similarity measurements. This is based on the observation that document image can be retrieved successfully if the similarity between the corresponding document vectors can be measured properly. We measure the document similarities by using the five sets of document images described in the last subsection that deal with four different topics. In addition, we evaluate the document similarity based on the document vectors converted by using the coding scheme III. The document similarity can be also evaluated based on the coding schemes I and II in the similar way.

As described in the last subsection, the five sets of document images are first converted into document vectors. Stop words are then removed based on the stop word list provided by the Cross-Language Evaluation Forum (CLEF).[18] Lastly, the document similarity shown in Table 4.6 is evaluated based on the processed document vectors. In particular, the diagonal items in Table 4.6 give the average similarities between documents of the same topic, which are evaluated as follows:

$$S = \frac{M \cdot (M-1)}{2} \sum_{i=1}^{M} \sum_{j=1}^{M} \text{sim}(DV_i, DV_j) \quad \forall i, j : j > i \qquad (4.7)$$

where M gives the number of the document vectors of the same topic. The function sim() is defined in equation 4.6.

The off-diagonal items in Table 4.6 are the average similarities between document of different topics, which are evaluated as follows:

$$S = \frac{1}{M \cdot N} \sum_{i=1}^{M} \sum_{j=1}^{N} \text{sim}(DV_i, DV_j) \qquad (4.8)$$

where M and N refer to the numbers of document vectors of the two different topics under study. As Table 4.6 shows, similarities between document vectors of different topics are normally smaller than 0.15, but similarities between those of the same topic reach over 0.25 in most cases. Document image can accordingly be retrieved by setting a similarity threshold lying between 0.15 and 0.25.

Table 4.6. Similarities between documents of the same and different topics evaluated based on the 80 text documents and the five sets of document images.

Text images	Class I	Class II	Class III	Class IV
Class I	0.3237	0.2439	0.0669	0.1007
Class II	0.2439	0.5931	0.0943	0.1482
Class III	0.0669	0.0943	0.2797	0.0307
Class IV	0.1007	0.1482	0.0307	0.2636
ASCII text	Class I	Class II	Class III	Class IV
Class I	0.3668	0.2891	0.1209	0.1572
Class II	0.2891	0.6690	0.0922	0.1683
Class III	0.1209	0.0922	0.3808	0.1205
Class IV	0.1571	0.1683	0.1205	0.3015

We also compare the word shape coding approach with the retrieval by using the electronic text. With electronic text, document vectors can be constructed in the similar way as described in Section 4.4.1. Several preprocessing operations including the stemming and the stop word removal are first implemented. Document similarity is then evaluated based on the constructed document vectors. Experimental results in Table 4.6 show that the retrieval by character-coded text performs a little better than the presented word shape coding approach. The better performance can be partially explained by the coding inaccuracy and the coding ambiguity of the presented coding schemes. More importantly, the retrieval degradation is mainly due to the word stemming, which can be easily accomplished over character-coded text but cannot be done properly over the converted word shape codes.

4.5.4. *Coding Scheme Selection*

Coding scheme selection is one of the key issues for the success of the document image retrieval by word shape coding. In most cases, there are three factors to consider while selecting a proper word shape coding scheme. The first two are the coding ambiguity and the coding robustness as discussed above. The last one is the coding speed, which may become equally important if fast processing is favored under some occasion. Therefore, the selection of the specific coding scheme is normally a trade-off among the three factors.

For the three word shape coding schemes described in Section 4.3, scheme III[5] obviously outperforms schemes I[4] and II[2,3] in term of coding ambiguity and coding robustness. However, it is disadvantageous in the coding speed due to the word image scanning column by column. The coding scheme I is significantly faster than the scheme III and also a bit faster than the coding scheme II. In addition, it is slightly superior to the coding scheme II in terms of the coding ambiguity and coding robustness as well shown in Tables 4.4 and 4.5. The main disadvantage of the scheme I lies with its susceptiblity to the document skew that widely exists within most scanned document images. Furthermore, the speed of the scheme II lies between the schemes I and III. And it is also much more tolerant to the document skew compared with the scheme I. Therefore, the scheme II may be chosen when the retrieval speed is critical and document images under study suffer from certain degree of the skew distortion.

4.6. Conclusion

This chapter presents a document image retrieval technique that searches imaged documents through word shape coding without OCR. Several word shape coding schemes are described, which convert a word image in a word shape code by using a few topological shape features such as character boundary extrema, character holes, and character water reservoirs. Document images can thus be converted into document vectors by capturing the word occurrence frequency information. Finally, document images can be retrieved based on the similarity between the converted document vectors. Experimental results show that the presented word shape coding approach is fast, robust, and capable of retrieving document images efficiently without OCR.

References

1. G. Salton, *Introduction to Modern Information Retrieval*. (McGraw-Hill, 1983).
2. S. Lu and C. L. Tan, Script and language identification in noisy and degraded document images, *IEEE Transaction on Pattern Analysis and Machine Intelligence*. **30**(1), 14–24, (2008).
3. S. Lu and C. L. Tan, Retrieval of machine-printed latin documents through word shape coding. *Pattern Recognition*. **41**(5), 1799–1809, (2008).
4. S. Lu and C. L. Tan. Identification of latin-base languages through character stroke categorization. In *International Conference on Document Analysis and Recognition* (September, 2007).

5. S. Lu, L. Li and C. L. Tan, Document image retrieval through word shape coding, *IEEE Transaction on Pattern Analysis and Machine Intelligence.* **30** (11), 1913–1918, (November 2008).

6. C. D. M. Lew, N. Sebe and R. Jain, Content-based multimedia information retrieval: State-of-the-art and challenges, *ACM Transactions on Multimedia Computing, Communication, and Applications.* **2**(1), 1–19, (2006).

7. D. S. Bloomberg and F. R. Chen. Extraction of text-related features for condensing image documents. pp. 72–88 (January, 1996).

8. F. R. Chen and D. S. Bloomberg, Summarization of imaged documents without OCR, *Computer Vision and Image Understanding.* **70**(3), 307–320 (June, 1998).

9. F. R. Chen, L. Wilcox, and D. Bloomberg. Detecting and locating partially specified keywords in scanned images using hidden markov models. pp. 133–138 (October, 1993).

10. J. Hull. Document image matching and retrieval with multiple distortion-invariantd descriptors. pp. 383–399 (October, 1994).

11. J. Hull and J. Cullen. Document image similarity and equivalence detection. pp. 308–312 (August, 1997).

12. T. Nakayama. Modeling content identification from document images. pp. 22–27 (October, 1994).

13. T. Nakayama. Content-oriented categorization of document images. pp. 818–823 (August, 1996).

14. A. L. Spitz, Determination of script and language content of document images, *IEEE Transaction on Pattern Analysis and Machine Intelligence.* **19** (3), 235–245 (March, 1997).

15. A. L. Spitz. Using character shape codes for word spotting in document images. pp. 382–389, (1995).

16. A. F. Smeaton and A. L. Spitz. Using character shape coding for information retrieval. pp. 974–978 (August, 1997).

17. C. L. Tan, W. Huang, Z. Yu, and Y. Xu, Image document text retrieval without ocr, *IEEE Transaction on Pattern Analysis and Machine Intelligence.* **24** (6), 838–844 (June, 2002).

18. http://www.unine.ch/info/clef/.

19. http://kdd.ics.uci.edu/databases/ reuters21578.

Chapter 5

Indexing and Retrieval of Handwritten Documents

Huaigu Cao* and Venu Govindaraju[†]

Center for Unified Biometrics and Sensors (CUBS)
Dept. of Computer Science and Engineering
University at Buffalo, Amherst, NY
*hcao3@cubs.buffalo.edu, [†]govind@cubs.buffalo.edu

Given that OCR accuracy is not yet adequate for handwritten scripts, specially with large lexicons, instead of indexing the OCR'ed text of handwriting for retrieval, various approaches based on other information from the document images have been proposed. In particular,information retrieval of handwritten documents has been dealt with in two ways: keyword spotting and document retrieval.

Keyword spotting methods can be performed by template-based or template-free approaches. The template-based approach is based on image matching and requires an image of the query word as a template. Therefore it is only applicable to constrained handwriting such as the handwriting of the same person or in case of small lexicons. In the template-free approach, the similarity between a word image and a query is measured by the recognition score given by a word recognizer. It is more robust for applications of unconstrained handwriting due to the training performed on large amount of data. To avoid the out-of-vocabulary problem, one can use the synthetic word templates (in template-based methods) or lexicon-free word recognition (for template-free methods) for spotting.

In document retrieval approaches, the most important problem is adjusting the term-weighting scheme of existing IR models by integrating more information produced by the underlying document analysis and recognition (DAR) systems. We present here a modified Vector Model for handwritten document retrieval. The term-weighting of this system is determined by word segmentation and recognition results.

Contents

5.1. Introduction

Automatic indexing and searching in handwritten documents is a very challenging task. The OCR driven technique is adequate only for applications of printed documents or hand-written documents of good image quality and relatively small lexicons. Thus, instead of indexing the OCR'ed text of handwriting for retrieval, approaches based on word spotting (image matching) and document image retrieval have been proposed.

Word spotting approaches search for query words within a date-set. After preprocessing of document images and word segmentation, feature vectors are extracted from word images and stored in a database. When a user provides a query word, the similarity between the query and the word image in the database is computed, and word images are returned in the decreasing order of similarities.

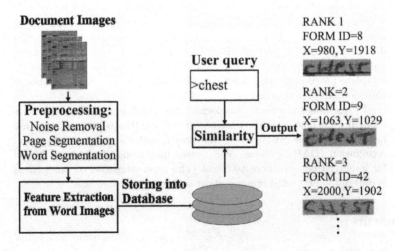

Fig. 5.1. Diagram of a keyword spotting system.

Keyword spotting methods can be template-based[2,8] or template-free.[5] In the template-based approach, an image of the query word is taken as a template and the similarity between the template and each word image in the database is calculated. Similarity[2,4] is achieved by Dynamic Time Warping (DTW) matching of profile features based on various definitions of distances[2-4,7] in the feature space. Similarity[8] is based on bitwise matching of the GSC features of two word images. The template-based approach is only applicable to constrained handwriting such as when dealing with a single writer or small lexicons. A mapping from query words to the word images are generated by indexing the database and suffers from the out-of-vocabulary problem.

Document retrieval approaches search for documents within a data-set that are relevant to the given query phrase. Different from a word spotting system, a document retrieval system computes doc-query similarity instead of word-query similarity. Performance is improved by integrating ranked OCR results into the term-weighting scheme.[9-12]

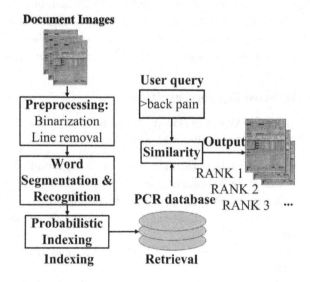

Fig. 5.2. Diagram of a handwritten document retrieval system.

This chapter is organized as follows. We introduce template-based keyword spotting techniques in Section 5.2. The DTW based method[2,4] and GSC based method[8] are described. We present a template-free approach to keyword spotting in Section 5.3. We use word recognition score as the similarity between the query and word image and use the word recognition method in a lexicon-free manner to solve the out-of-vocabulary problem. Gabor features are extracted from the grayscale images to improve the recognition and spotting performances on low-quality images. The template-free approach has been found to provide better performance for unconstrained handwriting. The handwritten document retrieval is described in Section 5.4. We conclude with a summary in Section 5.5.

5.2. Template-based keyword spotting

In a template-based keyword spotting system, word templates are usually generated by clustering and manually labelling a training set of word images. A query can't be performed if none of the word images of the query is in the training set. To avoid the out-of-vocabulary problem, synthetic word images are often used as query templates.[13]

Given the labelled templates, the similarity between a word image and the template image of the query is given by the matching score of the two images. Existing methods differ in the features representing the word images and matching schemes. In this section, we describe two template-based keyword spotting methods: DTW[4] and GSC,[8] respectively.

5.2.1. *DTW based keyword spotting*

In the Dynamic Time Warping (DTW) based method,[2,4] the following pre-processing steps are commonly performed.

(1) Word segmentation is performed and the background of every word image is cleaned by removing irrelevant connected components from other words that reach into the word's bounding box.
(2) Inter-word variations such as skew and slant angle are detected and eliminated.
(3) The bounding box of any word image is cropped so that it tightly encloses the word.
(4) The baseline of word images are normalized to a fixed position by padding extra rows to the images.

A normalized word image is represented by a multivariate time series composed of features from each column of the word image. These features include projection profile, upper/lower word profile, and number of background-to-foreground transitions.

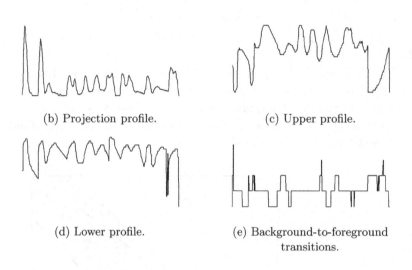

(a) A word image from George Washington's manuscripts.

(b) Projection profile.

(c) Upper profile.

(d) Lower profile.

(e) Background-to-foreground transitions.

Fig. 5.3.   The feature series used in DTW word spotting.

(1) Projection Profile. The projection profile of a word image is composed of the sums of foreground pixels in each columns.

(2) Upper/Lower Profiles. The upper profile of a word image is made of the distances from the upper boundary to the nearest foreground pixels in each column.

(3) Background-to-Foreground Transitions. The number of background pixels whose right neighboring pixels are foreground pixels is taken as the number of background-to-foreground transitions of the column.

Figure 5.3 shows the four feature series of a word image from the handwriting data set of George Washington's manuscripts (CIIR, University of Massachusetts[14]).

Suppose two word images w_A and w_B are represented by $\{f_A(1), f_A(2), ..., f_A(l_A)\}$ and $\{f_B(1), f_B(2), ..., f_B(l_B)\}$, respectively, where $f_A(i)$ is the feature vector of the i-th column of image w_A, $f_B(j)$ is the feature vector of the j-th column of image w_B, and l_A and l_B are the lengths of w_A, w_B, respectively. Then the DTW matching of w_A and w_B is given by the recurrence equation

$$\text{DTW}(i,j) = \min \left\{ \begin{array}{l} \text{DTW}(i-1,j) \\ \text{DTW}(i-1,j-1) \\ \text{DTW}(i,j-1) \end{array} \right\} + d(i,j) \tag{5.1}$$

where $d(i,j)$ is the square of the Euclidean distance between $f_A(i)$ and $f_B(j)$.

The time complexity of the DTW algorithm is in $O(l_A \cdot l_B)$. In order to speed up the computation, a global path constraint like the Sakoe-Chiba band (Figure 5.4 can be applied to force the paths to stay close to the diagonal of the DTW matrix. Another advantage of the path constraint is to prevent pathological warping.

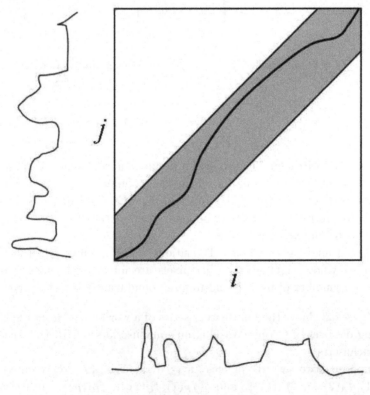

Fig. 5.4.   Sakoe-Chiba band.

The matching error of $f_A(i)$ and $f_B(j)$ is given by $\frac{1}{l}\text{DTW}(l_A, l_B)$ where l is length of the warping path recovered by DTW. The word images are ranked in the increasing order of the matching errors to the template image.

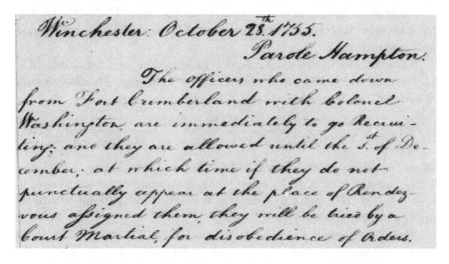

Fig. 5.5. A sample from George Washington's manuscripts.

The DTW based method has been tested on George Washington's manuscripts (Figure 5.5). The performance of keyword spotting was evaluated using the Mean Average Precision measure:[6]

(1) For each query, check the returned word images starting from rank1. Whenever a relevant word image is found, record the precision of the word images from the one with rank 1 to the current one. The average value of the recorded precisions for the query is taken as the Average Precision of the query.

(2) The mean value of the Average Precisions of all of the queries is the Mean Average Precision of the test.

A Mean Average Precision of 40.98% on 2372 word images of good quality and a Mean Average Precision of 16.50% on 3262 word images of poor quality were reported.[4]

5.2.2. *GSC feature based keyword spotting*

In the GSC feature based method,[8] a word image is represented by GSC features that consist of 512 bits corresponding to gradient (192 bits), structural (192 bits) and concavity (128 bits) features. A word image is divided into

32 regions (8 × 4) and 16 binary GSC features are extracted from each region. The gradient features are obtained by thresholding the results of Sobel edge detection in the 12 directions. The structural features consist of the presence of corners, diagonal lines, and vertical and horizontal lines in the gradient image, as determined by the 12 rules. The concavity features include direction of bays, presence of holes, and large vertical and horizontal strokes.

The similarity of two word images is measured by the bitwise matching of the respective GSC feature vectors of the two images. The dissimilarity of two GSC feature vectors X and Y is defined as

$$D(X,Y) = \frac{1}{2} - \frac{S_{11}S_{00} - S_{10}S_{01}}{2\sqrt{(S_{10} + S_{11})(S_{01} + S_{00})(S_{11} + S_{01})(S_{00} + S_{10})}} \qquad (5.2)$$

where S_{00}, S_{01}, S_{10}, and S_{11} are the numbers of 0-to-0, 0-to-1, 1-to-0, and 1-to-1 matches from X to Y, respectively. For example, the numbers of 0-to-0, 0-to-1, 1-to-0, and 1-to-1 matches between "0110110" and "0101001" are 1, 2, 3, and 1, respectively.

The GSC method has been tested on 9312 word images of 4 words ("been", "Cohen", "Medical", and "referred") written by 776 individuals. Each word was written three times by each individual. One of the three word images for every word written by any person is taken as a query template, and the remaining are taken for test. The performance of keyword spotting is evaluated by the recall and precision at different number of top matches. When the number of top matches of a query equals the number of relevant images, the recall value equals the precision value and is referred to as R-Precision.

The reults of both the GSC based method and the DTW based method are reported in.[8] The R-precision values of the above four queries using the GSC based method are 45.45%, 56.59%, 54.11%, and 62.04%, respectively. The R-precision values of the above four queries using the DTW based method are 35.53%, 38.65%, 44.39%, and 55.23%, respectively. Although the above results are obtained from a data set of multiple writers, the size of the lexicon is very small (containing only 4 words) and therefore the data set is not truly unconstrained.

5.3. Template-free keyword spotting

We have presented a template-free keyword spotting method in our prior work.[5] The similarity between query word w composed of n characters: $w =$

$c_1 c_2...c_n$ and word image I_w is defined as follows. Suppose a segmentation of I_w is represented by

$$s_{I_w} = [V_1 V_2 ... V_n], \qquad (5.3)$$

where $V_i (1 \leq i \leq n)$ is the feature vetor of the i-th character image of segmentation s_{I_w}, then the similarity between w and I_w:

$$\text{sim}(w, I_w) = \underset{[V_1 V_2 ... V_n]}{\text{argmax}} \left[\prod_{i=1}^{n} \Pr(c_i | V_i) \right]^{\frac{1}{n}} \qquad (5.4)$$

where $\prod_{i=1}^{n} \Pr(c_i | V_i)$ is the posterior probability that I_w is w given observation $[V_1 V_2 ... V_n]$.

5.3.1. *Segmentation of word image into character images*

A word image is normalized in two steps. First the image is re-sampled to make the height equal to 48 while preserving the aspect ratio. Then a margin of 8 pixels wide is added to the word image.

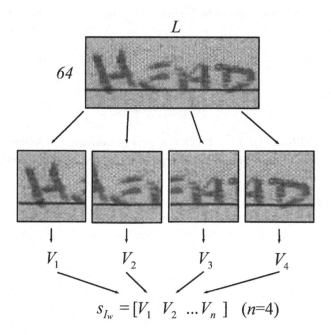

Fig. 5.6. Segmentation of a word image into four character images.

Given a normalized word image, denoted by $I_w[1 : L, 1 : 64]$ where L is the width and 64 is the height, and the number of characters n, I_w is divided into n 64×64 character images (Figure 5.6):

$$I_{c_i} = I_w[(x_0^i + \delta_i) : (x_0^i + \delta_i) + 63, 1 : 64], i = 1, 2, ..., n \qquad (5.5)$$

where

$$x_0^i = \frac{(n - i) + (i - 1)(L - 63)}{n - 1} \qquad (5.6)$$

and

$$\begin{cases} \delta_1, \delta_n \in \{0\}, & i = 1, n \\ \delta_i \in \{0, -8, 8\}, i = 2, ..., n - 1 \end{cases} \qquad (5.7)$$

The n character images may overlap or be separated from each other. This leads to 3^{n-2} combinations of $(\delta_1...\delta_n)$. Equation (5.4) is computed for all 3^{n-2} segmentations to find the maximum. $\delta_1 = ... = \delta_n = 0$ leads to a segmentation of constant interval between adjacent character images.

5.3.2. Extracting Gabor features from character image

The 2-D spatial function of the Gabor filter and its 2-D Fourier transform can be written as:[15]

$$g(x, y, F, \sigma_x, \sigma_y) = \frac{1}{2\pi\sigma_x\sigma_y} \exp[-\frac{1}{2}(\frac{x^2}{\sigma_x^2} + \frac{y^2}{\sigma_y^2}) + 2\pi j F x] \qquad (5.8)$$

$$G(u, v) = \exp\{-\frac{1}{2}[\frac{(u - F)^2}{\sigma_u^2} + \frac{v^2}{\sigma_v^2}]\} \qquad (5.9)$$

where $\sigma_u = 1/(2\pi\sigma_x)$, $\sigma_v = 1/(2\pi\sigma_y)$, and parameter F specifies the central frequency of interest. Gabor wavelet derived from Gabor filter in equation (5.8) is defined as

$$g_{mn}(x, y) =$$

$$a^{-m}g(a^{-m}(x\cos\theta + y\sin\theta), a^{-m}(-x\sin\theta + y\cos\theta), F, n\pi/K, \sigma_x, \sigma_y). \qquad (5.10)$$

In Equation (5.10), $m = 0, 1, ..., S - 1$ where S is the total number of scales, $\theta = n\pi/K$, and $n = 0, 1, ..., K - 1$ where K is the total number of orientations. The central frequency of interest is F. By varying m and n, we can apply filter $g_{mn}(x, y)$ to the input image (using 2-D convolution) to get features at different scale and orientation. The Gabor wavelet is non-orthogonal, thus there is redundant information in the filtered image. The following strategy is used to reduce the redundancy.[15] Let U_l and U_h denote the lower and upper center frequencies of interest. Then the filter parameters a, σ_u and σ_v are determined by

$$
\begin{cases}
a = (U_h/U_l)^{\frac{1}{S-1}} \\
\sigma_u = \frac{(a-1)U_l}{(a+1)\sqrt{2\ln 2}} \\
\sigma_v = \tan\left(\frac{\pi}{2K}\right)\left[U_l - \frac{2\ln 2\sigma_u^2}{U_l}\right]\left[2\ln 2 - \frac{(2\ln 2)^2\sigma_u^2}{U_l^2}\right]^{-\frac{1}{2}}
\end{cases}
\tag{5.11}
$$

The central frequency of interest should be set to $\frac{1}{2W}$ (where W is the stroke width) since it is the frequency of the signal perpendicular to the strokes. In 300 dpi document images, W usually varies from 5 to 8 pixels which corresponds to frequencies 0.1 and 0.0625, respectively. Our experiment is different from related work[16,17] in that instead of applying Gabor filter of only one scale, we have applied a Gabor wavelet for two different scales. The upper and lower frequencies of interest are $U_h = 0.1$, and $U_l = 0.05$ so the range of stroke width is completely covered. This is reasonable because the strokes tend to have a varying width.

Gabor wavelet transforms of two scales ($U_h = 0.1$, and $U_l = 0.05$) and four orientations are applied to 64×64 character images from the word images in our data-set. The histogram features,[16,17] *i.e.*, sums of signals for every quadrants from transformed image are extracted. First the 48×48 sub-image at the center of the 64×64 transformed image is divided into N by N blocks. For each block centered at (r, s), two histogram features $F_{r,s}^+$ and $F_{r,s}^-$ are calculated separately from the positive and negative real parts of the output weighted by a Gaussian function:[16]

$$
F_{r,s}^+ = \sum_{(u,v)\in n(r,s)} G(u - r, v - s) \times \max(0, F_r(u, v))
\tag{5.12}
$$

and

$$
F_{r,s}^- = \sum_{(m,n)\in n(r,s)} G(m - r, n - s) \times \min(0, F_r(m, n))
\tag{5.13}
$$

where $G(r, s) = \exp\{-(r^2 + s^2)/(2\tau^2)\}/(2\pi)$ is a Gaussian function, F_r is the real part output of Gabor filter, and $n(r, s)$ is the set of the coordinates of the pixels in the block centered at (r, s). For the scale $m=0$, N and τ are set to 4, 6 respectively; for the scale $m=0$, M and τ are set to 2, 12, respectively. The total number of features is $2 \times 4 \times (4 \times 4 + 2 \times 2) = 160$.

5.3.3. *Character classification probability* $\Pr(c_i|V_i)$

The Support Vector Machine (SVM) with RBF kernel is used in character recognition. The posterior probability $\Pr(C_i|V_i)$ in Equation (5.4) is modeled as a function of the decision value of the SVM classifier and estimated from the training set using the method in.[19] The estimated probabilities are stored in our database to speed up the execution of queries.

5.3.4. *Experimental results*

The template-free keyword spotting method has been tested on the New York State Pre-hospital Care Reports (PCR forms). The task is quite challenging for several reasons: (i) handwritten responses were very loosely constrained in terms of writing style, format of response, and choice of text due to irrepressible emergency situations, (ii) images are scanned from carbon copies and are very noisy (Figure 5.7), (iii) medical lexicons of words are very large (about 50,00 entries). This leads to difficulties in the automatic transcription of forms. The word recognition rate of the forms using Word Model Recognizer (WMR)[20] is about 20%.[21]

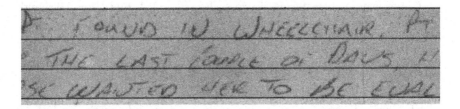

Fig. 5.7.   The text in a PCR form.

The experiments are performed on 12 PCR form images. We take 5295 character images from 10 form images for training the character recognizer, and perform spotting tests on 101 word images from 2 other form images. We use 6 keywords as queries.

The similarity in Equation (5.4) are compared with two other similarity functions using WMR[20] and DTW,[4] respectively. WMR is a word recognition algorithm based on chain-code features from binarized images and Euclidean-distance classification. The word recognition likelihood produced by WMR is taken as the similarity between the keyword and the word image. In the DTW approach 6 word images of the given query keywords are

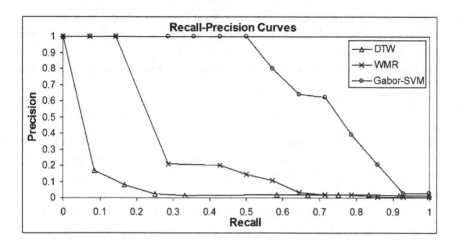

Fig. 5.8.   Recall-precision curves of three different similarity functions.

chosen from the training set as templates. Only the upper and lower profile features are extracted for DTW.

The recall-precision curve is used to evaluate the performance of keyword spotting. Given a threshold of the similarity or distance, the recall and precision are calculated by counting the retrieved word images and the genuine matches among the retrieved. The recalls and precisions are calculated at various thresholds (Figure 5.8). The template-free methods (Gabor-SVM, WMR) have better performance than the template-based method (DTW). The Gabor-SVM method has better performance than WMR.

5.4. Handwritten document retrieval

We can use a variant of the Vector IR Model for document retrieval.[12] In the classic Vector Model,[6] the documents are represented by the vector space of terms. A term is a word from the vocabulary of all of the documents. Given the vocabulary $\{t_i\}, 1 \leq i \leq N$, the term frequency of document d_j is defined by formula

$$\mathrm{tf}_{i,j} = \frac{\mathrm{freq}_{i,j}}{L}, \quad i = 1, ..., N \tag{5.14}$$

where $\mathrm{freq}_{i,j}$ is the number of occurrences of term t_i in document d_j and L is the total number of occurrences of all terms in document d_j, i.e., the length of d_j. For example, in a document d_j of 1000 words, term

t_i="diseases" occurs 3 times, then raw term frequency $\text{freq}_{i,j} = 3$ and term frequency $\text{tf}_{i,j} = 0.003$. Thus document d_j can be represented by vector $[\text{tf}_{1,j}, \text{tf}_{2,j}, ..., \text{tf}_{N,j}]$.

The inverse document frequency (IDF) of a term is defined by formula

$$\text{idf}_i = \log \frac{\#\{d_j\}}{\#\{d_j | \text{freq}_{i,j} > 0\}}, \quad i = 1, ..., N \tag{5.15}$$

where $\#\{\cdot\}$ denotes the number of elements in set $\{\cdot\}$. The IDF of a term shows the importance of the term based on the observation that a term that appears in most documents is less important than a term that appears in only a few documents.

A query is also represented by the vector of terms. The query term frequency (QTF) of query q is defined by

$$\text{tf}_{i,q} = \begin{cases} 1, & \text{if term } t_i \text{ is in } q \\ 0, & \text{otherwise} \end{cases} \quad i = 1, ..., N \tag{5.16}$$

and the query is represented by vector $[\text{tf}_{1,q}, \text{tf}_{2,q}, ..., \text{tf}_{N,q}]$.

The degree to which a document d_j is relevant to a query q is measured by the similarity between d_j and q:

$$\text{sim}(d_j, q) = \sum_{i=1}^{N} \text{tf}_{i,j} \cdot \text{idf}_i \cdot \text{tf}_{i,q}. \tag{5.17}$$

The raw frequency $\text{freq}_{i,j}$ is not immediately available from the document image and need to be estimated. Thus we use the modified definitions of TF and IDF:[12]

$$\begin{cases} \text{tf}'_{i,j} = \dfrac{E\{\text{freq}_{i,j}\}}{L} \\ \text{idf}'_i = \log \dfrac{\#\{d_j\}}{\#\{d_j | E\{\text{freq}_{i,j}\} > 0.5\}} \end{cases} \tag{5.18}$$

where $E\{\text{freq}_{i,j}\}$ is an estimation of $\text{freq}_{i,j}$.

Suppose document d_j is composed of an observational sequence of image features denoted by $\vec{o} = o_1 o_2 ... o_N$, and $\vec{w} = w_1 w_2 ... w_L$ is any segmentation of sequence $\vec{o}$ where $w_1, ..., w_L$ are word images. The MMSE estimation of $\text{freq}_{i,j}$ is

$$E\{\text{freq}_{i,j}\} = \sum_{\vec{w}} \Pr(\vec{w} | \vec{o}) \cdot \sum_{\vec{\tau}} \Pr(\vec{\tau} | \vec{w}) \cdot \#_{t_i}(\vec{\tau}) \tag{5.19}$$

where $\vec{\tau} = \tau_1...\tau_L$ is a sequence of terms. $\Pr(\vec{w}|\vec{\sigma})$ is the probability that $\vec{w}$ is a valid segmentation. $\Pr(\vec{\tau}|\vec{w})$ is the word sequence recognition probability. $\#_{t_i}(\vec{\tau})$ is the number of term t_i occurring in sequence $\vec{\tau}$. Given word segmentation probabilities, word recognition likelihood and the language model (n-gram), Equation (5.19) is solved using dynamic programming.

The word segmentation method is based on the distance between connected components. The segmentation probability is estimated non-parametrically from a training set of 1099 valid word gaps and 5138 non-valid word gaps. The Average Precision[6] of word gap classification is 69.79%. The word recognition likelihood is estimated from the matching distance of the word recognition algorithm.[20] The language model (bi-gram of 4670 English words) is learned from 783 PCR forms.

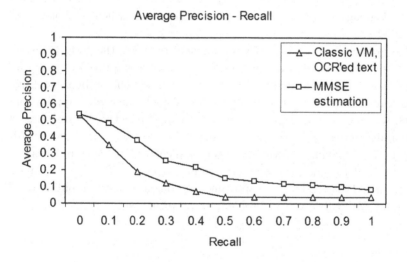

Fig. 5.9.   Precision-recall curve of the IR test.

We tested the search engine on 342 handwritten medical forms with 28 queries. We use the Mean Average Precision (MAP) and R-Precision[6] measurements to evaluate the performance of document retrieval. The MAP and R-Precision are 20.4% and 19.0%, respectively. For comparison, we run classic Vector Model on OCR'ed text obtained from the top-1 choices of word recognition results. The word recognizer is run on the word segmentation results obtained by connected component clustering using constant threshold. The MAP and R-Precision are 11.7% and 14.9%, respectively. The precision-recall curves of the two methods are shown in Figure 5.9. The MAP/R-Precision values and recall-precision curves show the improvement obtained by the modified Vector Model.

5.5. Summary

The template-based and template-free methods are two different approaches to keyword spotting. The template-based approach requires few training samples and is suitable for indexing document images by single writer. The template-free approach relies on OCR techniques and requires more training data. But it is more robust in applications of unconstrained handwriting. To avoid the OOV (out-of-vocabulary) problem, we usually adopt a lexicon-free word recognition technique. The performance can be improved by using grayscale image based features like the Gabor feature when the images are degraded.

For applications of handwritten document retrieval, the performance of traditional IR methods (Vector Model, *etc.* can be improved by accurate estimation of raw term frequencies. A furture direction can be to combine word spotting and document retrieval into a single integrated application. When we index the document images, we can also index the positions of (potential) words and highlight the words in the retrieved documents. Although this indexing process has been implemented in text retrieval, it is non-trivial to index the document images due to the time and space constraints. Existing keyword spotting methods are based on online word matching. We will solve this problem in the future work.

References

1. R. Manmatha, C. Han, E. M. Riseman, and W. B. Croft, *Indexing handwriting using word matching*, in 1st ACM International Conference on Digital Libraries , Bethesda, MD, March 20-23, pp. 151-159 (1996).
2. S. Kane, A. Lehman, and E. Partridge, *Indexing George Washington's handwritten manuscripts*, Technical Report MM-34, Center for Intelligent Information Retrieval, University of Massachusetts Amherst (2001).
3. S. Belonge, J. Malik, and J. Puzicha, *Shape matching and object recognition using shape contexts*, IEEE Trans. on PAMI 24: 24 (2002) 509-522 (2002).
4. R. Manmatha and T. M. Rath, *Indexing of handwritten historical documents-recent progress*, in Symposium on Document Image Understanding Technology (SDIUT), pp. 77-85 (2003).

5. Huaigu Cao and Venu Govindaraju, *Template-Free Word Spotting in Low-Quality Manuscripts*, the Sixth International Conference on Advances in Pattern Recognition (ICAPR), Calcutta, India, 2007.
6. J. van Rijsbergen, *Information Retrieval*, Butterworth, London, England, 1979.
7. J. L. Rothfeder, S. Feng, and T. M. Rath, *Using corner feature correspondences to rank word images by similarity*, CIIR Technical Report MM-44 (2003).
8. B. Zhang, S. N. Srihari, and C. Huang, *Word image retriecal using binary features*, in Document Recognition and Retrieval XI, SPIE vol. 5296, pp. 45-53 (2004).
9. Toni M. Rath and R. Manmatha and Victor Lavrenko, *A search engine for historical manuscript images*, in Proceedings of the 27th annual international ACM SIGIR conference on research and development in information retrieval, 2004.
10. Nicholas R. Howe and Toni M. Rath and R. Manmatha, *Boosted decision trees for word recognition in handwritten document retrievals*, in Proceedings of the SIGIR, pp. 377–383, 2005.
11. Duk-Ryong Lee and Woo-Youn Kim and Il-Seok Oh, *Hangul Document Image Retrieval System Using Rank-based Recognition*, in Proceedings of the International Conference on Document Analysis and Recognition, pp. 615–619, 2005.
12. H.Cao and V. Govindaraju, *Vector Model Based Indexing and Retrieval of Handwritten Medical Forms*, in Proceedings of the Ninth International Conference on Document Analysis and Recognition, 2007.
13. Basilios Gatos, Thomas Konidaris, Kostas Ntzios, Ioannis Pratikakis, and Stavros J. Perantonis, *A Segmentation-free Approach for Keyword Search in Historical Typewritten Documents*, pp. 54-58, ICDAR 2005.
14. http://ciir.cs.umass.edu.
15. B.S. Manjunath, W.Y. Ma, *Texture features for browsing and retrieval of image data*, IEEE Transactions on Pattern Analysis and Machine Intelligence, Volume: 18, Issue: 8, Pages: 837 - 842 (1996).
16. Xuewen Wang, Xiaoqing Ding, Changsong Liu, *Optimized Gabor Filter Based Feature Extraction for Character Recognition*, ICPR (4) 2002: 223-226 (2002).
17. Xuewen Wang, Xiaoqing Ding, Changsong Liu, *Gabor filters-based feature extraction for character recognition*, Pattern Recognition 38(3): 369-379 (2005).
18. T.-F. Wu, C.-J. Lin, and R. C. Weng, *Probability estimates for multi-class classification by pairwise coupling*, Journal of Machine Learning Research, 5:975-1005 (2004). URL: http://www.csie.ntu.edu.tw/cjlin/papers/ svmprob/svmprob.pdf.
19. Chih-Chung Chang and Chih-Jen Lin, *LIBSVM: a library for support vector machines*, (2001). Software available at http://www.csie.ntu.edu.tw/cjlin/libsvm.

20. G. Kim and V. Govindaraju, *A lexicon driven approach to handwritten word recognition for real-time applications*, IEEE Transactions on Pattern Analysis and Machine Intelligence, Volume: 19, Pages: 366 - 379 (1997).
21. Robert Milewski, Venu Govindaraju, *Extraction of Handwritten Text from Carbon Copy Medical Form Images*, Document Analysis Systems 2006, pp. 106-116 (2006).

Chapter 6

Comprehensive Check Image Reader

M. Shridhar, G. F. Houle, Ron Bakker, F. Kimura

University of Michigan-Dearborn, MI 48128, USA,
Kappa Image LLC, Oakland, CA 94612, USA,
Dia Europe BV, Netherlands,
Mie University, Tsu, Japan
mals@engin.umd.umich.edu

A check contains more than just an amount. The fields of interests are courtesy and legal amounts, date, check number, MICR line, payer, payee, memo, signature, signature instruction, fractional validation numbers, endorsement, security features, etc. In fact a bank can literally construct a very meaningful profile of the account holder from an analysis of the checks written and received by an account holder. Since October, 2005 the "Check 21" law defines an image of a check as being as valid as the original document. The agreement between banks is that a binary image at $200 - 240$ dpi is the most practical format to use. Since most banks are now creating images and must be able to handle incoming images, it creates a need for new image tools to validate the quality and readability of each field. This chapter describes the challenges in finding and recognizing the fields of interest on the broad document types. These fields contain machine printed and handwritten words. The chapter will focus on handwritten legal line recognition which remains the most challenging field.

Contents

6.1. Introduction

Extracting all information on a check is a challenging endeavor. Whether we need to extract machine printed text like a payer block or a legal line, or handwritten fields like a date or a courtesy amount, many preprocessing steps are required to handle artifacts such as skew and poor image quality. Because of the lack of standards in the US, locating the fields of interest requires adaptive registration of the image. We briefly describe the challenges in processing machine printed checks, and then handwritten checks. Then the remainder of the chapter provides technical details on recognizing the handwritten field.

6.2. Check Preprocessing

Because of the wide variation in document quality, the problem of adjusting a camera to reach the highest recognition rate will always be an issue (see Fig. 6.1).

Fig. 6.1. Image quality problem.

Ideally a gray-level image should be captured, but for Check 21 the decision to go with 200 − 240 dpi binary images for exchange purposes has been adopted. The next generation of document processing undoubtedly will use gray level information, but current solutions need to work well with binary images.

An important distinction between checks and other documents is the multi-pass printing of checks. First, the check itself (background and text) is created with a high print quality. The text regions will appropriately have various font types and sizes. Then, in a different printing process, the check will be filled out. It can then be expected that the quality and the type of printed text will vary over the same check. For example, the legal amount shown in Fig. 6.2 has broken characters that might require dilation to repair. In some other areas (e.g., payer name) the characters are touching and might require erosion to improve the performance of the classifier. Such potential problems dictate the use of locally adaptive image analysis.

Other problems associated with multi-pass printing are skewed text regions (Fig. 6.2) and overlapping characters. Furthermore, the image analysis needs to selectively remove any noise (i.e. scanning noise, background scenes and textures, etc.) without affecting the text information. To these problems we can add typical character recognition problems (e.g. line/-word/character segmentation, font variations, reverse video, broken and touching characters, line going through the characters, etc.)

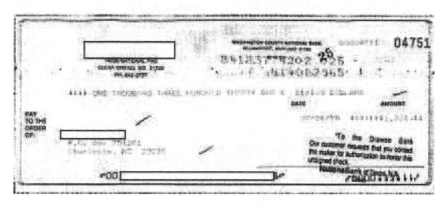

Fig. 6.2. Challenges in reading checks.

The first step in handling any type of document consists of defining the linguistic context associated with it. The Brown Corpus was created by entering words found in newspapers and calculating frequencies of each word. The same idea can be done by processing 100,000 checks from several banks. The keywords like "PAY TO THE ORDER OF" can be labeled as a place holder to find special fields like payee, legal line amount, courtesy amount, etc.

6.2.1. *Check processing challenges*

In check processing typically five target fields need to be identified and recognized: signature presence, payee name, legal and courtesy amounts, and date. Contextual analysis is critical to controlling the error rate. The contextual information in each field can be expressed by a set of specific rules. For instance, when the recognized legal and courtesy amounts agree, then the combined result can be assumed to have a very low error rate. The error rate can be further reduced if an external source such as spoken amount is available to corroborate against the legal and/or courtesy amounts. For the date field, contextual information could be the current year, the current day of the year, or the date distribution read with confidence from previous checks. The MICR line number at the bottom of the check could be used to identify the payer and its list of valid payee names. Using the MICR line information, we could even have a list of check numbers (beginning of MICR line number and also at the top right corner of the check) supplied by the payer. Thus, once the payer name has been recognized along with the check number, we could verify that the amount and the date match. This assumes that the payer has electronically supplied the bank with their list of transactions, which is frequently the case with large lockbox customers. In this scenario, the bank would send back the same list with an indicator for each check processed and validated. The challenge of locating and recognizing the five semantic types typically found in remittance applications is now described.

6.2.1.1. *Legal amount recognition challenge*

On most personal checks and some business checks, the legal amount is handwritten (Fig. 6.3), posing a major challenge. Machine-printed keywords can often be used to locate the legal line, which can then be treated as a phrase. Also, some business checks do not contain the legal amount (Fig. 6.4) and this poses an additional challenge. Section 6.4 of this chapter describes how legal line phrases can be successfully recognized.

When the legal amount is not fully spelled out (e.g., Fig. 6.5), the recognition accuracy drops due to lack of redundancy.

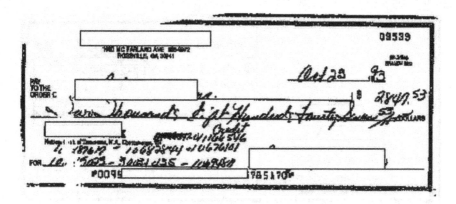

Fig. 6.3. Handwritten legal amount.

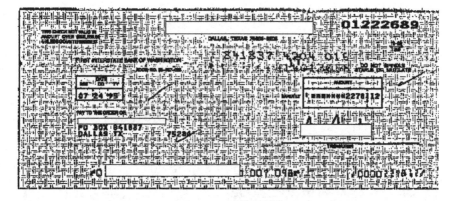

Fig. 6.4. Check with no legal amount.

6.2.1.2. *Check processing challenges*

The courtesy amount is the numerical character representation of the amount on the check. While the legal amount may not be present on all checks, the courtesy amount should (in theory) always be present. Finding the courtesy amount on personal checks is not difficult since these items tend to follow the ANSI standard location. However, business checks do not conform to the ANSI specification, and their courtesy amount locations vary widely (Fig. 6.6). Moreover, not all amounts have a currency delimiter (Dollar sign or asterisks) associated with them.

Other issues that affect recognition of courtesy amount in a handwritten personal check are the extraction and recognition of the cents portion.

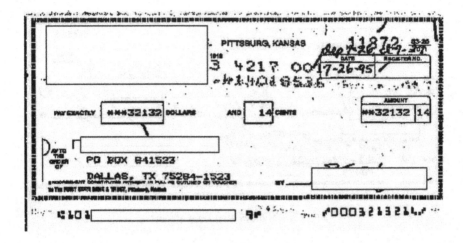

Fig. 6.5.　Digit-type legal amounts.

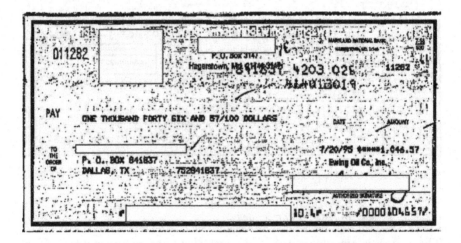

Fig. 6.6.　Example of courtesy amount fused with date field.

Many writers often include the "/100" or "/xx" in expressing the cents portion (Fig. 6.7) and very often we have one connected component that renders recognition almost impossible.

Another troublesome aspect is the way the double zero "00" is written. The double zero is often recognized as "50" or "60" because of the connecting link at the top (Fig. 6.8). Our approach has relied on using two recognition engines – one for the dollar part (variable string length)

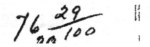

Fig. 6.7. Courtesy Amount with /100.

and the other for the cents part (string of two characters), assuming that we have successfully detected and removed the "/100". Recognition of numeral strings is based on presegmentation followed by concurrent concatenation and recognition using dynamic programming optimization for the final recognition.

Fig. 6.8. Samples of "00" that cause misrecognition.

6.2.1.3. *Date recognition challenge*

The date field is the most difficult target to isolate for several reasons: it has only a few characters; it can be located practically anywhere in the upper region of a check; and it may be fused (in almost any spatial orientation) with the courtesy amount. Once isolated, character recognition engines have problems recognizing short fields because of lack of field-level statistics. Furthermore, the date format varies from a numeric format (07-20-95) to an alphanumeric format (Jul. 20, 1995).

6.2.1.4. *Payee name recognition challenge*

Machine printed payee name field is the easiest field to locate and to recognize, as it usually exhibits a clean background and good quality characters. This is explained by the fact that the payee address block (which might be used for mailing purposes) tends to follow USPS Publication 28, which gives recommendations to ensure proper delivery of the mail piece. Fig. 6.9 illustrates an example in which the payee name is above the legal amount line. A purely geometric-based location algorithm would have misidentified the two strings. Such cases require semantic clues to correctly parse the fields.

Fig. 6.9.   Payee name example.

6.2.1.5. *Signature detection challenge*

Signature detection on checks can be done with high accuracy for two reasons: first, the signature location is reasonably well constrained, and second, the system is only looking for presence of a signature (as opposed to fraud detection which requires recognition of the signature shape). However, signature detection is not as trivial as simply counting pixels in a given area. A density factor and a regularity measure (i.e., text has small components of similar width and height, etc., and signature has long smooth curves) must be computed. Stamped directives (see Fig. 6.2) should also be reliably detected. Fig. 6.10 illustrates an example where signature detection will (and probably should) fail. A human operator will have to determine this check's negotiability.

6.2.1.6. *Courtesy amount field*

To handle handwritten courtesy amount successfully, some specialized tools were also designed. First, we have ensured robust recognition of the dollar sign "$" since it is a reliable anchor, especially on personal checks where it characteristically has an edge bracket to its left as shown in Fig. 6.11.

With the "$" sign identified, a cleanup of the field is needed to remove graphic frames which were not removed successfully during the document layout analysis. For the machine printed amounts, the asterisk '*' symbol is also of great help in finding the courtesy and the legal amount; a string of one or more asterisks is essentially a currency symbol when the check is a business check.

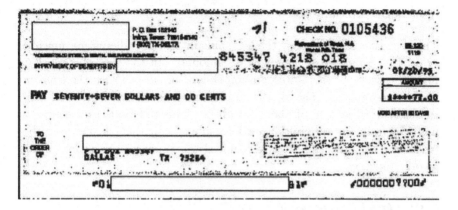

Fig. 6.10. Signature detection challenge.

Fig. 6.11. Dollar sign registration.

The cents part of the courtesy amount is by far the most challenging piece, and will have the biggest impact on the overall accuracy of the field. For this reason, it is worth spending major effort to have a specialized tool to detect the slash since, if present, it will clearly identify the cents and the boundary of the amount. If two connected components are found over the slash, we can disregard the information below the slash. However, in several cases of touching digits, the recognition of "100" is also a great help in assigning confidence to the segmentation. Finally, other specialized tools recognize "xx" and connected "00", each as a single entity (i.e., no segmentation required).

The results of the courtesy amount need to convey specific information about the format ($DD.cc or $DD cc/100) to allow for separate confidence for dollars and cents. Also, since the resulting amount will be used in corroboration with the legal amount, more than one field result is expected. In the case of handwritten personal checks, the courtesy amount choices will be passed to the legal amount phrase recognizer for validation as explained in the next section. With separate confidence for dollars and cents, the workflow manager will be able to request in some cases only cents keying to complete a transaction.

6.3. Legal Amount Recognition

The approach to recognizing the legal amount is quite different for machine printed as compared to handwritten amounts. In the case of a machine printed legal amount, the recognition is done in parallel with the courtesy amount recognition. The algorithm used is based on spotting words from the legal word lexicon of about 40 words. This technique uses confusion matrices from the recognition engine (single engine or corroboration between two engines). Then the recognized words must be parsed to obtain a correct syntax.

6.3.1. *Legal line parsing*

Legal line recognition produces a set of numeric hypotheses with associated digit confidences. This is done so that corroboration between the legal and courtesy amounts be performed with both sets of results in a normalized form. To do so, each of the most likely interpretations of the legal amount are parsed, using a grammar describing the valid constructs found in legal amounts, and each successful parse used for a syntax directed translation of the legal amount string. The output of the translation is the set of digits and confidences that constitute the numeric equivalent of the legal line. To illustrate this process further, consider the recognition results from a legal amount field shown below:

	1st Result	Conf	2nd Result	Conf	3rd Result	Conf
Word#1	FOUR	98				
Word#2	THOUSAND	92				
Word#3	TWENTY	76	TWELVE	64	TEN	51
Word#4		99				
Word#5	FOUR	92				
Word#6	DOLLARS	88				
Word#7	AND	96				
Word#8	SIXTY	72	FIFTY	67		
Word#9		98				
Word#10	SEVEN	91				
Word#11	CENTS	83	SEVEN	52		

Only the top three candidates for the ranked lexicon for each word are considered in order to reduce the number of cases that have to be parsed. Each of the twelve possible combinations is passed as input to a recursive descent parser that incorporates a syntax directed translator. The grammar was obtained through several thousand legal lines from ground-truthed business checks. It incorporates the common prefixes found in legal amounts, such as "PAY EXACTLY" or "THE SUM OF".

Only two of the twelve possibilities survive through the parser:

"FOUR THOUSAND TWENTY - FOUR DOLLARS AND SIXTY - SEVEN CENTS"

"FOUR THOUSAND TWENTY - FOUR DOLLARS AND FIFTY - SEVEN CENTS"

Each word is an input symbol to the parser, and each symbol is assigned two numeric attributes: its recognition confidence and its numeric value if it is a number word, or a zero otherwise. The translator uses these attributes to generate output in the form of digit/confidence pairs. For the above two examples the output is:

4 (98)	0 (99)	2 (76)	4 (92)	6 (72)	7 (91)
4 (98)	0 (99)	2 (76)	4 (92)	5 (67)	7 (91)

Note that the value of the hundreds of dollars place is zero and that the confidence is arbitrarily assigned to 99. Also note that the non-number words in the legal line do not contribute to the confidence of any of the digits.

6.3.1.1. *From word to legal line phrase matching*

For handwritten amounts, the legal phrase recognition is in a more experimental stage. In an effort to integrate the handwritten legal phrase recognizer in a production system, it was decided to use it as a validation to reinforce or reduce the confidence of the courtesy amount. To appreciate the major challenge associated with reading legal amounts, a detailed technical description is now presented starting at the word level and evolving towards phrase recognition.

6.3.2. *Legal line recognition for handwritten checks*

Legal phrase matching is an extremely challenging task for several reasons. First, most legal lines are written using a full cursive style as opposed to hand printed style. Second, word separation is often ambiguous when using projection or profile analysis. Before attempting recognition, the legal phrase image needs some special processing (Fig. 6.12). In addition to overhangs from the previous line, one must consider the removal of various artifacts associated with this legal field. Some issues to consider are (1) removal of underline without deleting portions of writing, (2) removal of the numeric portion of the monetary amount, (3) removal of long strokes to fill any gaps in the field. Correct processing will lead to a second stage which includes noise suppression and slant correction and the final stage in which all the words of the phrase are clearly identified.

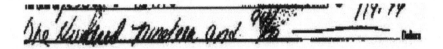

Fig. 6.12.   Legal line with artifacts.

Once the image has been prepared, legal line phrase matching can be accomplished in two modes. First, in a parallel mode, the legal field is recognized using a fixed size word lexicon consisting of numeric words "one" through "twenty", "thirty" through "hundred" in steps of 10, and "thousand". This assumes that clear word boundaries can be found, which is not always the case. The second mode which is the serial mode uses results from CAR (courtesy amount recognizer) to generate a reduced size lexicon of possible legal phrases. Any errors in CAR will almost certainly lead to errors in LAR (legal amount recognizer) and hence this approach is generally avoided.

The advantage in using a parallel mode is to obtain an independent (unbiased) contribution to the recognized amount. Should the legal amount then agree with the courtesy amount, the confidence would be such that an extremely low error rate could be achieved. Also, if no recognition results from the courtesy amount, the legal line recognition and proper parsing would be the only possible result. Finally, ambiguities in CAR (e.g. 100 vs. 700) can be resolved with LAR processed in a parallel mode.

The disadvantage is speed. If the check amount is large, say $1253.76, then the legal expression might read

One thousand (and) two hundred and fifty-three dollars (and)

Thus as many as ten words may be written on a line of about four inches. The connector word "and" often appears at the end to connect with the fractional amount. In this case, gaps between words might become too small to correctly determine the word boundaries (and thus to extract words). Thus, in many cases the full, independent result desired from the parallel mode may not actually be generated. An added complication is the presence of misspelled words like FOURTY instead of FORTY.

Recognition of legal amount proceeds in three stages. The first stage is the removal of overhangs, artifacts and salt-pepper noise. This stage also includes slant correction, smoothing, deriving estimates of word boundaries and segmentation of words into characters and/or sub-characters. The second stage involves the recognition of all possible words in a scan from left to right, using the estimated word boundaries as starting points for words. The third stage involves the construction of valid legal phrases using the list of recognized words. In this stage, for each phrase a confidence value is derived. Legal phrases with the highest confidences are then used to compare with the results of CAR for a final decision.

6.3.3. *Handwritten word recognition*

Legal amounts in checks contain less than forty words starting with "ONE" through "TWENTY" , "THIRTY" through "HUNDRED", "THOU-SAND", "AND", "DOLLARS", "ONLY" and the character '&'. These words are used as the lexicon for word recognition. The steps needed to perform this include the following: A) Slant estimation, correction and smoothing, B) Presegmentation to segment a word image into characters and/or sub-characters, C) Word matching to evaluate the likelihood value for each word in the lexicon,[9] D) Post-processing to refine the final selection (if feasible).

Fig. 6.13 shows the initial image of SEVENTEEN and the final segmented slant corrected image.

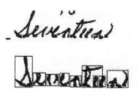

Fig. 6.13.   Initial and final steps in word recognition.

6.3.3.1. Slant correction

The binary image is then slant estimated and corrected (Fig. 6.14 and Fig. 6.15). The slant correction algorithm utilizes the chain code of the word contour. Horizontal chain elements can be neglected from border chains and the borders are divided into slant chain segments. As illustrated in Fig. 6.14, the orientation of each chain segment is given by

$$\theta = \tan^{-1}((n_1 + n_2 + n_3)/(n_1 - n_3)) \qquad (6.1)$$

where n_i is the number of chain elements at an angle of $i \times 45°$ (/ or — or \\). It is easy to show that the average orientation over all chain segments is also given by Eqn. (6.1).

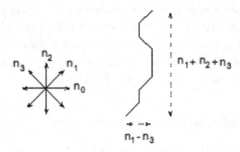

Fig. 6.14.   Orientation of a chain segment.

6.3.3.2. Character segmentation

Character segmentation is the process of extracting characters from a word/phrase image. There are several approaches to character segmentation: a) Contour analysis, b) Profile analysis, c) Run-length analysis, d) Disjoint box segmentation. In the contour analysis approach, possible segmentation points are detected in terms of local extrema analysis of the upper contour of a word. Among the local minima, those that are not deep enough from the adjacent local maxima are sequentially removed. To obtain characters separated by vertical lines, segmentation points may be shifted horizontally.

For the profile analysis, instead of the upper contour of a word, the upper profile is analyzed. The upper profile is a set of the topmost foreground pixels in each column. Post processing is required to find some segmentation points overshadowed by character segments such as the long "T" bar. Fig. 6.16 illustrates the segmentation procedure.

Fig. 6.15. (a) Input word image, (b) non-horizontal, border pixels, (c) slant corrected word image.

In the run length analysis, ligatures between "on", "or", "ve", etc. occasionally do not have a valley point in the upper contour. To detect and split these ligatures, a single-run stretch (Fig. 6.17) is detected and split at the middle point. A run is a vertical streak of one or more black pixels, and the single-run is the unique run on a single vertical line. Fig. 6.18 shows the result of segmenting the image and enclosing these in disjoint boxes.

6.3.3.3. *Word matching algorithm*

A lexicon directed algorithm is used for word matching algorithm. The number of the boxes (or segments) obtained by the disjoint box segmentation is generally greater than the number of characters in the word. In order to merge these segments into characters and find the optimal character segmentation, dynamic programming (DP) is applied using the total likelihood of characters as the objective function.

The likelihood of each character is given by a discriminant function described later. To apply DP, the boxes are sorted left to right according to the location of their centroids. If two or more boxes have the same x coordinates at the centroids, they are sorted top to bottom. Numbers above or below the boxes in Fig. 6.18 show the order of the sorted boxes. It is worth observing that the disjoint box segmentation and the box sorting

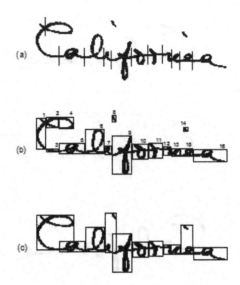

Fig. 6.16.   (a) Example of pre-segmentation points, (b) disjoint box segmentation, (c) optimum character segmentation.

Fig. 6.17.   Single-run stretch between 'o' and 'r'.

Fig. 6.18.   Disjoint box segmentation.

process reduce the segmentation problem to a simple Markov process, in most cases. For example, boxes 3 and 4 correspond to letter "v" of Seventeen, box 5 to "e", box 6 to "n" ... and so on. These assignments of boxes to letters are represented, for example, by

i	1	2	3	4	5	6	7	8	9
A_i	S	e	v	e	n	t	e	e	n
$j(i)$	1	2	4	5	6	8	9	11	13

where i denotes the letter number, $j(i)$ denotes the number of the last box corresponding to the i-th letter. Note that the number of the first box corresponding to the i-th letter is $j(i-1)+1$. Given $[j(i), i = 1, 2, \cdots, n]$ the total likelihood of character is represented by

$$L = \sum_{i=1}^{n} l(i, j(i-1)+1, j(i)) \tag{6.2}$$

where $l(i, j(i-1)+1, j(i))$ is the likelihood for i-th letter.

In the lexicon directed algorithm, an ASCII lexicon of possible words is provided and the optimal character segmentation is found for each lexicon word. All lexicon words are then ranked according to their optimal likelihood per character $(L*/n)$ to select the best candidate word. The optimal assignment (the optimal segmentation) which maximizes the total likelihood is found by applying the dynamic programming technique as follows. The optimal assignment $j(n)^*$ for n-th letter is the one such that

$$L^* = L(n, j(n)^*)_{j(n)} = \max L(n, j(n)) \tag{6.3}$$

where $L(k, j(k))$ is the maximum likelihood of partial solutions given $j(k)$ for the k-th letter, which is defined and calculated recursively by

$$L(k, j(k)) = \max_{j(1), j(2), \ldots, j(k-1)} \sum_{i=1}^{k} l(i, j(i-1)+1, j(i)) \tag{6.4}$$

$$
\begin{aligned}
L(k, j(k)) &= \max_{j(1), j(2), \ldots, j(k-1)} \sum_{i=1}^{k} l(i, j(i-1)+1, j(i)) \\
&= \max_{j(1), j(2), \ldots, j(k-1)} [l(k, j(k-1)+1, j(k)) + \sum_{i=1}^{k-1} l(i, j(i-1)+1, j(i))] \\
&= \max_{j(k-1)} [l(k, j(k-1)+1, j(k)) + \max_{j(1), j(2), \ldots, j(k-1)} \sum_{i=1}^{k-1} l(i, j(i-1)+1, j(i))] \\
&= \max_{j(k-1)} [l(k, j(k-1)+1, j(k)) + L(k-1, j(k-1))] \tag{6.5}
\end{aligned}
$$

and

$$L(0, j(0)) = 0 \tag{6.6}$$

for $j(0) = 1, 2, .., m$.

Starting from Eqn. (6.5), all $L(k, j(k))'s$ are calculated for $k = 1, 2, ..., n$ using Eqn. (6.4) to find $j(n)^\star$. The rest of $j(k)^\star$ ($k = n - 1, n - 2, ..., 1$) are found by back tracking a pointer array representing the optimal $j(k - 1)^\star$ which maximizes $L(k, j(k))$ in Eqn. (6.4).

Character likelihood is calculated using a modified quadratic discriminant function (MQDF)[12] which is less sensitive to the estimation error of the covariance matrix and requires less computation time and storage than the ordinary quadratic discriminant function (QDF). It is given as follows:

$$g(X) = \{|X - M|^2 - \sum_{i=1}^{k} \frac{\lambda_i}{\lambda_i + h^2} [\phi_i^T (X - M)]^2\}/h^2 \tag{6.7}$$

In Eqn. (6.7), X denotes the input feature vector, M denotes the sample mean vector for each character class, and λ_i and ϕ_i denote the eigenvalues and eigenvectors of the sample covariance matrix. Values of constants h^2 and k are selected experimentally to achieve the best performance. Given a feature vector, $g(X)$ is calculated for a character class specified by the word lexicon. The MQDF is derived from the Baye's decision rule for unknown Gaussian distribution.[16]

The histograms of the chain codes of the contour elements are used as the feature vector. The rectangular frame enclosing character contours is divided into 4×4 rectangular regions. In each region, a local histogram of the chain codes is calculated. The feature vector is composed of these local histograms. Since contour orientation is quantized to one of 4 possible values ($0°, 45°, 90°, 135°$) a histogram in each region has four components. Thus the feature vector has 64 components when all the 16 regions are included. Fig. 6.19 illustrates the extraction of chain-code features, where the histogram features of a region are shown on the right.

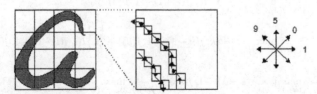

Fig. 6.19.   Feature extraction (chain code histogram).

j\i	0	1	2	3	4	5	6	7	8	9
0	0	0	0	0	0	0	0	0	0	0
1	0	0	0	0	0	0	0	0	0	0
2	0	0	1	1	1	1	0	0	0	0
3	0	0	0	0	0	0	0	0	0	0
4	0	0	0	0	1	1	1	1	1	0
5	0	0	0	0	0	0	0	0	0	0

One critical point in segmentation based recognition techniques, using dynamic programming, is the speed of feature extraction, because the correct segmentation points have to be determined in optimization process with respect to the total likelihood of the resultant characters. The use of the cumulative orientation histogram enables one to realize high speed feature extraction. Border following and orientation labeling are performed only once to an input word image, and the orientation feature vector of a rectangular region including one or more boxes is extracted by a small number of arithmetic operations. Each border pixel has one of four labels standing for horizontal, vertical, and two diagonal orientations. These pixels constitute four separate border pixel images, each of which is processed independently as follows. The cumulative orientation histogram is defined as

$$C(i,j) = C(i-1,j)+C(i,j-1)+C(i-1,j-1)+c(i,j), C(i,0) = C(0,j) = 0 \tag{6.8}$$

where $c(i,j) = 1$ denotes a border pixel image. Using this cumulative histogram, the number of border pixels within a specified rectangular region is calculated as

$$n(i_{min}, j_{min}, i_{max}, j_{max}) = C(i_{max}, j_{max}) - C(i_{min} - 1, j_{max})$$
$$- C(i_{max}, j_{min} - 1) + C(i_{min} - 1, j_{min} - 1) \tag{6.9}$$

where (i_{min}, j_{min}) and (i_{max}, j_{max}) are the coordinates of left upper corner and right lower corner of the rectangular region. For example, the number of border pixels in the rectangular region $(4, 2) - (8, 4)$ in the following example is calculated by $n(4, 2, 8, 4) = 9 - 0 - 2 + 0 = 7$.

Note that the calculation involves only one addition and two subtractions for any rectangular region with an arbitrary size.

j\i	0	1	2	3	4	5	6	7	8	9
0	0	0	0	0	0	0	0	0	0	0
1	0	0	0	0	0	0	0	0	0	0
2	0	0	1	2	3	4	4	4	4	4
3	0	0	1	2	3	4	4	4	4	4
4	0	0	1	2	4	6	7	8	9	9
5	0	0	1	2	4	6	7	8	9	9

6.3.3.4. *Legal line phrase matching*

The word extraction algorithm yields a list of words derived from the estimated word boundaries. From this, valid legal line phrases are extracted by eliminating improbable word sequences such as "Thirty Forty", "Ten Fourteen", "Eight Thirteen" etc. Using the confidences associated with individual words, an overall confidence value is derived for each valid legal phrase that can be constructed. Some examples are shown below.

6.4. Experimental Results for CAR and LAR

It is difficult to give comparable results with respect to the results obtained by other researchers and commercial software suppliers like A2IA, ParaScript etc. due to lack of a uniform benchmark and confidentiality clauses. This is even more so with handwritten checks since data on handwritten checks is not readily available. In general, overall accuracy is dependent on a) accuracy of field extraction for courtesy amount, b) accuracy of field extraction for legal amount, c) accuracy of field extraction for the dollar portion of courtesy amount, d) accuracy of field extraction for the cents portion of courtesy amount, e) recognition accuracies for the dollar part of CAR, cents part of CAR and the accuracy of legal amount and f) resolution of discrepancies between LAR and CAR. It is generally well known that recognition accuracy for LAR is considerably lower compared to recognition accuracy for CAR. We used 25,000 business checks and 10,000 personal checks to derive the results presented below.

Some comments are in order with regard to the above performance figures. It is very clear that we should develop new strategies to significantly improve the performance of CAR. Areas needing improvement include

- accurate extraction of the dollar and cents portion of CAR (currently at 86%).

Fig. 6.20. Example.

- improving accuracy of extracting cents amount when "/100" is part of the cents field.
- improving the accuracy of cents recognition (especially those involving "00").
- improving the accuracy of LAR field extraction (stripping of the cents part in LAR field).
- improving the accuracy of LAR (a formidable challenge).

It is also interesting to note that we have significantly outperformed the commercial vendor in the area of LAR recognition.

Business (Machine printed) checks:			Personal (Handwritten) Checks		
CAR (dollars & cents performance)	Commercial Vendor: 88.9%	Shridhar & Houle: 78.1%	*CAR (dollars & cents performance)*	Commercial Vendor: 68.7%	Shridhar & Houle: 43.5%
LAR (dollars & cents performance)	Commercial Vendor: 39.2%	Shridhar & Houle: 56.6%	*LAR (dollars & cents performance)*	Commercial Vendor: 32.2%	Shridhar & Houle: 46.1%
Combined (LAR + CAR for dollars & cents	Commercial Vendor: 90.1%	Shridhar & Houle: 95.5%	*Combined (LAR + CAR for dollars &*	Commercial Vendor: 79.1%	Shridhar & Houle: 70.5%
Shridhar & Houle combined (LAR+CAR) with commercial vendor: 98.60% (at 1% error)			Shridhar & Houle combined (LAR+CAR) with commercial vendor: 85.80% (at 1% error)		

6.5. Automatic Signature Verification

The primary motivation for this study arose from the need of financial institutions to stem the rising tide of significant losses due to fraudulent financial instruments. The financial institutions needed a verification system that would reject at least 80% of fraudulent checks or giros (financial instrument used in some European countries) while rejecting no more than 10-12% of all genuine checks.

In real life production when using one or two signature references (i.e. signatories) the false positive rate is too high to detect skilled forgery. In applications such as check or giro processing, extracting a clean signature is often a challenge because of the printed text added by transport to mark and track items. Recent efforts by some financial institutions have led to collection of historical data to better capture signature variations for a specific account. It may contain one or more signature writers, and it may contain instances where more than one signature is required on the given documents, depending on the amount or other account parameters.

Keeping more than two signatories is a concern because of the memory requirements (2K-5K per snippet) and privacy issues. Furthermore current image-based signature verification are too slow (0.5-2 sec per verification) to consider using a large number of references. This leads to the proposed approach where each reference signature is converted to a small number of pre-computed features resulting in verification speeds in excess of 60 verifications per second.

A survey of existing literature reveals a vast amount of research directed towards automatic signature verification (ASV) with a focus on detection of forgeries. There are far too many papers to cite in this area.[19-33] However, the authors refer the reader to the works of Sabourin et al,[19] Fang et al,[20] Plamondon et al[22-25] for some insightful ideas and methodologies. It is difficult to do a fair comparison unless a common signature reference database is provided. Most researchers have created databases using "controlled"/"ideal" conditions, which serves some analytical purposes. However, the current study is entirely based on real fraud cases that caused major losses to US banks. In successful fraud cases, most of the signatures are skilled forgeries, where the forgers practice to achieve a genuine representation of the account holder's signature.

Fig. 6.21. Images that have signature fields with artifacts (Masked for privacy).

In this study the authors emphasize the importance of using multiple references to capture the inherent signature variations that a signer normally exhibits when signing a document. Fig. 6.21, illustrates typical signature artifacts that may be present in the field. The major challenge with addressing detection of forgeries starts with the capture of a "clean" signature image from a given document without including overhangs from other fields in a document, printed text that overlaps with the signature and other artifacts introduced by the processor of checks or giros.

6.5.1. *Feature-based ASV*

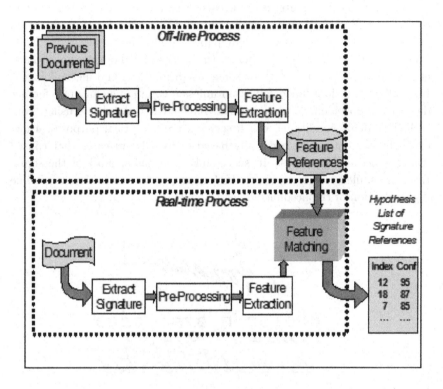

Fig. 6.22.   Feature-based ASV adapted to each account.

A big challenge faced by financial institutions is that would-be fraud perpetrators may find ways to acquire critical image data containing valuable information about the account holder, such as images of legitimate signatures. This data exists primarily because machine recognition of signatures and other fields in a document necessarily requires storage of document images in computers that are subject to unauthorized access. Furthermore, current ASV methods of detecting forgeries by comparing signatures to multiple reference images is generally slow, often limited to one or two verifications per second. A novel solution to the problem is now presented. If only features derived from signature reference images rather than the signature images themselves are stored in the computers, then the actual signatures are not exposed to unauthorized access. Forgers have very little use for feature data since those features do not help them to make signature forgeries. Secondly, since only the features from a test signature are required to be computed, automatic recognition with multiple reference signatures is much faster and more reliable. Finally, the amount of storage required to store the features from a large number of signature references is no larger than a typical image snippet for a single signature.

6.5.1.1. *Description of features*

The selection of features from a given signature is very critical to the overall performance of the verification system. A survey of existing literature reveals a wide diversity of features that have been proposed for signature matching. These include regional features such as

- pixel distribution in a rectangular grid superimposed on the image
- chain code distribution in a rectangular grid superimposed on the image
- top and bottom profiles of the signature image
- height distribution across the image
- white run distribution in a horizontal scan of the image
- peaks in the top and bottom profile
- distribution of zero crossings in the binarized signature image
- curvature distribution in the binarized image

In addition to regional features, global features also play a key role in verification. These include

- an estimate of the slant of the signature
- aspect ratio of the signature image
- overall pixel density
- maximum zero crossing in horizontal scans
- presence or absence of underlines in the signature image

While many of these features work well if the signature images are relatively clean, they generally perform poorly if the images include artifacts that are not part of the signature. Also, global features are generally only useful for rejecting a signature providing little help in a decision to accept a signature as legitimate. It is also important to realize that some form of normalization (either in the image space or the feature space) is often required to compensate for the size variations of test and reference signatures. The underlines that frequently appear in the signature areas of documents may often have to be erased from the images if bottom profiles of the signature are to be extracted. The study described here deals with signature images extracted from bank checks. The reference signatures are extracted from previously processed checks which were confirmed to be legitimate. The binary images were generated by a camera with a resolution set at 240 dpi. The main observation with regard to the captured images is the presence of significant noise and artifacts in the signature area. It is therefore very important that these artifacts be suppressed as much as is feasible prior to signature verification processing. Another observation is the inconsistency in the signature patterns. These inconsistencies may stem from the mood of the writer when the check was signed. The actual features used in this study consisted of regional features and global features as listed below:

- pixel distribution in a rectangular grid superimposed on the image
- edge (or chain code) distribution in a rectangular grid superimposed on the image
- slant
- pixel density
- aspect ratio

The global features (slant, pixel density and aspect ratio) were only used to decrease the verification confidence, based on observed differences. Dynamic warping was used to match the signature being analyzed against the reference signatures before a verification score was derived. A score was derived for each of the features and a composite score was then obtained as a weighted average of the individual scores.

6.5.2. *ASV based on dynamic feature matching*

We now describe the match function $f(x, y)$ between a reference and an unknown. The features used are labeled as follows:

(1) Pixel distribution over a grid of (MxN) - PixRef[i, j] and PixTest[i, j] for i = 1,2, , M and j = 1, 2, , N
(2) Four-directional chain code distribution over a grid of (KxL) - EdgeRef[i, j] and EdgeTest[i, j] for i = 1,2, , M and j = 1, 2, , N
(3) Pixel Density across image -PixRef and PixTest
(4) Aspect Ratio - AspRef and AspTest
(5) Slant of image - SlantRef and SlantTest

Fig. 6.23 shows the signature image with superimposed grid. All the images were normalized to a standard size of (75x300) pixels before the

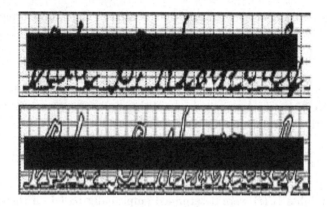

Fig. 6.23. Signature Image with a Superimposed Grid for Extraction of Pixel and Chain Code Features (Signature Masked for Privacy).

features were extracted from the images. The features for reference images were pre-computed and stored for use in verification. Pre-computing the reference image features resulted in considerable savings of CPU time during ASV processing.

For the pixel distribution features dynamic warping was used to derive a cost which was normalized to the range 0 - 1000. For the chain-code features, both weighted and Euclidean distances were computed and normalized to the range of 0 - 1000. The weighted and Euclidean distances are defined as :

$$g(X) = \sum_{i=1}^{k} \{\phi_i^T (X - M)\}^2 / \lambda_i \qquad (6.10)$$

$$d(X) = \|X - M\|^2 \qquad (6.11)$$

Here X denotes the test feature vector, M denotes the reference feature vector and λ_i and ϕ_i denote the eigenvalues and eigenvectors of the feature covariance matrix, ϕ_i is the i-th eigen value and k is the number of eigen vectors used. The global features were compared to derive a score in the range of 0 - 1000 as follows:

$PixDensity Cost = 2000*abs (PixRef-PixTest)/(PixRef+PixTest)$

$AspRatio Cost = 2000*abs (AspRef-AspTest)/(AspRef+AspTest)$

The slant feature was used only to penalize the final measure of similarity between the test and reference signatures if the relative difference is larger than 15%. For each feature that is used in this study, a measure of similarity was derived as

$$\text{Similarity}[i] = 100 * (1 - \text{Cost}[i]/1000), i = 1, 2, 3, 4.$$

Thus, if the two signatures are identical, then we would obtain a similarity measure of 100%. A weighted sum of the similarity scores was computed to obtain the overall similarity measure:

$$\text{Total Score} = \sum_{i=1}^{4} W(i) * \text{Similarity}(i), \quad \sum_{i=1}^{4} W(i) = 1 \qquad (6.12)$$

The weights $W(i)$ were determined empirically based on the effectiveness of each feature used in this study.

6.5.3. Multi-references ASV matching function

Now that we have a function $f(x, y)$ to match a reference against an unknown signature, we need to formulate how we use all the reference signatures to come up with a final score. For instance, we could use the maximum match values between the unknown and all the references but it may be sub-optimal compared to account specific adaptive measures as we present below. Also, an important question that we have answered here is whether or not all the reference signatures should be used. Some of the references may be poorly extracted and thus reduce the match value. So, some selection criteria has to be devised and formalized. Let R_k^x $(k = 1, 2, \cdots, K)$ be a subset of the genuine reference signatures from account x $(x = 1, 2, \cdots, X)$. Then let T_j^x $(j = 1, 2, \cdots, J)$ be the test signatures for account x. A match value can then be calculated by the average match to the references, i.e.

$$M_j^x = \frac{\sum_{k=1}^{K} f(T_j^x, R_k^x)}{K} \qquad (6.13)$$

where $f(x, y)$ is the signature matching function between x and y described earlier. It returns a match value between 0 (reject) to 100 (excellent). Since we have up to $K = 20$ possible reference signatures per account we can calibrate the match value and renormalize the match based on the average match and standard deviation for that account. In other words, we apply Eqn. (6.13) on the reference values, i.e.,

$$N_j^x = \frac{\sum_{k=1, k \neq j}^{K-1} f(R_j^x, R_k^x)}{(K - 1)} \qquad (6.14)$$

We can then compute the average and standard deviation of the values.

$$\overline{G}^x = \sum_{j=1}^{K} N_j^x / K \text{ and } \sigma_{G^x}^2 = \sum_{j=1}^{K} (N_j^x - \overline{G}^x)^2 / K \qquad (6.15)$$

With the a priori knowledge of the average and standard deviation of the reference match values, we can normalize the distribution as:

$$\widetilde{M}^x = (M^x - \overline{G}^x) / \sigma_{G^x} \qquad (6.16)$$

We then have a distribution with average 0 and standard deviation of 1. To remap this value to a value between 0 and 100 we applied a linear mapping so that 2 (i.e., average match + 2 times the standard deviation) becomes 90 and -5 (i.e., average match - 5 times the standard deviation) becomes 0.

$$M^x = 64.28 + 12.85 \bullet \widetilde{M}^x \qquad (6.17)$$

Clearly this value may be less than 0 for very bad match and above 100 for extremely good match. The match value was truncated to be between 0 an 100. Finally, it is important to mention that the number of references (i.e., K) is a parameter that varies from 2 to 20. The selection criterion used to pick the next reference is the most centered (based on Euclidean distance) of the remaining references.

6.5.4. *Results*

A total of 85 accounts (50 of which contained real fraudulent signatures) were used in this test. For each account, at least 20 genuine signatures were available for the reference set and 5 to 30 signature images were available for testing. Ideally a genuine match should get a match value computed from Eqn. (6.17) closer or above 100 and a fraudulent signature should be closer or below 0. One of the interesting finding depicted in Fig. 6.24 is that above 12 references the performance degraded. In all there were 1778 genuine signatures and 151 confirmed fraudulent signatures. The genuine signatures had an average match and standard deviation of 66.25 and 22.6, respectively. The fraudulent signatures had an average match and standard deviation of 15.96 and 20.0, respectively. Even though 20 or more reference signatures were available from the TRAINING set, we wanted to determine the impact on verification accuracy as we increased the number of references used in matching. We set the false negative rate at 10% (no more than 10% of the actual fraud items is accepted as legitimate) and then measured the false positive rate as we increased the number of reference signatures.

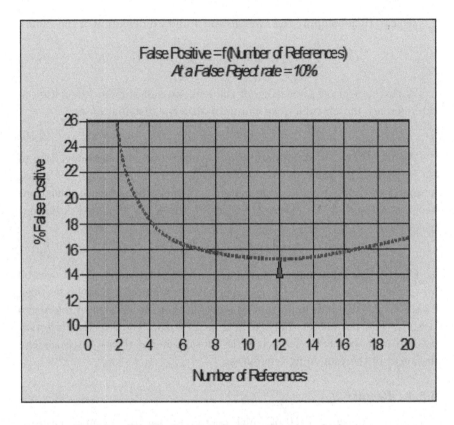

Fig. 6.24.   False Positive as a function of number of references.

Fig. 6.24 clearly shows that using more than 12 references does not help in reducing the false positive percentage. In fact, the false positive rate may increase when using more references. This may appear abnormal but after further analysis of the 20 possible references, some available candidates may be of such poor quality that they may allow bad input signatures to be accepted. Once the optimal number of 12 references has been discovered we then measured the performance as a function of the reference threshold. Accordingly, Fig. 6.25 shows the cumulative distributions for genuine and fraudulent signatures when using 12 references. For example at a threshold of about 30, almost 80% of the actual fraudulent signatures are identified while only about 10% of the genuine signatures are identified as forgery suspects (false positives). At a threshold of 48, almost 90% of the fraudulent signatures are identified while the number of genuine signatures identified

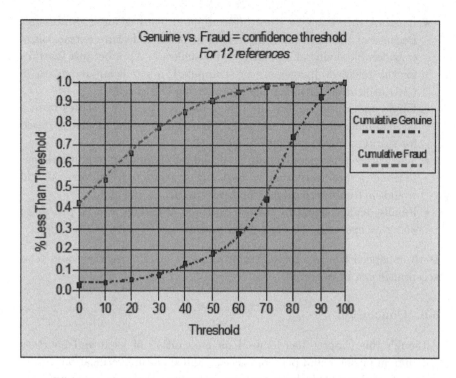

Fig. 6.25. Cumulative Distributions for Genuine and Fraud Signatures.

as forgery suspects increases to 16% of the total genuine signatures. Various strategies outside the scope of this study are available to reduce the number of forgery suspects identified for review. The overall measure is computed for a given matching threshold T below which the signature is rejected. For those above or equal to T, we can calculate the false positive rate FP = flagged-fraud / flagged. It is noteworthy to observe that 12 feature references fits in less than 2 kilobytes. It is interesting to observe that 40% of the fraudulent signatures are identified at the threshold setting of zero. Due to the normalization that is performed, thresholds would have to be set to negative values to falsely accept forged signatures. Similarly, almost 1.2% of the genuine signatures are also falsely rejected at the threshold setting of zero. The main advantages of the proposed technique are summarized below.

- The proposed ASV allows matching against a large number of signature references, thus increasing the accuracy.

- It is only necessary to store pre-computed features for each account. Because of the inherent compression involved in feature extraction, a considerable saving of storage space is achieved. Also, because features for the reference images are pre-computed, a significant reduction in CPU utilization for much faster processing is realized.
- Furthermore, the amount of storage required to store features from a large number of reference signatures is about the same as that required for storing a single reference image.
- The feature references contain no visual representation of potential use to fraud perpetrators, thereby reducing exposure to fraud losses should would-be fraud perpetrators find ways to access this data.
- Finally, binary signature images captured at 240 dpi can be processed at a rate exceeding 60 images per second.

With enhanced features further improvements in false rejection and false acceptance can be achieved.

6.6. Conclusion

Although this chapter has focused on recognition of legal and courtesy amounts in business and personal checks, and signature verification, recognition of all the fields in both business and personal checks is our ultimate goal. This will allow financial institutions to construct a profile for each account holder and will allow for fraud prevention which is a major source of revenue loss. We have shown that even though our performance in some areas are below what is commercially available, the combination of our system with the commercially available recognition systems enable the achievement of cost effective automation of check processing.

Acknowledgments

The authors would like to acknowledge Jim Mason (president of Kappa Image LLC) for his valuable suggestions.

References

1. Prince, Cheryl J, "Check Imaging's Uphill Battle," Bank Systems & Technology Vol. 32, No. 8, pp. 34- 38, Aug. 1995.
2. Mentis Corporation, "1995 Banking Systems & Technology Database - Check Processing & Imaging," 40 pages.

3. DataPro, "Document Imaging System" Report No. 6010, December 1994, pp. 1-6.

4. Dixon, James D., "Check-processing Efficiency," Bank Management, pp. 53-55, Jul./Aug. 95

5. Y. Y. Tang, C. Y. Suen, C. D. Yan, and M. Cheriet, "Document Analysis and Understanding: A Brief Survey," ICDAR '91, St-Malo France, pp. 17-31.

6. G. F. Houle and K. B. Eom, "On The Use of A Priori Knowledge In Character Recognition," SPIE-1992,1661-14

7. International Conference on Document Analysis and Recognition, Vol. I and II, Montreal, Quebec, August 14-16, 1995.

8. T. Paquet, Y. Lecourtier, "Handwriting Recognition: Application on Bank cheques," Proceedings of 1st Intl. Conf. Document Anal. and Recog., p. 749, St. Malo, France, Sept. 1991

9. J. Salome, M. Leroux, J. Badard, "Recognition of Cursive Script Words in a Small Lexicon," Proc. 1st Int. Conf. Document Analysis Research, 1991, pp.774-782.

10. N. Gorsky, "Off-line Recognition of Bad Quality Handwritten Words Using Prototypes," Fundamentals in Handwriting Recognition, S. Impedovo (Ed), NATO ASI Series F: Computer and Systems Sciences, Vol. 124, Springer-Verlag, 1994.

11. F. Kimura, M.Shridhar, and Z. Chen "Improvements of a Lexicon Directed Algorithm for Recognition of Unconstrained Handwritten Words", Proc. of 2nd ICDAR Conf. pp. 18-22 (1993).

12. F. Kimura, S. Tsuruoka, Y. Miyake, M. Shridhar, "A Lexicon Directed Algorithm for Recognition of Unconstrained Handwritten Words," IEICE Trans. Inf. & Syst., Vol. E77-D, No. 7, pp. 785-793, July 1994.

13. E. Lecolinet, J. P. Crettez, "A Grapheme-Based Segmentation Technique for Cursive Script Recognition," Proc. of 1st ICDAR, pp. 740-748 (1991).

14. C. K. Chow, "Optimal Read / Error Tradeoff" (invited presentation), Proceedings of 3rd Annual Symposium on Document Analysis and Information Retrieval, ISRI, Las Vegas, 1994.

15. R. M. K. Sinha, B. Prasada, G. F. Houle, and M. Sabourin, "Hybrid Contextual Text Recognition with String Matching," IEEE Trans. on PAMI-15, 9, Sep. 1993.

16. F. Kimura, M. Shridhar, "Handwritten numeral recognition based on multiple algorithms," Pattern Recognition, Vol. 24, No. 10, pp. 969-983, 1991

17. G. Kim, V. Govindaraju, "A lexicon driven approach to handwritten word recognition for real-time applications," IEEE Transactions on Pattern Analysis and Machine Intelligence, Vol. 19, No. 4, PP. 366-379, 1997

18. G.F. Houle, "Handwritten word segmentation." Fundamentals in Handwriting Recognition, Springer-Verlag Berlin Heidelbert 1994, pp. 228-232

19. M. Shridhar, G.F. Houle, R. Bakker, F. Kimura, "Real-time feature-based automatic signature verification," Proceeding of IWFHR-10, La Baule, France on October 23-26, 2006.

20. Edson J. R. Justino, A. El Yacoubi, F. Bortolozzi and R. Sabourin, "An Off-Line Signature Verification System Using HMM and Graphometric Features", DAS 2000.

21. Robert Sabourin: Off-line signature verification: recent advances and perspectives. 84-98, Brazilian Symposium on Document Image Analysis (BSDIA 1997).
22. F. Bauer, and B. Wirtz, "Parameter Reduction and Personalized Parameter Selection for Automatic Signature Verification", ICDAR-1995 183-186 pp
23. R. Plamondon and G. Lorette, "Automatic Signature Verification and Writer Identification - The State of the Art", Pattern Recognition, Vol. 22, No. 2, pp. 107-131, 1989.
24. F. Leclerc and R. Plamondon, "Automatic Signature Verification: The State of the Art - 1989-1993", International Journal of Pattern Recognition and Artificial Intelligence, Vol. 8, No. 3, pp. 643-660, 1994.
25. R. Plamondon and S. Srihari, "On-Line and Off-Line Handwriting Recognition: A Comprehensive Survey", IEEE Transactions on PAMI, Vol. 22, No. 1, pp. 63-84, 2000.
26. J-J. Brault and R. Plamondon, "Segmenting Handwritten Signatures at Their Perceptually Important Points", IEEE Transactions on PAMI, Vol. 15, No. 9, pp. 953-957, 1993.
27. A. Zimmer and L. L. Ling, "Preprocessing: Segmenting by Stroke Complexity", Proceedings of the VI Iber-American Symposium on Pattern Recognition, pp. 89-94,.Florianpolis, Brazil, 2001.
28. W. Guerfali and R. Plamondon, "The Delta LogNormal Theory for the Generation and Modeling of Cursive Characters", Proceedings of the ICDAR, Vol. 2, pp. 495-498, 1995.
29. L. O'Gorman, "Curvilinear Feature Detection from Curvature Estimation", Proceedings of the 9th International Conference on Pattern Recognition, pp. 1116-1119, 1988.
30. R. Sabourin. and G. Genest, "An extended Shadow-Code Based Approach for Off-Line Signature Verification: Part I - Evaluation of the Bar mask Definition", Proceedings of the IAPR, pp. 450-455, Jerusalem, Israel, 1994.
31. K. V. Mardia, "Statistics of Directional Data", Academic Press, 1972.
32. J. P. Drouhard, R. Sabourin and M. Godbout, "Neural network approach to off-line signature verification using directional PDF", Pattern Recognition, Vol. 29, No. 3, pp. 415-42, 1996
33. Jinhong K. Guo, David Doermann, Azriel Rosenfeld, "Off-Line Skilled Forgery Detection Using Stroke and Sub-Stroke Properties," icpr, p. 2355, 15th International Conference on Pattern Recognition (ICPR'00) - Volume 2, 2000.

Chapter 7

Statistical Deformation Model for Handwritten Character Recognition

Seiichi Uchida

Faculty of Information Science and Electrical Engineering
Kyushu University, Fukuoka-shi, 819-0395 Japan,
uchida@is.kyushu-u.ac.jp

This paper introduces statistical deformation models for offline and on-line handwritten character recognition problems. Those models utilize eigen-deformations, which are deformations frequently observed in a certain category. Eigen-deformations are learned from actual character patterns by combining two technologies, i.e., elastic matching and principal component analysis (PCA). The learned eigen-deformations can improve performance of the handwritten character recognition tasks, as established through experimental results.

Contents

S. Uchida

7.1. Introduction

One of the main problems of offline and online handwritten character recognition is how to deal with the deformations in characters. A promising strategy to this problem is the incorporation of a deformation model. If recognition can be done with a reasonable deformation model, it may become tolerant to deformations within each character category.

There have been proposed many deformation models and some of them were designed in an empirical manner. Recognition methods based on elastic matching have often relied on a continuous and monotonic deformation model.[1-5] This is a typical empirical model and has been developed according to the observation that character patterns often preserve their topologies. Affine deformation models[6-8] and local perturbation models (or image distortion models[9]) are also popular empirical deformation models.

While the empirical models generally work well in handwritten character recognition tasks, they are not well-grounded by actual deformations of handwritten characters. In addition, the empirical models are just approximations of actual deformations. In addition, they cannot incorporate category-dependent deformation characteristics. In fact, the category-dependent deformation characteristics exist. For example, in category "M", two parallel vertical strokes are often slanted to be closer. In contrast, in category "H", however, the same deformation is rarely observed.

Statistical models are better alternatives to the empirical models. The statistical models learn deformation characteristics from actual character patterns. Thus, if a model learns the deformations of a certain category, it can represent the category-dependent deformation characteristics.

Hidden Markov model (HMM) is a popular statistical model for handwritten characters (e.g., Ref. 10–15). HMM has not only a solid stochastic background, but also a well-established learning scheme. HMM, however, has a limitation on regulating global deformation characteristics; that is, HMM can regulate local deformations of neighboring regions due to its Markovian property.

This chapter is concerned with another statistical deformation model of offline and online handwritten characters. This deformation model is based on a combination of elastic matching and principal component analysis (PCA) and also capable of learning actual deformations of handwritten characters. Different from HMM, this deformation model can regulate not only local deformations but also global deformations. In the following, the contributions of this chapter are summarized.

7.1.1. *Contributions of this Chapter*

The first contribution of this chapter is to introduce a statistical deformation model for *offline* handwritten character recognition. The model is realized by two steps. The first step is the automatic extraction of the deformations of character images by elastic matching. Elastic matching is formulated as an optimization problem of the pixel-to-pixel correspondence between two image patterns. Since the resulting pixel-to-pixel correspondence represents the displacement of individual pixels, i.e., the deformation of one character image from another. The second step is a statistical analysis of the extracted deformations by PCA. The resulting principal components, called *eigen-deformations*, represent intrinsic deformations of handwritten characters.

The second contribution is to introduce a statistical deformation model for *online* handwritten character recognition. While the discussion is similar to the above offline case, it is different in several points. For example, deformations often appear as the difference in pattern length. Consequently, online handwritten character patterns have rarely been handled in a PCA-based statistical analysis framework, which assumes the same dimensionality of subjected patterns. In addition, online handwritten character patterns often undergo heavy nonlinear temporal/spatial fluctuation. Elastic matching to extract the deformation between two patterns solves these problems and helps to establish a statistical deformation model.

7.2. Statistical Deformation Model of Offline Handwritten Character Recognition

7.2.1. *Extraction of Deformations by Elastic Matching*

The first step for statistical deformation analysis of handwritten character images is the extraction of deformations of actual handwritten character images and it can be done automatically by elastic matching. Elastic matching is formulated as the following optimization problem. Consider an $I \times I$ reference character image $\boldsymbol{R} = \{\boldsymbol{r}_{i,j}\}$ and an $I \times I$ input character image $\boldsymbol{E} = \{\boldsymbol{e}_{x,y}\}$, where $\boldsymbol{r}_{i,j}$ and $\boldsymbol{e}_{x,y}$ are d-dimensional pixel feature vectors at pixel (i,j) on $\boldsymbol{R}$ and (x,y) on $\boldsymbol{E}$, respectively. Let $\boldsymbol{F}$ denote a 2D-2D mapping from $\boldsymbol{R}$ to $\boldsymbol{E}$, i.e., $\boldsymbol{F} : (i,j) \mapsto (x,y)$. As shown in Figure 7.1, the mapping $\boldsymbol{F}$ determines the pixel-to-pixel correspondence from $\boldsymbol{R}$ to $\boldsymbol{E}$. Elastic matching between $\boldsymbol{R}$ and $\boldsymbol{E}$ is formulated as the minimization

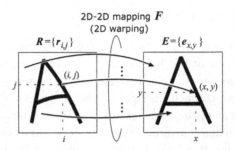

Fig. 7.1.   Elastic matching between two character images.

problem of the following objective function with respect to $\boldsymbol{F}$:

$$J_{R,E}(\boldsymbol{F}) = \|\boldsymbol{R} - \boldsymbol{E}_F\|, \tag{7.1}$$

where $\boldsymbol{E}_F$ is the character image obtained by fitting $\boldsymbol{E}$ to $\boldsymbol{R}$, i.e., $\boldsymbol{E}_F = \{\boldsymbol{e}_{x_{i,j}, y_{i,j}}\}$, and $(x_{i,j}, y_{i,j})$ denotes the pixel of $\boldsymbol{E}$ corresponding to the (i,j)th pixel of $\boldsymbol{R}$ under $\boldsymbol{F}$. On the minimization, several constraints (such as a smoothness constraint and boundary constraints) are often assumed to regularize $\boldsymbol{F}$.

Let $\tilde{\boldsymbol{F}}$ denote the mapping $\boldsymbol{F}$ which minimizes $J_{R,E}(\boldsymbol{F})$ of (7.1). This mapping $\tilde{\boldsymbol{F}}$ represents the relative deformation of the input image $\boldsymbol{E}$ from the reference image $\boldsymbol{R}$. Specifically, the deformation of $\boldsymbol{E}$ is extracted as the following $2I^2$-dimensional vector, called *deformation vector*,

$$\boldsymbol{v} = ((1-x_{1,1}, 1-y_{1,1}), \ldots, (i-x_{i,j}, j-y_{i,j}), \ldots, (I-x_{I,I}, I-y_{I,I}))^T. \tag{7.2}$$

Note that $\boldsymbol{v}$ is a discrete representation of $\tilde{\boldsymbol{F}}$.

The constrained minimization of (7.1) with respect to $\boldsymbol{F}$ (i.e., the extraction of $\boldsymbol{v}$) is done by various optimization strategies. If the mapping $\boldsymbol{F}$ is defined as a parametric function, iterative strategies and exhaustive strategies are often employed for optimizing the parameters of $\boldsymbol{F}$. In contrast, if the mapping $\boldsymbol{F}$ is a non-parametric function, combinatorial optimization strategies, such as dynamic programming, local perturbation, and deterministic relaxation, are employed. Various formulations and optimization strategies of the elastic matching problem are summarized in.[16]

7.2.2. *Estimations of Eigen-Deformations*

Eigen-deformations of a category are intrinsic deformations of the category and defined as M principal axes $\{\boldsymbol{u}_1, \ldots, \boldsymbol{u}_m, \ldots, \boldsymbol{u}_M\}$ which span an M-

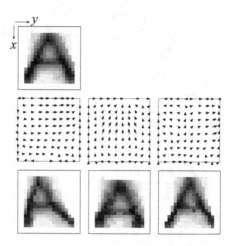

Fig. 7.2.   Eigen-deformations of handwritten characters.

dimensional subspace in the $2I^2$-dimensional deformation space. The eigen-deformations can be estimated by applying PCA to $\{v_n | n = 1, \ldots, N\}$, where v_n is the extracted deformation between R and E_n. Specifically, the eigen-deformations are obtained as the eigen-vectors of the covariance matrix $\Sigma = \sum_n (v_n - \bar{v})(v_n - \bar{v})^T / N$, where $\bar{v}$ is the mean vector of $\{v_n\}$.

Figure 7.2 shows the first three eigen-deformations estimated from 500 handwritten characters of the category "A". The first eigen-deformation u_1, that is, the most frequent deformation of "A", was the global slant transformation. The second was the vertical shift of the horizontal stroke and the third was the width variation of the upper part. Consequently, this figure confirms that frequent deformations of "A" were extracted successfully.

Note that in this experiment, the dimensionality of the deformation vector v was 74 though the size of the character image pattern was 20×20 (i.e., $I = 20$ and $2I^2 = 800$). This is because a "sparse" EM was used where the displacements of 3 pixels (leftmost, middle, and rightmost) were optimized at every row. The displacements of the other pixels were given by linear interpolation.

Figure 7.3 shows the patterns R deformed by the first three eigen-deformations u_1, u_2, and u_3 with the amplification with $k\sqrt{\lambda_m}$ ($k = -2, -1, 0, 1, 2$), where λ_m is the eigenvalue of the mth eigenvector. This figure also show that frequent deformations were extracted as the eigen-deformation at each category.

S. Uchida

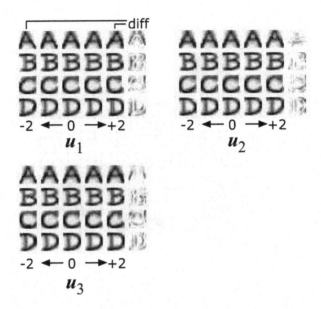

Fig. 7.3.   Reference pattern R deformed by top three eigen-deformations, u_1, u_2, and u_3.

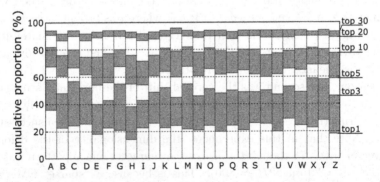

Fig. 7.4.   Category-wise cumulative proportion $\rho(M)$ of eigen-deformations at $M = 1, 3, 5, 10, 20$, and 30. Note that $\rho(M) = 100\%$ at $M = 74$.

Figure 7.4 shows the cumulative proportion of each category. The cumulative proportion by the top M eigen-deformations is defined as $\rho(M) = \sum_{m=1}^{M} \lambda_m / \sum_{m=1}^{74} \lambda_m$. In all categories, the cumulative proportion exceeded 50% with the top $3 \sim 5$ eigen-deformations and 80% with the top $10 \sim 20$ eigen-deformations. Thus, the distribution of deformation vectors was not isotropic and can be approximated by a small number of eigen-deformations. In other words, there existed a low-dimensional and efficient subspace of deformations.

7.2.3. *Recognition with Eigen-Deformations (1)*

The eigen-deformations can be utilized for recognizing handwritten character images. A direct use of the eigen-deformations for evaluating a distance between two characters R and E is as follows:

$$D_{\text{disp}}(R, E) = (v - \overline{v})^T \Sigma^{-1}(v - \overline{v}) = \sum_{m=1}^{2I^2} \frac{1}{\lambda_m} \langle v - \overline{v}, u_m \rangle^2, \qquad (7.3)$$

where E is an unknown input image and v is the deformation extracted by the elastic matching between R and E. This is the well-known Mahalanobis distance and evaluates the statistical divergence of the estimated deformation on E from the deformations which usually appear in the category of R. If the estimated deformation v gives a large distance value, the result of elastic matching between E and R is somewhat abnormal and therefore the category of R will not become a candidate of the correct category of E.

The recognition performance by $D_{\text{disp}}(R, E)$ alone, however, is not satisfactory. This is because the distance $D_{\text{disp}}(R, E)$ completely neglects the distance of pixel features. This fact will be certified through an experimental result in 7.2.5.

An alternative and reasonable choice is the linear combination of the distance in the pixel feature space and the distance in the deformation space,[17] that is,

$$D_{\text{hybrid}}(R, E) = (1 - w)D_{\text{feat}}(R, E) + wD_{\text{disp}}(R, E), \qquad (7.4)$$

where $D_{\text{feat}}(R, E)$ is the elastic matching distance in the pixel feature space, i.e.,

$$D_{\text{feat}}(R, E) = J_{R,E}(\tilde{F}), \qquad (7.5)$$

and w is a constant $(0 \leq w \leq 1)$ to ballance two distances.

In practice, the modified Mahalanobis distance[18] is employed instead of (7.3). Specifically, the higher-order eigenvalues λ_m $(m = M + 2, \ldots, 2I^2)$

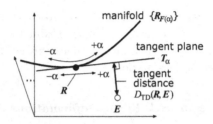

Fig. 7.5.   Manifold $\boldsymbol{R}_\alpha$, its tangent plane $\boldsymbol{T}_\alpha$, and tangent distance $D_{\mathrm{TD}}(\boldsymbol{R}, \boldsymbol{E})$.

are replaced by λ_{M+1}, to suppress the estimation errors of higher-order eigenvalues in (7.3). According to this replacement, (7.3) is reduced to

$$D_{\mathrm{disp}}(\boldsymbol{R}, \boldsymbol{E}) \sim \frac{1}{\lambda_{M+1}} \|\boldsymbol{v} - \overline{\boldsymbol{v}}\| + \sum_{m=1}^{M} \left(\frac{1}{\lambda_m} - \frac{1}{\lambda_{M+1}} \right) \langle \boldsymbol{v} - \overline{\boldsymbol{v}}, \boldsymbol{u}_m \rangle^2. \quad (7.6)$$

The parameter M is to be determined experimentally, for example, considering the cumulative proportion $\rho(M)$.

7.2.4.   *Recognition with Eigen-Deformations (2)*

The above recognition method has a weak-point that two heterogeneous distances D_{feat} and D_{disp} are added naively to create the single distance D_{hybrid}. In contrast, the following method[19] can avoid this weak-point by embedding the eigen-deformations into an elastic matching procedure.

Consider that the mapping $\boldsymbol{F}$ is defined as a linear combination of eigen-deformations, i.e.,

$$\boldsymbol{F}(\alpha) = \sum_{m=1}^{M} \alpha_m \boldsymbol{u}_m, \quad (7.7)$$

where $\alpha = (\alpha_1, \ldots, \alpha_m, \ldots, \alpha_M)^T$. Then an elastic matching problem with $\boldsymbol{F}(\alpha)$ can be formulated as the minimization problem of the following objective function:

$$J_{\boldsymbol{R},\boldsymbol{E}}(\alpha) = \|\boldsymbol{R}_{\boldsymbol{F}(\alpha)} - \boldsymbol{E}\|, \quad (7.8)$$

where $\boldsymbol{R}_{\boldsymbol{F}(\alpha)}$ is the reference pattern deformed by the mapping $\boldsymbol{F}(\alpha)$.

The set of deformed reference patterns, $\{\boldsymbol{R}_{\boldsymbol{F}(\alpha)} | \forall \alpha\}$, will form an M-dimensional manifold in an $(I^2 \cdot d)$-dimensional pixel feature space. Thus the minimum value of $J_{\boldsymbol{R},\boldsymbol{E}}(\alpha)$ is equivalent to the shortest distance between the M-dimensional manifold and $\boldsymbol{E}$.

Fig. 7.6.   Tangent vectors of the category "A", derived from R and eigen-deformations u_1, u_2, and u_3.

The minimization problem (7.8) with respect to α is hard to solve directly. This is because the M-dimensional parameter vector α to be optimized is involved in the nonlinear function R. Thus, some approximation is required to solve the optimization problem.

In,[19] the approximation scheme used in the tangent distance method[20] has been employed for the above minimization problem. As shown in Fig. 7.5, the minimum distance $\min_\alpha J_{R,E}(\alpha)$ can be approximated by the following *tangent distance*,

$$D_{\mathrm{TD}}(R, E) = \min_\alpha \|T_\alpha - E\|, \qquad (7.9)$$

where T_α is the tangent plane of the manifold at $\alpha = 0$. The tangent plane is an M-dimensional hyperplane in the feature space and linear with respect to α. Thus the minimization problem of (7.9) has a closed-form solution. Intuitively speaking, the distance $D_{\mathrm{TD}}(R, E)$ is the Euclidean distance between the input E and its closest point on the tangent plane. Figure 7.6 shows three tangent vectors which span the tangent plane of the category "A".

7.2.5. *Recognition Result*

Figure 7.7 shows results of a handwritten character recognition experiment using 26 (categories) × 1,100 (samples) isolated handwritten English upper-case character images from the standard character image database ETL6. The first 100 samples of each category were simply averaged to create one reference pattern R and the next 500 samples were used as training samples E_n to estimate the eigen-deformations. The remaining 500 samples ($13,000 = 26 \times 500$ samples in total) were used as test samples E.

The highest recognition rate (99.47%) was attained by D_{hybrid} with its best weight w. The recognition rate by D_{disp}, i.e., the recognition rate by evaluating only the deformation v, was not sufficient. Thus, the pixel features (i.e., appearance features) should not be neglected for evaluating

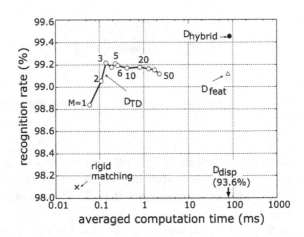

Fig. 7.7.   Relation between computation time (ms) and recognition rate (%).

the distance of two character images. The recognition rates by D_{TD} were saturated around $M = 3$. This result is supported by the fast saturation of the cumulative proportion of Fig. 7.4.

7.2.6.   Related Work

The original idea of the eigen-deformations, i.e., principal components of deformations, can be found in the point distribution models (PDM), which has been proposed by Cootes et al.[21] and applied to various patterns. Shen and Davatzikos[22] have introduced an automatic deformation collection scheme into the PDM. PDM for curvilinear patterns has been applied to face recognition,[23] Chinese character recognition,[24] and hand posture recognition.[25] Uchida et al.[17] have extended the PDM to deal with fully 2D deformations and have applied to an elastic matching-based handwritten character recognition system.

Iwai et al.[26] have applied PCA to interframe motion vector fields obtained by block matching, which can be considered as the simplest elastic matching. Bing et al.[27] have proposed a face expression recognition method based on a subspace of face deformations. Naster et al.[28] have analyzed a deformation vector extended to deal with the variation of the pixel feature value. Those ideas will be promising for recognizing handwritten character images.

The eigen-deformations are the principal axes spanning a subspace of the $2I^2$-dimensional deformation space. Any point on the subspace rep-

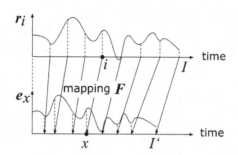

Fig. 7.8.   Elastic matching between two online handwritten character patterns.

resents a deformation F. On the other hands, we can consider a subspace on the $(I^2 \cdot d)$-dimensional pixel feature space. Any point on the subspace represents an $I \times I \times d$ image pattern. The axes spanning this subspace are derived as dominant eigen-vectors of the covariance matrix $\Sigma = \sum_n (E_n - \overline{E})(E_n - \overline{E})^T / N$, where $\overline{E}$ is the mean vector of $\{E_n\}$. There are huge research attempts about the latter subspace.[29,30] Eigenface[31] and parametric eigenspace[32,33] are famous examples of those attempts.

While the latter subspace also can represent a set of deformed character patterns, the former subspace will represent the set in a more compact manner. Consider a character image R and a set of character images created by translating R. The number of the eigen-deformations estimated from the set is two; one will represent horizontal shift and the other vertical shift. In contrast, the number of the principal eigen-vectors in the pixel feature space will be far larger than two. This superiority will hold for other geometric deformations and thus the subspace of deformations can be a more efficient representation than the subspace of the pixel features.

7.3. Statistical Deformation Model of Online Handwritten Character Recognition

7.3.1. *Extraction of Deformations by Elastic Matching*

Consider two online handwritten character patterns, $R = r_1, r_2, \ldots, r_i,$ $\ldots, r_I$ and $E = e_1, e_2, \ldots, e_x, \ldots, e_{I'}$. The former is a reference character pattern and the latter is an input character pattern. Their elements r_i and e_x are d-dimensional feature vectors representing the features at i and x; they are often 3-dimensional vectors comprised of x-coordinate, y-coordinate, and local direction.

S. Uchida

Let F denote a 1D-1D mapping from R to E, i.e., $F : i \mapsto x$. Figure 7.8 depicts F. Elastic matching between R and E is formulated as the minimization of the following objective function with respect to F,

$$J_{R,E}(F) = \|R - E_F\|, \qquad (7.10)$$

where E_F is the character pattern obtained by fitting E to R, i.e., $E_F = e_{x_1}, \ldots, e_{x_i}, \ldots, e_{x_I}$, where x_i represents the $i - x$ correspondence under F. On the minimization, several constraints (such as the monotonicity and continuity constraint defined as $x_i - x_{i-1} \in \{0, 1, 2\}$ and boundary constraints $x_1 = 1$ and $x_I = I'$) are often assumed to regularize F. This constrained minimization problem can be solved effectively by a DP algorithm, called dynamic time warping or DP matching, and its detail are omitted here.

The deformation of E from R is represented by the following $(I \cdot d)$-dimensional deformation vector,

$$v = (e_{x_1} - r_1, \ldots, e_{x_i} - r_i, \ldots, e_{x_I} - r_I)^T. \qquad (7.11)$$

It should be noted that the dimension of the above deformation vector v is fixed at $(I \cdot d)$ and independent of the length of E, i.e., I'. This property is very important to apply various statistical methods, such as PCA, to sequential patterns.

Also note that it is possible to define v as

$$v = (1 - x_1, \ldots, i - x_i, \ldots, I - x_I)^T.$$

Although this definition is a straightforward modification of the deformation vector of (7.2), we will use v of (7.11) as a deformation vector here. This is because in online character recognition, r_i and e_x are often spatial features and thus their difference represents a deformation.

7.3.2. *Estimation of Eigen-Deformations*

Eigen-deformations of online handwritten character patterns are also estimated by the procedure of 7.2.2; that is, they can be estimated as dominant eigen-vectors of the covariance matrix of v.

Eigen-deformations of online handwritten digits were estimated by using about 1,000 samples from UNIPEN Train-R01/V07 database (1a).[34] Figure 7.9 shows character patterns generated by $R + \bar{v} \pm 2\sqrt{\lambda_m}u_m$ ($m = 1, 2$).[35] That is, those patterns are reference patterns deformed by their mean deformation vector $\bar{v}$ and the first two eigen-deformations u_m. Note that the effect of $\bar{v}$ was not significant because R was set around the center

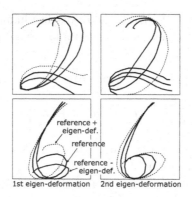

Fig. 7.9. Reference character pattern deformed by the first two eigen-deformations of "2" and "6".

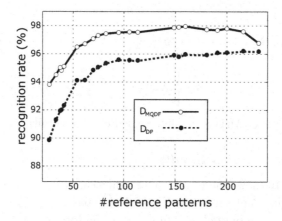

Fig. 7.10. Accuracy of online character recognition based on eigen-deformations.

of the set of the training samples by a clustering technique and thus the norm of $\bar{v}$ was small.

Figure 7.9 shows that deformations frequently observed in actual characters were estimated as eigen-deformations. For example, the first eigen-deformation of "6" represents the vertical variation of its loop part, and the second one represents the horizontal variation of the loop part.

7.3.3. Recognition with Eigen-Deformations

For online handwritten character recognition based on the eigen-deformations, the following quadratic discrimination function (QDF) is a possible choice.[35] The QDF is the Bayes discrimination function under the assumption that the deformation vectors have a Gaussian distribution and defined as

$$D_{\mathrm{QDF}}(\boldsymbol{R}, \boldsymbol{E}) = (\boldsymbol{v} - \overline{\boldsymbol{v}})^T \Sigma^{-1}(\boldsymbol{v} - \overline{\boldsymbol{v}}) + \log |\Sigma| + (I \cdot d) \log 2\pi$$

$$= \sum_{m=1}^{I \cdot d} \frac{1}{\lambda_m} \langle \boldsymbol{v} - \overline{\boldsymbol{v}}, \boldsymbol{u}_m \rangle^2 + \log \prod_{m=1}^{I \cdot d} \lambda_m + (I \cdot d) \log 2\pi. \quad (7.12)$$

The last term, $(I \cdot d) \log 2\pi$, cannot be omitted here because each category has a different dimension of $\boldsymbol{v}$ (i.e., $I \cdot d$).

As noted 7.2.3, the estimation errors of higher-order eigenvalues are amplified in (7.12). Thus, the modified quadratic discriminant function (MQDF)[18] was employed, where the higher-order eigenvalues λ_m ($m = M+1, \ldots, I \cdot d$) are replaced by λ_{M+1}, i.e.,

$$D_{\mathrm{MQDF}}(\boldsymbol{R}_c, \boldsymbol{E}) \sim \frac{1}{\lambda_{M+1}} \|\boldsymbol{v} - \overline{\boldsymbol{v}}\|^2 + \sum_{m=1}^{M} \left(\frac{1}{\lambda_m} - \frac{1}{\lambda_{M+1}} \right) \langle \boldsymbol{v} - \overline{\boldsymbol{v}}, \boldsymbol{u}_m \rangle^2$$

$$+ \log \left\{ (\lambda_{M+1})^{I \cdot d - M} \prod_{m=1}^{M} \lambda_m \right\} + (I \cdot d) \log 2\pi. \quad (7.13)$$

The parameter M is to be determined experimentally.

7.3.4. Recognition Results

Figure 7.10 shows the results of an online character recognition experiment using digit samples from the UNIPEN database. Recognition rates attained by D_{MQDF} are plotted as a function of the total number of reference patterns, which are created by a clustering technique. The recognition rates attained by the conventional DP-matching distance (D_{DP}), which equals to the minimum value of (7.10), are also plotted.

As shown in Fig. 7.10, MQDF with the eigen-deformations outperformed the DP-matching distance. This will be because elastic matching results $\boldsymbol{F}$ which were deviated from the distribution of the deformations of the category were penalized by the eigen-deformations in MQDF. Thus, the above recognition method can avoid misrecognitions due to overfitting, which is the phenomenon that the distance between $\boldsymbol{E}$ and $\boldsymbol{R}$ of a wrong category is underestimated by unnatural mapping $\boldsymbol{F}$.

This result also proves that D_{MQDF} outperforms that statistical dynamic time warping (SDTW),[5] which is a recent and sophisticated online character recognition technique. In fact, it has been reported in[5] that

SDTW attained 97.10% on the same UNIPEN data set by 150 reference patterns.

7.3.5. Related Work

Sequential patterns, such as online handwritten character patterns, are often re-sampled to have the same dimension in advance to applying PCA or other statistical analysis techniques. For example, Deepu et al.[36] have proposed an online character recognition technique based on a subspace method where all online character patterns are re-sampled to have a constant number of data points. The online character recognition technique by Zheng et al.[37] is more radical because they used only two points (i.e., the start point and the end point) for each character stroke segment. In the handwriting synthesis technique by Wang et al.,[38] online cursive handwritings are firstly aligned to be the same dimension and then PCA is applied to them. PCA-based gesture/motion analysis techniques[39–41] also re-sampled gesture patterns to have the same dimension. An exception is Martens and Claesen,[42] which employed elastic matching to extract a fixed-dimensional deformation vector from online signatures.

7.4. Conclusion

Statistical deformation models of handwritten character images and online handwritten character patterns have been introduced. The body of those models are eigen-deformations, which are deformations frequently observed in a certain category and span a subspace in a deformation space of the category. For estimating the eigen-deformations, elastic matching and principal component analysis (PCA) were employed. The former was utilized to extract deformations of target patterns automatically. For the online patterns, elastic matching was also utilized to adjust difference in their lengths. The latter was utilized to derive the eigen-deformations as the principal components of the extracted deformations.

The usefulness of the statistical deformation models with eigen-deformations has been confirmed experimentally. The estimated eigen-deformations could represent frequently observed deformations in each character category. In addition, the eigen-deformations were useful for improving accuracy in both of offline and online character recognition tasks.

S. Uchida

Acknowledgment

The author thanks Emeritus Professor Hiroaki Sakoe for his invaluable supervision.

References

1. Y. Fujimoto, S. Kadota, S. Hayashi, M. Yamamoto, S. Yajima, and M. Yasuda, "Recognition of handprinted characters by nonlinear elastic matching," Proc. ICPR, pp. 113–118, 1976.
2. K. Yoshida and H. Sakoe, "Online handwritten character recognition for a personal computer system," IEEE Trans. Consumer Electronics, vol. CE-28, no. 3, pp. 202–209, 1982.
3. D. J. Burr, "Designing a handwriting reader," IEEE Trans. PAMI, vol. PAMI-5, no. 5, pp. 554–559, 1983.
4. S. D. Connell and A. K. Jain, "Template-based online character recognition," Pattern Recognit., vol. 34, no. 1, pp. 1–14, 2001.
5. C. Bahlmann and H. Burkhardt, "The writer independent online handwriting recognition system flog on hand and cluster generative statistical dynamic time warping," IEEE Trans. PAMI, vol. 26, no. 3, pp. 299–310, 2004.
6. T. Wakahara, "Shape matching using LAT and its application to handwritten numeral recognition," IEEE Trans. PAMI, vol. 16, no. 6, pp. 618–629, 1994.
7. T. Wakahara and K. Odaka, "On-line cursive Kanji character recognition using stroke-based affine transformation," IEEE Trans. PAMI, vol. 19, no. 12, pp. 1381–1385, 1997.
8. T. Wakahara, Y. Kimura, and A. Tomono, "Affine-invariant recognition of gray-scale characters using global affine transformation correlation," IEEE Trans. PAMI, vol. 23, no. 4, pp. 384–395, 2001.
9. D. Keysers, C. Gollan, and H. Ney, "Local context in non-linear deformation models for handwritten character recognition," Proc. ICPR, vol. 4, pp. 511–514, 2004.
10. R. Nag, K. H. Wong, and F. Fallside, "Script recognition using hidden Markov models," Proc. ICASSP, vol. 3, pp. 2071–2074, 1986.
11. J. Hu, M. K. Brown, W. Turin, "HMM based on-line handwriting recognition," IEEE Trans. PAMI, vol. 18,no. 10, pp. 1039–1045, 1996.
12. M. Nakai, N. Akira, H. Shimodaira, and S. Sagayama, "Substroke approach to HMM-based on-line Kanji handwriting recognition," Proc. ICDAR, pp. 491–495, 2001.
13. W. Cho, S. -W. Lee, and J. H. Kim, "Modeling and recognition of cursive words with hidden Markov models," Pattern Recognit., vol. 28, no. 12, pp. 1941–1953, 1995.
14. H. -S. Park and S. -W. Lee "A truly 2-D hidden Markov model for off-line handwritten character recognition," Pattern Recognit., vol. 31, no. 12, pp. 1849–1864, 1998.

15. S. S. Kuo and O. E. Agazzi, "Keyword spotting in poorly printed documents using pseudo 2-D hidden Markov models," IEEE Trans. PAMI, vol. 16, no. 8, pp. 842–848, 1994.
16. S. Uchida and H. Sakoe, "A survey of elastic matching techniques for handwritten character recognition," IEICE Trans. Inf. & Syst., vol. E88-D, no. 8, pp. 1781–1790, 2005.
17. S. Uchida and H. Sakoe, "Eigen-deformations for elastic matching based handwritten character recognition," Pattern Recognit., vol. 36, no. 9, pp. 2031–2040, 2003.
18. F. Kimura, K. Takashina, S. Tsuruoka, "Modified quadratic discriminant functions and the application to Chinese character recognition," IEEE Trans. PAMI, vol. 9, no. 1, pp. 149-153, 1987.
19. S. Uchida and H. Sakoe, "Handwritten character recognition using elastic matching based on a class-dependent deformation model," Proc. ICDAR, vol. 1 of 2, pp. 163–167, 2003.
20. P. Simard, Y. Le Cun, J. Denker, and B. Victorri, "An efficient algorithm for learning invariances in adaptive classifier," Proc. ICPR, vol. 2, pp. 651–655, 1992.
21. T. F. Cootes, C. J. Taylor, D. H. Cooper, and J. Graham, "Active shape models - their training and application," Comput. Vis. Image Und., vol. 61, no. 1, pp. 38–59, 1995.
22. D. Shen and C. Davatzikos, "An adaptive-focus deformable model using statistical and geometric information," IEEE Trans. PAMI, vol. 22, no. 8, pp. 906-913, 2000.
23. A. Lanitis, C. J. Taylor, and T. F. Cootes, "Automatic interpretation and coding of face images using flexible models," IEEE Trans. PAMI, vol. 19, no. 7, pp. 743–756, 1997.
24. D. Shi, S. R. Gunn, and R. I. Damper, "Handwritten Chinese radical recognition using nonlinear active shape models," IEEE Trans. PAMI, vol. 25, no. 2, pp. 277–280, 2003.
25. T. Ahmad, C. J. Taylor, A. Lanitis, and T. F. Cootes, "Tracking and recognising hand gestures, using statistical shape models" Image Vis. Computing, vol. 15, pp. 345–352, 1997.
26. Y. Iwai, T. Hata, M. Yachida, "Gesture recognition based on subspace method and hidden Markov model," Proc. IROS, vol. 2 of 2, pp. 960–966, 1997.
27. Y. Bing, C. Ping, and J. Lianfu, "Recognizing faces with expressions: within-class space and between-class space," Proc. ICPR, vol. 1 of 4, pp. 139–142, 2002.
28. C. Naster, B. Moghaddam, and A. Pentland, "Flexible images: matching and recognition using learned deformations," Comput. Vis. Image Und., vol. 65, no. 2, pp. 179–191, 1997.
29. E. Oja, Subspace Methods of Pattern Recognition, Research Studies Press and J. Wiley, 1983.
30. Proceedings of Subspace2007. http://www.viplab.is.tsukuba.ac.jp/ss2007

31. M. Turk and A. Pentland, "Eigenfaces for recognition," Journal of Cognitive Neuroscience, vol. 3, no. 1, pp. 71–86, 1991.
32. H. Murase and S. K. Nayar, "Illumination planning for object recognition using parametric eigenspace," IEEE Trans. PAMI, vol. 16, no. 12, pp. 1219–1227, 1994.
33. H. Hase, T. Shinokawa, M. Yoneda, C. Y. Suen, "Recognition of rotated characters by eigen-space," Proc. ICDAR, vol. 2, pp. 731–735, 2003.
34. I. Guyon, L. Schomaker, R. Plamondon, M. Liberman, and S. Janet, "UNIPEN project of on-line data exchange and recognizer benchmarks," Proc. ICPR, pp. 29–33, 1994.
35. H. Mitoma, S. Uchida, and H. Sakoe "Online character recognition based on elastic matching and quadratic discrimination," Proc. ICDAR, vol. 1 of 2, pp.36–40, 2005.
36. V. Deepu, S. Madhvanath, A. G. Ramakrishnan, "Principal component analysis for online handwritten character recognition," Proc. ICPR, vol. 2 of 4 , pp. 327–330, 2004.
37. J. Zheng, X. Ding, Y. Wu, and Z. Lu, "Spatio-temporal unified model for on-line handwritten Chinese character recognition," Proc. ICDAR, pp. 649–652, 1999.
38. J. Wang, C. Wu, Y.-Q. Xu, and H.-Y. Shum, "Combining shape and physical models for online cursive handwriting synthesis," Int. J. Doc. Ana. Recog., vol. 7, no. 4, pp. 219–227, 2005.
39. T. D. Sanger, "Optimal movement primitives," Advances in Neural Info. Proc. Systems, vol. 7, pp. 1023–30, 1995.
40. Y. Yacoob and M. Black, "Parameterized modeling and recognition of activities," Comput. Vis. Image Und., vol. 73, no. 2, pp. 232–247, 1999.
41. A. Fod, M. Mataric,and O. C. Jenkins, "Automated derivation of primitives for movement classification," Autonomous Robots, vol. 12, no. 1, pp. 39–54, 2002.
42. R. Martens and L. Claesen, "On-line signature verification by dynamic time-warping," Proc. ICPR, pp. 38–42, 1996.

Chapter 8

Robust Word Recognition for Museum Index Cards with the SNT-Grid

Simon M. Lucas* and Alejandro Foullon-Pérez†

University of Essex, Department of Computing and Electronic Systems
Wivenhoe Park, Colchester, CO4 3SQ, United Kingdom
*sml@essex.ac.uk, †afoull@essex.ac.uk

The scanning n-tuple (SNT) grid provides an extremely efficient way to apply a character classifier to all possible locations within in image. This makes it a natural choice for segmentation free (convolutional) OCR. This paper reports the first attempt to build a practical word recognition system based on the SNT-grid. The system is designed for recognizing type-written words on museum archive cards. The raw recognition outputs of the SNT-grid are post-processed using a priority queue best-first word recognition system. Precision and recall results are reported for this task, together with the combined standard F measure of approximately 93%. These results show that the system is significantly better for this task than a leading commercial general purpose OCR system.

Contents

175

8.1. Introduction

Optical Character Recognition (OCR) has been a field of research for over 50 years. However, recognizing text in historical documents still represents a difficult challenge. These documents exhibit a group of characteristics that make it hard to design a general solution, and while general purpose commercial OCR systems have been consistently improving at this task, they still fail to achieve sufficient accuracy for many purposes. Difficulties include a mixture of machine printed and handwritten characters, smears, hand-made strokes, slants in text rows, uneven ink thickness, touching or broken characters etc. The focus of this paper is to retrieve machine printed words in museum archive cards containing these characteristic problems.

A common feature of most OCR methods is to segment the image into character regions prior to the character recognition phase. If this segmentation is done in a strict way then it becomes hard to recover from segmentation errors, since the appropriate character regions might never be passed to the recogniser. An extreme alternative is to design segmentation free OCR methods, applying a classifier at all locations in an image. This results in a huge number of character hypotheses and necessitates a post-processing of these using contextual methods.

The approach taken in this paper is to have a balance between these two ideas. On one hand, we locate possible text areas with a simple, fast and robust process. On the other hand, we apply a classifier through all positions of the areas extracted. In the word recognition method used, the whole character hypothesis graph located in the text area is passed to the algorithm.

The system uses a scanning n-tuple (SNT) grid[1] for the segmentation-free recognition stage, and a priorty-queue dictionary search algorithm[2] for the contextual stage. These methods for chosen for two main reasons. First, the SNT-grid offers an extremely efficient way to apply a recogniser it to all possible image locations. Second, the Priority Queue Method is a fast technique to obtain the in best-first order the probabilities of all words in a lexicon that exceed a specific threshold given a character hypotheses graph.

As part of the research, we also investigated how synthetically created training data can best be used for training an SNT-Grid classifier, and show that contextual training is necessary in order to get best performance for this word recognition task.

8.2. Synthetic Training Data

The model we use to create the synthetic training data set is the one proposed by Baird.[3] It is based on the physical deformations produced in printing and scanning/imaging processes. This model operates on the gray level values of an image, and is parameterized in ten different ways. However, there are some deformations that were not necessary for our experiments. For example, the misplacement in the vertical and horizontal direction of the character. Baird suggests the values of the parameters, but we tuned them to match the variations observed in our museum card data, by visual inspection. The parameters we use are:

- Width and Height: we obtain the factors to scale the image in width and height with a normal distribution with mean 1.0 and standard deviation of 0.02.
- Rotation - Skew: we rotate by a random number of degrees, draw from a Gaussian with zero mean and standard deviation of 2.
- Blur: The blur refers to the point spread in the ink or scanning process. A Gaussian filter models this and in our experiments we use σ normally distributed with mean 0.9 and standard deviation 0.13.
- Sensitivity: One of the physical deformations in the scanning process is due to the variations in the sensitivity of photo sensors. This is modeled in two stages. First, the value of *sensitivity* for each character are normally distributed with mean 0.125 and standard deviation 0.04. Secondly, we add to each pixel random noise normally distributed with mean 0 and standard deviation equal to the *sensitivity*.
- Binarization: This is a critical step in OCR. We will explain below the details of how we implemented the binarization process.

The last stage in the deforming process is the binarization of the image. In this case we explored various methods. We tried different local adaptive algorithms that have been proven to be the fastest with convincing performance. A comprehensive literature review about different methods can be found in 4, 5, 6, and 7. Although Niblack's method[8] is the fastest, White's algorithm[9] is better in terms of discriminating background noise after binarization. One big advantage of having a clear background is that we don't need to create it synthetically. White's method can be simplified by the following expression:

$$y = \begin{cases} 1 \text{ if } m_{w \times w}(i,j) < I(i,j) * \text{bias} \\ 0 \text{ otherwise} \end{cases} \tag{8.1}$$

where $m_{w \times w}(i, j)$ is the local mean over a $w = 10$ sized window, bias $= 1.1$, and $I(i, j)$ is the centre pixel gray value of the window.[7]

A typewriter font[a] is considered as the ground truth, and some minor adjustments were necessary in cases where the font character was dissimilar to the character images in the cards. Some resulting deformations produced by the model can be seen in Fig. 8.1.

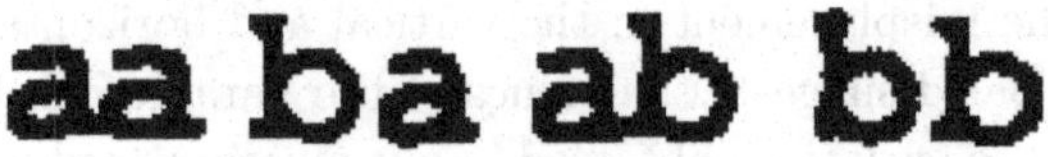

aa ba ab bb

Fig. 8.1.   Randomly deformed character pairs.

8.3. The Scanning N-Tuple Grid

Before describing the SNT-grid, we first give a brief summary of n-tuple classifiers. N-Tuple networks date back to the late 1950s with the optical character recognition work of Bledsoe and Browning.[10] More detailed treatments of standard n-tuple systems can be found in[11] and.[12] They work by randomly sampling the input space with set of n points. If each sample point has m possible values, then the sample point can be interpreted as an n digit number in base m, and used as an index into an array of weights, also called a Look-Up Table (LUT). There are many varieties of n-tuple systems. Original n-tuple systems were often implemented in hardware, since the indexed look-up process is easy to implement using RAM chips. The very simplest of these used a 1-bit wide memory configuration, also known as binary n-tuples. Each memory location in a binary n-tuple records whether an address has occurred during training or not. Such systems suffer the risk of *saturation*, where excess training can make test-set performance worse, since given noisy training data, all addresses will eventually occur. For this reason, modern n-tuple systems tend to store continuous value weights, or probabilities. When trained on supervised data, probabilistic n-tuple systems can be trained using single-pass maximum likelihood techniques, where the probability of each address occurring is estimated as the number of times it occurred during training, divided by the number of occurrences of all addresses in the n-tuple.

More recently Lucas[13] introduced a back-propagation training rule based on optimizing a cross-entropy measure, and was able to improve

---

[a]TrueType font technology

performance compared to the standard maximum likelihood method. The current work uses maximum likelihood training, but it may be possible to obtain improved results by optimizing a cross-entropy measure instead.

The SNT-Grid is based on scanning n-tuple (SNT) classifiers, but applied to two-dimensional rather than one-dimensional signals. SNT classifiers were introduced in 14–15. The principal advantage was to extend the standard n-tuple classifiers to patterns of variable lengths. The experiments have shown that this method is both fast and accurate.

Figure 8.2 illustrates how the SNT-Grid is applied to an image. A scanning window is slid through all positions assigning to it the address encoded. In our example, from left to right, top to bottom and taking black pixels as 1 and white pixels as 0, the corresponding binary address at that position is: 0000 1111 1110 0011.

Fig. 8.2.   SNT-Grid example.

The parameters of the SNT-Grid are: the number of sample points in the horizontal direction n_x, and their spacing g_x; the number of sample points in the vertical direction n_y and their spacing g_y. Thus, the correct nomenclature is SNT-Grid(n_x, n_y, g_x, g_y).

8.3.1. Training and recognition of the SNT-Grid

To estimate the probability of an address we use the maximum likelihood method. Let $m_k(a)$ be the counter of how many times the address a for class k is found in the training stage. Each address is then normalized by dividing this count by the sum of all addresses determined through all training input patterns. A common practice is to calculate the log probabilities to facilitate posterior operations. Thus, the log probabilities can be expressed as:

$$l_k(a) = \log\left(\frac{m_k(a) + \varepsilon}{\sum_{j=0}^{N-1} m_k(j)}\right) \tag{8.2}$$

where $N = 2^{(n_x \cdot n_y)}$ and ε is a constant to prevent zero probabilities. Usually ε takes small values, we set it in our experiments to 0.5. This process is similar to the add-one discounting technique using in n-gram based statistical language models.

At a specific location of the image, we define:

$$l_k(I) = \sum_{i \in I} l_k(a(i)) \tag{8.3}$$

as the log-likelihood of a region I in the image for a class k. This is calculated with the sums of all log likelihoods of each address $a(i)$ at all positions $i \in I$. This can be calculated very efficiently using the integral image method of Viola and Jones,[16] Eq. (8.3). The calculation depends only on the integral values at the four corners of the required rectangle within in image, and does not depend on the size of the rectangle.

8.3.2. Fast encoding with a two pass templates

A critical step for the calculations explained before is to have an address encoded image. In Ref. 1, Lucas and Cho propose a fast indexing by performing a two one-dimension passes over the entire image in the vertical and horizontal directions. The result is a significant computational time saving compared to a naive implementation.

The main advantage of this method is that its computational cost is linear with respect to the number of pixels in an image. A naive approach would cost $O(whWH)$, where W and H are the width and height of the image respectively, and w and h refer to the width and height of the grid. The cost can be reduced to $O(WH)$ if the addresses are obtained with the fast two-pass method.

Figure 8.3 shows how the first pass calculates the vertical addresses. For this example we use a SNT-Grid(2,2,2,2). The first and vertical swap of the standard n-tuple, will have numbers in the range of 0 to $2^{n_y} - 1$. This array will be called the column features. In the example there are two different positions of the vertical samples of the grid and their respective vertical address. The number between colons is the binary string representation of the pixels.

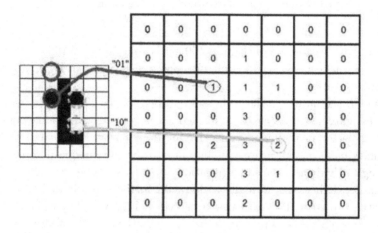

Fig. 8.3. Vertical one-dimension encoding of the original bitmap.

Over this array, the horizontal scan takes place and it is mixed with the row features. The binary strings are combined to produce the final address. The final range of addresses is from 0 to $2^{n_y \times n_x} - 1$. Figure 8.4 shows the final address array, and how they should be merged.

8.4. Isolated Characters Results in Cards with Synthetic Data

In this section we show the results of recognition of isolated characters in the museum cards using our synthetic training data. We trained the system to recognize all the uppercase and lowercase letters in the alphabet including the 10 digits (62 classes in total). For characters considered as the targets,

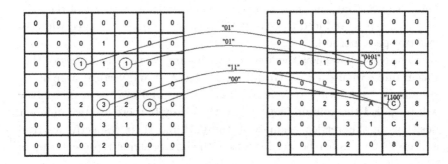

Fig. 8.4. Second and horizontal one-dimension encoding for use in training and recognition.

we manually located all of them in 150 cards containing 10,196 characters. We tried various SNT-Grid configurations and a SNT-Grid(4,4,2,3) gave the best results.

Due to the nature of the addresses encoded by the classifier, we wanted to investigate how the system performed when we used surrounding context for each letter in training. Note that addresses that are located on the left margin of the character will contain information outside its bounding rectangle. Evidently, the same situation appears with the top margin, but we ignored it because normally a character in the cards is well separated from the top row. This is better observed in Fig. 8.2. The right bottom corner of the SNT-Grid in that position, where the encoded address will be located, is inside character "H" bounding region. However, some "tuples" on the left margin of the grid are collecting information of its neighbour character "C".

One possible way to attack this problem is to train each character with all possible characters to its left (context). Table 8.1 shows a comparison between training with and without context. A similar idea was used for the recognition set where characters were completely isolated or were processed with context. In these experiments region I was defined as the whole isolated image.

We can conclude from Table 8.1 that the recognition of characters ignoring its context does not depend on the type of training. Both results are very similar. However, on the other hand, it does affect significantly when we are trying to recognize them including their surrounding character.

Although the results are not impressive, they are quite acceptable if we consider some special cases. We inspected the confusion matrix and

Table 8.1. Comparison of different types of training and recognition.

	Recognition without context	Recognition with context
Isolated Training	89.88%	82.74%
Context Training	89.64%	89.57%

we could observe that there were many misrecognitions in characters that were much alike than other classes. For example, the digit 1 is confused as lowercase l in many occasions; as well as uppercase O with digit 0. Some not so obvious confusions are between the uppercase and lowercase versions of P and W, respectively. The reason is because the classifier tolerates slight invariances in size. If we consider these special cases, the accuracy can improve to 95%.

Naturally, these confusions increase as the number classes do. However, when the system performs in smaller groups of classes, and the similarity between them is not close, the classifier trained synthetically performs excellent in the cards. This is the case in the recognition of exclusively the digits. The accuracy in these isolated digits is 99.58% when trained and recognized with context.

8.5. Priority Queue Method

The SNT-Grid is a fast classifier that can be efficiently applied at all positions in an image. However, the classification graph implicitly produced by this will be huge and the performance of the system to retrieve words from a lexicon, if performed naively, could be unacceptably slow. Therefore, efficient data structures are required for searching the best paths. The following description is adapted with minor modifications from.[2]

The Priority Queue Method[2] is a collection of data structures and objects that efficiently finds lexicon entries that form paths in a graph of containing character hypotheses. The algorithm is a type of Stack Decoding algorithm.[17,18] Before listing the algorithm in pseudo-code, we describe the other data structures and object classes used.

A *CharHypothesis* is an element in the recognition graph that gives its x-position, its character class and its confidence. We treat these confidences here as independent probabilities, and compute the likelihood of a path as the product of its individual character confidence values (calculated by summing the log-likelihoods).

The *Priority Queue* is a standard data structure that offers ordered access to a set of objects It provides three methods of interest to us here: hasMore(), returns true if the queue is not empty, false if it is; add() adds an object to the queue; pop() returns and removes the first item from the queue. Note that all items in the queue must be comparable with each other. The queue is maintained in order of highest confidence objects (i.e. paths) first.

The *trie* is a data structure that stores all lexicon words in a prefix tree. Ours is implemented using a Hash table indexed on the next character to store the references to the next nodes in the trie. Each node has a boolean flag to indicate whether this node represents a complete word. Each node also holds a reference to the previous node in order to retrieve the word represented by that node by performing a back-trace to the root of the trie. Our trie has two methods of relevance to the *wordSearch* function: follow(char c) returns the node reached from the current node by following character c. The function next() returns the set of all characters that can follow the current node in the trie.

The *Path* class stores the node in the trie reached by this path, the column in the graph (x-position) that this path ends at, and the confidence of this path. *Path* implements the *Comparable* interface such that more likely paths are pushed to the front of the priority queue.

The *PathLut* (Look-Up Table) class offers efficient access to the best paths to each node (column) in the graph. This is implemented as an array of hashtables. The hashtable for each column contains a set of paths, indexed on the trie node reached by the end of the path. This allows us to determine very efficiently whether a newly extended path should be extended any further.

This brings us to the *extensionsOf* function. This takes a path, the recognition graph and the pathLut. This function gets the set of possible extensions of the trie node of the path, and considers extending each one. First the confidence of that character in that position is looked up in the recognition graph. We can allow some spatial variation at this stage, by looking for characters in the recognition graph that lie in the inclusive range of *gap* between *minGap* to *maxGap* from the current end point of the path. The decision is made as follows. If pathLut[path.x + gap] already holds a better (more likely) way of reaching that trie node at that column in the graph, then there is no need to extend it further - otherwise it should be extended. We also prune paths that fall below some likelihood threshold, for reasons of efficiency. There is a trade-off however, as over-aggressive pruning can lead to the optimal solution being missed.

The pseudo-code is the following:

```
PriorityQueue wordSearch(RecGraph recGraph,Trie words,int n){

    // Declare variables
    PriorityQueue activeQueue;
    PriorityQueue completed;
    PathLut pathLut;

    // initialise
    activeQueue = new PriorityQueue();
    completed = new PriorityQueue();

    pathLut = new PathLut(recGraph.width);

    for each CharHypothesis ch in recGraph {
        Path path = new Path(words.follow(ch.char),ch.x,ch.p);
        activeQueue.add(path);
    }

    // do the search
    while (activeQueue.hasMore() AND completed.size() < n){
        Path curPath = activeQueue.pop();
        Set extensions = extensionsOf(curPath,recGraph,pathLut);
        for each Path extended in extensions {
            if (extended is complete){
                completed.add(extended)
            }
            activeQueue.add(extended);
        }
    }
    return completed;
}
```

8.6. Experimental Results

We manually located the words contained in 50 museum cards. The total number of words in them is 491 and these were considered as the ground truth (targets) for the evaluation of our system. The dictionary was built with approximately 8,000 words of common proper names. All of the cards have proper names. Scientific terms for moths are also included (approximately 3,000 terms). The names and terms that were not included from databases we added them manually to the lexicon. The whole dictionary contains 11,141 different words.

Among the words in the lexicon some of them are substrings of others. For the experiments in this paper we added some characters as delimiters for each word to the left and right of it in order to eliminate the detection of substrings in the cards. These delimiters should be characters that are not contained in the original set of words. The main reason for doing this is that we lacked an overall language model for entire cards (or entire text-rows). Given a higher-level context, word delimiting would at least in theory be unnecessary, since the recognition of short word substrings would be unlikely to form part of an overall high-confidence solution.

We define D as the set of valid delimiters:

$$D = \left\{ \text{" "}, \text{"."}, \text{":"}, \text{","} \right\} \tag{8.4}$$

Let be P_D the set containing all possible permutations from D, where the size of each permutation is 2 and the size of the set, D, from which elements are permuted is 4. This is:

$$P_D = \left\{ p_1, p_2, ... p_{\binom{4}{2}} \right\} \tag{8.5}$$

Equation (8.6) is applied to every word in the dictionary. Let be p_i^n be the i-th character of the n-th permutation contained in P_D, where $i = 1, 2$ and $n = 1, 2, \ldots, \binom{4}{2}$. The set W contains all unique words in the lexicon, and w is an element in that set. Therefore each delimited word is added to the final lexicon and obtained by:

for $\forall\, w \subset W$ and for $\forall\, p^n \subset P_D$: delimited word $= p_1^n + w + p_2^n$ (8.6)

The information retrieval field uses three widely known measurements for this kind of experiment evaluations. These are precision, recall and F-measure or harmonic mean:

$$\text{precision} = \frac{c}{e} \tag{8.7}$$

$$\text{recall} = \frac{c}{t} \tag{8.8}$$

$$F = \frac{2 \cdot (\text{precision} \cdot \text{recall})}{(\text{precision} + \text{recall})} \qquad (8.9)$$

where t is the total targets (words) in the card's set, e is the number of words estimated and c the number of words correctly recognized. The F-measure provides a way to penalize a low value of either precision or recall. This punishes trivial strategies such as *return every possible thing*, which would have perfect recall but very low precision.

Our first approach was to implement a complete segmentation free method. This is, all positions of the image were classified and were included in the word recognition algorithm. Figure 8.5 depicts an original image together with an interpretation for the top classification for characters in each pixel.

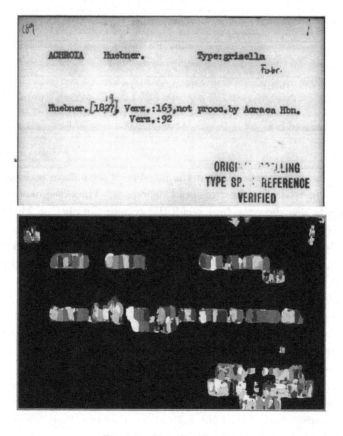

Fig. 8.5. Top classification.

Each color belongs to a different class containing the biggest probability in the recognition graph. It may not be necessary to find the absolute best path for an entry lexicon to retrieve a word. This assumption permits us to try different ways to optimize the speed of the system. One of them is to set the minGap and maxGap parameters with the same value in the Priority Queue Method. We observed that each character is evenly distributed by a distance of 13 pixels wide and decided to set minGap = maxGap = 13. Once a word is detected in a row, the method searches for a higher probability of the same word in its surroundings within a window. Naturally, the minimum threshold of the probability of the retrieved words affects the behaviour of the precision, recall and speed[b] of the system. Table 8.2 shows these variations.

Table 8.2.   Results in a complete segmentation free method.

Priority Queue Threshold	0.0001	0.001	0.01	0.05
Targets	491	491	491	491
Correct	460	457	440	409
Estimates	1663	880	545	445
Recall	**93.68%**	93.07%	89.61%	83.29%
Precision	27.66%	51.93%	80.73%	91.91%
F-measure	42.71%	66.66%	84.93%	87.39%
Speed (sec./card)	42.9	38.3	37.6	37.1

A natural consequence is that the number of seconds to process a complete card increases as the threshold decreases. These segmentation free experiments also show the best recall the system can obtain. This is highlighted in the table.

We observed that there are many incorrect estimates with a low probability and length ≤ 4. One way to reduce the number of estimates is to create a heuristic rule to cut off estimates with short length and low probability.

These images contain a considerable amount of locations where text is not located. This is shown in Fig. 8.5 as black areas, where *background* is the dominating class. To eliminate processing of background areas we propose to go through a robust and simple segmentation of text areas by dilating the foreground in the binarized image. The positions in these blobs are the only ones participating in the classification and word recognition steps. A consequence is that the system speed improves significantly.

---

[b]All of the times shown are based on a pc with a Pentium 4 3.2GHz processor and 1.5 GB in RAM

Following the assumption that it is unessential to retrieve the best word found in a surrounding window, we can process only a certain amount of lines in the text areas. Table 8.3 shows the results of processing a line and setting a gap in the vertical direction Gap_y, where Gap_y = 1 means to process all lines. The overall system performance is not affected and some results improve as it is shown. The threshold is set to 0.001 for these experiments and estimates with length $\leq$ 4 and probability $\leq$ 0.05 are discarded. This heuristic rule was set by analyzing the set of incorrect estimates and their length.

Table 8.3.   Results in text areas and some lines.

Gap_y	1	2	3	4	5	6	7
Targets	491	491	491	491	491	491	491
Correct	443	442	440	441	438	433	427
Estimates	468	463	460	457	455	450	443
Recall	**90.22%**	90.02%	89.61%	89.81%	89.2%	88.18%	86.96%
Precision	94.65%	95.46%	95.65%	**96.49%**	96.26%	96.22%	96.38%
F-measure	92.38%	92.66%	92.53%	**93.03%**	92.60%	92.02%	91.43%
Speed (sec./card)	13.8	8.9	6.7	5.7	5.0	4.6	4.2

A previous paper has shown results in isolated words,[19] with the same type of cards, and the accuracy reported is 85%. This can be broadly compared to our best recall 91.85% form Table 8.2. Other type of experiments are shown in Ref. 2 and the accuracy obtained is 93.1%. However, these classified only digits and retrieved strings from a 300 lexicon of valid years. The difference in trying to classify digits (10 classes) and our 62 classes makes a direct comparison difficult. However, our methods offer competitive performance.

Downton et al.[20] built a complete system including document image analysis, separating the image into text fields. Nevertheless, in their experiments they show results without this step. The accuracy reported is 83.1% for species/genus text field and author names.

Finally, to make a direct comparison with a commercial leader of OCR software (ABBY Fine Reader 8.0), we manually counted the estimates and correct targets retrieved by it on the same 30 cards that were used to test our system. A total of 296 target words were on them. We included the specialized dictionary in the software and the F-measure obtained was 60.6%. The recall (69%) was better than the precision (54%). Our method performs better because they were designed for these types of cards and

trained on specially designed synthetic data, while the commercial package
is a general purpose OCR system.

8.6.1. *Mis-recognized examples*

The words that were not recognized by our methods fall into one of the three
following categories. The first one is if the word image contains smears or
handwriting in its immediate surroundings, degrading recognition of delimiter characters. The reason for the second error is because the word
contains an invalid delimiter. Finally if the font is similar but sufficiently
different the system fails; this is a consequence of the training data being
based on a single font. Figure 8.6 shows each of these cases:

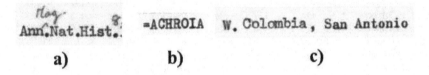

a)   b)   c)

Fig. 8.6. Missed recognitions. (a) handwriting invading delimiters bounding box (b)
invalid delimiters (c) different font in the case of "San Antonio".

8.6.2. *Correctly recognized examples*

This subsection exemplifies cases where our system performs good under
uncommon circumstances. Figure 8.7 shows specific words that were correctly retrieved.

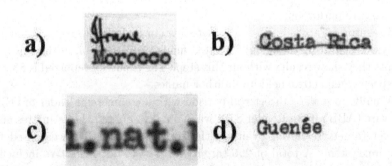

Fig. 8.7. Good recognitions. (a) slight invasion of handwriting (b) hand-made underlining (c) scanning deformation (d) accents.

Figure 8.7-(a) shows that if the handwriting is not strongly invading the bounding box of a character, the word is retrieved correctly. This example also demonstrates that even if the characters are similar (o,c) and touching each other the system still performs well. Figure 8.7-(b) presents a hand-made stroke suggesting an underlining. Nevertheless the features are strong enough to identify both words. Sometimes, due to the scanning processing, characters have noticeable variations. This is the case of Fig. 8.7-(c). Finally there might be cases where a character can contain an accent. Most of the cases the system will be able to pick them up.

Finally Fig. 8.8 depicts a card with a significant amount of handwriting. The words detected are highlighted with blue labels. From this image we can appreciate that the system's precision is not diminished.

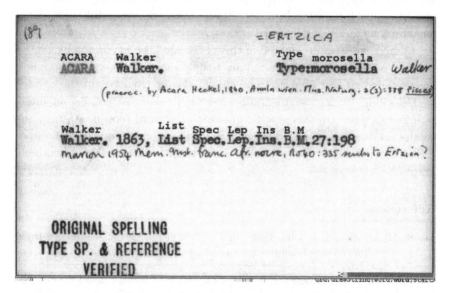

Fig. 8.8.   Good precision example.

8.7. Discussion and Conclusions

This paper reported the first attempt to build a practical word recognition system based on the SNT-grid. The system was tailored for recognizing type-written words on museum archive cards. The features of this problem that make it attractive for our technique are:

• Words are type-written in a restricted range of fonts.

- The fonts are mono-spaced: this made the graph-search easier.
- General purpose commercial systems still perform poorly on this task.

The raw recognition outputs of the SNT-grid are post-processed using a priority queue best-first word recognition system. Although the original aim was to apply the character classifier to all possible locations in the image, we made some compromises in developing the system. In particular, we did not apply the full classifier to parts of the image identified as background, and we also found that best performance could be achieved without applying the dictionary search to all lines in the image.

The combined standard F measure of approximately 93% was significantly better for this task than a leading commercial general purpose OCR system, although we are keen to point out that the commercial OCR system has a much harder job, in that it aims to work reasonably well across an enormous range of document styles.

All SNT-grid results quoted in this paper used the maximum likelihood training method. On other scanning t-tuple tasks, cross-entropy training has provided greater accuracy, and should also be tried for this task.

Designing efficient segmentation-free OCR systems remains an interesting challenge. On this specific museum card word recognition task our results are very promising, but there is much scope for future work, especially in how best to construct and search these large character hypothesis graphs.

References

1. S. M. Lucas and K. Cho. Fast convolutional ocr with the scanning n-tuple grid. In *International Conference on Document Analysis and Recognition*, pp. 799–803, (2005).
2. S. M. Lucas, G. Patoulas, and A. C. Downton. Fast lexicon-based word recognition in noisy index card images. In *International Conference on Document Analysis and Recognition*, pp. 462–466, (2003).
3. H. S. Baird. Document image defect models. In ed. N. Y. Springer-Verlag, *Structured Document Image Anaylisis. In H. Baird, H. Bunke, and K. Yamamoto (Eds.)*, pp. 546–556, (1992).
4. B. Sankur, A. T. Abak, and U. Baris. Assessment of thresholding algorithms for document processing. In *Image Processing, 1999. ICIP 99. Proceedings. 1999 International Conference on*, vol. 1, pp. 580–584 (October, 1999).
5. O. D. Trier and A. K. Jain, Goal-directed evaluation of binarization methods, *IEEE Trans. Pattern Anal. Mach. Intell.* **17**(12), 1191–1201 (December, 1995).

6. O. D. Trier and T. Taxt, Evaluation of binarization methods for document images, *IEEE Trans. Pattern Anal. Mach. Intell.* **17**(3), 312–315 (March, 1995).

7. M. Sezgin and B. Sankur, Survey over image thresholding techniques and quantitative p erformance evaluation, *Journal of Electronic Imaging.* **13**(1), 146–165, (2004).

8. W. Niblack, *An Introduction to Digital Image Processing.* (Prentice Hall, Englewood Cliffs, N.J., 1986).

9. J. White and G. D. Rohrer, Image thresholding for optical character recognition and other image thresholding for optical character recognition and other applications requiring character image extraction., *IBM J. Res. Develop.* **27** (4), 400–411 (July, 1983).

10. W. W. Bledsoe and I. Browning. Pattern recognition and reading by machine. In *Proceedings of the Eastern Joint Computer Conference,* pp. 225–232. (1959).

11. J. Ullman, Experiments with the n-tuple method of pattern recognition, *IEEE Transactions on Computers.* **18**(12), 1135–1137 (December, 1969).

12. R. Rohwer and M. Morciniec, A theoretical and experimental account of n-tuple classifier performance, *Neural Computation.* **8**, 629 – 642, ((1996)).

13. S. Lucas. Discriminative training of the scanning n-tuple classifier. In *Lecture Notes in Computer Science (2686): Computational Methods in Neural Modelling,* pp. 222 – 229. Springer-Verlag, Berlin, ((2003)).

14. S. M. Lucas. High performance ocr with syntactic neural networks. In ed. L. IEE, *Proceedings of IEE 4th International Conference on Artificial Neural Networks,* pp. 133–138, (1995).

15. S. M. Lucas and A. Amiri. Statistical syntactic methods for high performance ocr. In *IEE Proceedings on Vision, Image and Signal Processing,* vol. 143, pp. 23–30, (1996).

16. P. Viola and M. J. Jones, Robust real-time face detection, *International Journal of Computer Vision.* **57**, 137–154, (2004).

17. F. Jelinek, Fast sequential decoding algorithm using a stack, *IBM Journal of Research and Development.* **13**, 675–685, (1969).

18. F. Jelinek. Continous speech recognition by statistical methods. In *Proceedings of IEEE,* pp. 532–556, (1975).

19. S. M. Lucas, A. C. Tams, S. Cho, S. Ryu, and A. C. Downton. Robust word recognition for museum archive card indexing. In *International Conference on Document Analysis and Recognition,* pp. 144–148, (2001).

20. A. C. Downton, J. He, and S. M. Lucas, User-configurable ocr enhancement for online natural history archives, *Int. Journal on Document Analysis and Recognition, special issue on Analysis of Historical Documents.* **9**(2-4), 263–279, (2007).

Chapter 9

Historical Handwritten Document Recognition

S. L. Feng* and R. Manmatha[†]

Department of Computer Science, University of Massachusetts, Amherst, MA-01007, USA, *slfeng.umass@gmail.com,* [†]*manmatha@cs.umass.edu*

Historial handwritten manuscripts contain much valuable information but till recently little attempt has been made to recognize such documents. We compare a number of classification and sequence models for recognizing such manuscripts. Experiments are shown on a small corpus of documents from the George Washington collection

Contents

---

*S. L. Feng is now at the Siemens Corporate Research Center, Princeton, NJ.

9.1. Introduction

In this chapter, we discuss historical handwritten document recognition. We describe and compare the application of various classification and sequence models to the recognition task.

In particular, our historical handwritten document recognition is performed at the word level, i.e. the recognition units are word images. Character segmentation on degraded historical handwritten document is still a difficult problem. To avoid the errors introduced by character segmentation, recognition in this work is directly done on the word level where historical handwritten documents are first segmented into word images. Word segmentation is much easier to do than character segmentation. Once features are extracted from each word image, machine learning techniques may be employed to label each feature by learning over transcribed documents. For the purpose of fair comparisons between different models, this chapter employs the same dataset and the same features for experiments with those used by.[1]

This chapter is devoted to the investigation of various statistical models on word image recognition for historical handwritten documents. Most of the models discussed in this chapter, including support vector machines, maximum entropy, naive Bayes with kernel density estimate, and conditional random field, have been employed for this task for the first time. Although Hidden Markov models (HMMs) have been widely used for this problem, we proposed two different ways to improve the recognition performance with HMMs. One is the smoothing of the probabilities of feature generation and the other is the combination of HMM and kernel density estimates. The recognition results may be used for retrieval. To do this, we can directly use a text retrieval model over the automatically generated transcripts of the handwritten images.

In this chapter, classification models are first discussed followed by sequence models. Finally, experiments over these models are reported and compared.

9.2. Related Work on Historical Handwritten Document Recognition and Retrieval

Handwriting recognition is a classical computer vision problem which generally can be categorized into online recognition and offline recognition, depending on whether the recognition is performed online and synchronized with the actually writing. Benefiting from the dynamic information obtained in strokes using special input devices like tablets, online handwriting recognition has advanced to the level of commercial application. One can refer to[2] for a comprehensive survey of online handwriting recognition approaches. Historical handwritten document recognition is an offline recognition process given that no dynamic information is available.

Offline handwriting recognition[2-4] has only been successful in small-vocabulary and highly constrained domains, such as postal code recognition in automatic mail sorting and bank check reading.[4-6] Only very recently have people started to look at offline recognition of large vocabulary handwritten documents.[7] A Hidden Markov Model (HMM) is a popular model used for handwritten document recognition. Rath *et al.*[1] described an approach to recognizing historical handwritten manuscripts using simple HMMs with one state for each word. By adding word bigrams from similar historical corpora they showed that the performance could approach a word level recognition accuracy of 60%. Marti *et al.*[8] proposed the use of a HMM for modern handwriting recognition. Each character is represented using a Hidden Markov model with 14 states. Words and lines are modelled as a concatenation of these Markov models. A statistical language model was used to compute word bigrams and this improved the performance by 10%. Edwards *et al.*[9,10] described an approach to recognizing medieval Latin manuscripts using generalized-HMMs, where each state is a character or the space between characters. A similar generalized-HMM was used by Chan and Forsyth[11] for Arabic printed and handwritten documents recognition.

Recently, other models like dynamic programming techniques[12] and boosted decision trees[13] have also been proposed for handwritten document recognition. Based on the unit of recognition, handwritten document recognition can be classified into segmentation based[2,3,8] and holistic analysis methods.[1,5,13,14] The former relies on segmentation word images into smaller units, like characters, strokes and image columns.[2,3,15] The latter[1,5,13,14] takes word images as recognition units and requires no further segmentation. More details on handwritten recognition may be found in survey articles by Steinherz *et al.*,[3] Plamondon *et al.*[2] and Vinciarelli.[4]

Direct retrieval approaches have also been proposed for document image retrieval without involving an explicit recognition procedure. Manmatha *et al.*[16-18] proposed the word spotting idea for handwritten document retrieval. Word spotting first clusters words in a collection of handwritten documents via a word image matching algorithm,[19,20] then automatically selects candidate clusters for indexing. Rath and Manmatha[19,21,22] investigated a number of different approaches for word matching and clustering, including SSD, shape context,[23] index approach[24] and dynamic time warping (DTW).[19] Tan et al.[25] represent both textual queries and document image words with features, then retrieve printed documents by matching these features. Gatos et al.[26] proposed a similar technique which retrieves historical typewritten documents through matching synthetic word images created from query words with automated segmented document words. After the first run of retrieval for each query, they refined the ranked list through user's relevance feedback. Inspired by the use of eigenface in face recognition,[27] Terasawa et al.[28] proposed an eigenspace method for matching word images which are represented as sequences of small slits. Balasubramanian et al.[29] proposed a DTW based word matching scheme for printed document image retrieval.

More recently, Rath et al.[30] proposed relevance model based probabilistic approaches for automatic annotation of historical handwritten document images. They developed the first automatic retrieval system for historical manuscripts based on the joint occurrence of annotation and word images in cross-modal retrieval models. Howe et al.[13] proposed boosted decision trees for historical handwritten word recognition. They augmented the word classes with a very few training samples to deal with the skewed distribution of class frequencies and substantially improved the recognition performance.

In this chapter, we explore recognition approaches for historical handwritten manuscript. Our recognition approaches consist of two main aspects. First, we thoroughly investigate different classification models for handwritten word recognition. In particular, we compare support vector machines, conditional maximum entropy models and Naive Bayes with Gaussian kernel density estimates.[31] Second, we explore the use of sequence models for whole word recognition, e.g. conditional random field models and HMMs.[32]

9.3. Classification Models for Handwritten Word Recognition

We investigate a number of different classification models for historical handwritten word recognition - both discriminative and generative. The model selection is based on their general classification performance and their usefulness to our recognition problem.

9.3.1. *Support Vector Machines*

Originally introduced as a binary linear classifier, support vector machines (SVMs) attempt to find an oriented hyper-plane which separates the linear separable space defined by the training data while maximizing the margin. The margin is the distance of each training instance to the hyperplane.

To extend this to classifying nonlinear separable data, SVM uses a *kernel* function K to map the training data to a higher Euclidean space, in which the data may be linearly separable. The kernel function is defined as : $K(x_i, x_j) = <\phi(x_i), \phi(x_j)>$, where $\phi(x)$ is some mapping. For dealing with nonseparable data and avoiding overfitting, SVM's usually use a soft margin which allows some instances to be misclassified. A SVM classifier solves the optimization problem:

$$\min_{\xi,\mathbf{w},b} <\mathbf{w}, w> +C \sum_{i=1}^{N} \xi_i \qquad (9.1)$$

such that $y_i(<\mathbf{w}, \phi(x_i)> +b) \geq 1 - \xi_i$, and $\xi_i \geq 0$. Here **w** is a vector pointing perpendicularly to the separating hyper-plane and b is the offset parameter of this hyper-plane. $y_i \in \{-1, 1\}$ is the label of instance x_i. The slack variable ξ_i measures the degree of misclassification of the datum x_i and the capability C determines the cost of margin constraint violations.

SVM has shown a powerful classification capability in many applications.[33] In the handwritten word recognition scenario, x_i is a feature vector representing a word image and $y_i \in \{-1, 1\}$ is an indicator of whether that word image is labeled as a particular word. To adapt the original SVM to the multiple-class case, we adopt the max-win strategy, which uses k binary SVMs for the k-class problem. Each of these binary SVMs separates the word images of a particular class/label w and the non-w word images. For a test word image, the class/label with the highest value wins. Since the max-win has to train k binary SVMs for k classes (labels), the complexity of SVM training is high for recognition at the word level, since the vocabulary may be very large.

9.3.2. *Conditional Maximum Entropy Models*

Maximum Entropy models have been recently widely applied in domains involving sequential data learning, e.g. natural languages,[34,35] biological sequence analysis,[36] and very promising results have been achieved. Since maximum entropy models utilize information based on the entire history of a sequence, unlike HMMs whose predictions are usually based only on a short fixed length of prior emissions, we expect maximum entropy models to work well for handwritten document recognition problems since in our case each page may be taken as a long sequence of words, each of which emits a set of observations represented as word image features.

The goal of conditional maximum entropy models is to estimate the conditional distribution of label y given data x, say $P(y|x)$. The framework is fairly straightforward. It basically specifies that the modeled distribution should be as uniform as possible, while being consistent with the constraints that are given by the features of the training data. Given a set of predicates.[a] $f_i(x, y)$, which may be real or binary values and represent some observation properties (e.g. co-occurrence) of the input x and output y, the constraints are that for each predicate its expectation value under the model $P(y|x)$ should be the same as its expectation under the empirical joint distribution $\tilde{P}(x, y)$, i.e.

$$\sum_{x,y} \tilde{P}(x)P(y|x, \lambda)f(x, y) = \sum_{x,y} \tilde{P}(x, y)f(x, y) \qquad (9.2)$$

With these constraints, the maximum conditional entropy principle picks the model maximizing the conditional entropy:

$$H(P) = - \sum_{x \in X, y \in Y} \tilde{P}(x)P(y|x, \lambda) \log P(y|x, \lambda) \qquad (9.3)$$

It has been shown[37] that there is always a unique distribution that satisfies the constraints and maximize the conditional entropy. This distribution has the exponential form:

$$P(y|x, \lambda) = \frac{1}{Z} e^{\sum_i \lambda_i f_i(x,y)} \qquad (9.4)$$

where Z is a normalization constant such that $\sum_y P(y|x, \lambda) = 1$ and λ_i is the weight of predicate f_i in the model.

The maximum entropy model's flexibility comes from the ability to use arbitrary predicate definitions as constraints. These feature definitions represent knowledge learned from the training set. So our test of conditional maximum entropy modeling on our task focuses on the aspect of predicate definitions and their effects on performance. Both discrete predicates and continuous predicates are investigated in our work.

---

[a]We use the term predicates rather than features to differentiate these from image features.

9.3.2.1. *Discrete Predicates*

We do a linear vector quantization (VQ) on the original continuous features measured from the images and discretize each of them into a fixed number of bins. We define two types of binary predicates for the maximum entropy model based on the discrete features extracted from word images and the corresponding label sequence:

(1) **Unigram Predicates** The frequency of a discrete feature x and the current word w:

$$f_i^u(x, w) = \begin{cases} 1 \text{ if the feature set of } w \text{ contains } x \\ 0 \text{ otherwise} \end{cases} \quad (9.5)$$

(2) **Bigram Predicates** We define two sets of bigram predicates, which intuitively represent the statistical properties of a word and the features of this word's neighboring word images. For example, if in the training set the word *"force"* always follows the word *"Fredericksburgh's"*, then in the test set it will increase the probability of the current word being recognized as "force" given that its previous word image is very long. One set of bigram predicates we define is the joint frequency of the word w and a discrete feature x which appears in the feature set of the word image preceding word w:

$$f_i^{bf}(x, w) = \begin{cases} 1 \text{ if the feature set of the word image preceding } w \text{ contains } x \\ 0 \text{ otherwise} \end{cases}$$

$$(9.6)$$

and the other set is the frequency of word w and a discrete feature x which appears in the feature set of the word image following word w:

$$f_i^{bb}(x, w) = \begin{cases} 1 \text{ if the feature set of the word image following } w \text{ contains } x \\ 0 \text{ otherwise} \end{cases}$$

$$(9.7)$$

9.3.2.2. *Continuous Predicates*

Since the VQ process causes loss of information from the raw continuous features and there is little literature on maximum entropy models using continuous predicates, we are interested in investigating continuous features for maximum entropy models.

(1) **Raw Predicates** In theory, the raw continuous features can be directly fed into the maximum entropy models, defining the predicate as the

values of feature φ (feature name, e.g. width, height...) of word w:

$$f_i^{cr}(\varphi, w) = x \tag{9.8}$$

i.e. the feature φ of w has value x

(2) **Distance Predicates** Maximum entropy models have a problem with the raw predicates. Note that in Equation 9.4, the conditional probability of a label given the observed features is formulated as an exponential function of the predicates. This exponential form implies that the conditional probability is basically monotonically non-decreasing over each predicate. In the case of raw predicates, since each predicate is an observed feature, the label probability is monotonically non-decreasing with each feature. However we know that the distribution of a visual feature over a specific class/label is usually not a single monotonic function but more complicated (e.g. it may be modeled as a Gaussian mixture which is not monotonically non-decreasing). For example, word image length is a real-valued visual feature widely used for word recognition. In the case of raw predicates, the probability of a word is non-decreasing with the increasing of the word image length, which is apparently not in accordance with reality. To solve this problem, we use distance predicates.

The intuition for using distance predicates is to convert the raw features to some predicates so tht the label probability is truly non-decreasing as predicate values increase. Assuming that each kind of visual features of a label is subject to a certain Gaussian distribution whose mean is the average value of the features, then the larger the distance of an observed feature distance to this mean, the smaller the probability of that label given that observed feature. So one approach to computing distance predicates is to first calculate the centers of each set of features which is labeled as the same word, then use the distances of each raw feature to all these centers as the new feature set substituting for the original raw feature. However if the number of class labels (the size of the vocabulary in our case) is too large , this method will generate too many features to let the maximum entropy models finish all the runs in reasonable time.

An alternative idea is to use k-means to cluster each feature into a fixed number of categories (for simplicity, 5 in our experiments) and calculate the distances of each feature to the centers of every category instead of to the centers of each word class. This distance predicate for maximum entropy is defined as the negative of the distance of each feature of each word to every center:

$$f_i^{cd}(\varphi_c, w) = -d \qquad (9.9)$$

i.e. the negative of the distance of feature φ of w to the c-th center is d.

9.3.3. Naive Bayes with Gaussian Kernel Density Estimate

Since our dataset is from letters which use natural language it is unbalanced. That is, since word frequencies follow a Zipfian-like distribution their frequencies vary widely. On the other hand the dataset also provides us with reasonable prior probabilities of words in the document corpus. So instead of discriminative models like SVMs and maximum entropy, we want to use some kind of generative probability density model like Naive Bayes.

The Naive Bayes framework is pretty simple:

$$P(w|\mathbf{x}) = \frac{P(\mathbf{x}|w)P(w)}{\sum_w P(\mathbf{x}|w)P(w)} \qquad (9.10)$$

where $\mathbf{x}$ is the feature vector of a word image and w a transcription word. We estimate the prior probability of word w directly as its relative frequency in the training set. We calculate the probability of the visual features of a word image given a word w using a non-parametric Gaussian kernel density estimate:

$$P(\mathbf{x}|w) = \frac{1}{\|w\|} \sum_{i=1}^{\|w\|} \frac{\exp\{-(\mathbf{x} - \mathbf{x}_i)^T \Sigma^{-1}(\mathbf{x} - \mathbf{x}_i)\}}{\sqrt{2^k \pi^k |\Sigma|}} \qquad (9.11)$$

This equation arises out of placing a Gaussian kernel over the feature vector $\mathbf{x}_i$ of every word image labeled as word w. $\|w\|$ denotes the number of word images labeled as "w". $\mathbf{x}_i$ is a feature of the i-th word image labeled as "w". Each kernel is parameterized by the feature covariance matrix Σ. We assumed $\Sigma = \beta \cdot I$, where I is the identity matrix and β plays the role of kernel bandwidth, which determines the smoothness of $P(\mathbf{x}|w)$ around the support points $\mathbf{x}_i$. The value of β is selected empirically on a validation set.

9.4. Sequence Models for Word Recognition

This section investigates machine learning sequence models for the task of handwritten document recognition. Although HMMs have been widely used for this task, most of them estimate the probability of an image feature generated by a label using a Gassian distribution in the continuous feature space. Instead, we discussed the probability estimation in the discrete feature space and also propose combining kernel density estimates with HMMs for more accurate estimates in the continuous feature space. The conditional random field (CRF) is a recently developed graphical model for information extraction. This work introduces CRFs for historical handwritten document recognition for the first time. This is also the first application of CRF on a large state space.

9.4.1. Word Recognition with Discrete HMMs

We first test a HMM based on discrete features. As a generative model, a HMM estimates the joint probability of a hidden state sequence and a given observation sequence, which in our task are a sequence of words $S =< s_1, s_2, \ldots, s_T >$ and a sequence of discrete feature vectors $O =< o_1, o_2, \ldots, o_T >$ extracted from word images respectively:

$$P(S, O) = \prod_{t=0}^{T} P(s_t|s_{t-1})P(o_t|s_t) \tag{9.12}$$

where T denotes the length of the sequences, and both transition probabilities $P(s_t|s_{t-1})$ and generative probabilities $P(o_t|s_t)$ are assumed to be subject to multinomial distributions. For each discrete feature in the feature vector $o_t =< o_{t1}, o_{t2}, \ldots, o_{tm} >$ extracted from the t-th word image, we assume it is independent of others given a hidden word s_t. Thus we have $P(o_t|s_t) = \prod_{i=0}^{m} P(o_{ti}|s_t)$. Given labeled handwritten documents as a training set τ, these probabilities can be easily computed using maximum likelihood estimation (MLE). Let w and v be two arbitrary words from vocabulary V, the transition probabilities are calculated as:

$$P(s_t = w|s_{t-1} = v) = \frac{\sharp(\text{word pair}(v,\, w) \text{ occurs in } \tau)}{\sharp(\text{word } v \text{ occurs in } \tau)} \tag{9.13}$$

Let I_w denotes all the word images labeled as w in the training set τ, then the generative probabilities are calculated as

$$P(o_{ti}|s_t = w) = \frac{\sharp(\ o_{ti} \text{ occurs as a feature of } I_w\ )}{\sharp(\text{all features of } I_w\ )} \tag{9.14}$$

The estimation of transition probabilities is done as in[1] and includes an averaging over the background distributions of these labels to smooth the probabilities:

$$\hat{P}(s_t = w | s_{t-1} = v) = \frac{1}{2} P(s_t = w | s_{t-1} = v)$$

$$+ \frac{1}{2} P(s_t = w) \tag{9.15}$$

where $P(s_t)$ is the background probability of label s_t in the collection τ and calculated as:

$$\hat{P}(s_t = w) = \frac{1}{2} \cdot \frac{\sharp(w \text{ in } \tau)}{\sharp(\text{all words in } \tau)} + \frac{1}{2} \cdot \frac{1}{|V|} \tag{9.16}$$

where $|V|$ is the size of the whole vocabulary.

Experiments in section 9.5 show this model doesn't perform that well.

9.4.1.1. *Feature Probability Smoothing for HMMs*

We explore using smoothing techniques to improve the performance of our original HMM model in section 9.4.1 - note that we are smoothing the features here not just the words as is usually done. The maximum likelihood estimate for generative probabilities in equation 9.14 is prone to be biased when the sample size is relative small. To alleviate this bias we smooth the generative probabilities using background probabilities of discrete features. In stead of a direct averaging as in,[1] we tune the weight to optimize the likelihood on a held-out portion of a training sample. The formulation for feature probability smoothing has a linear form as follows:

$$\hat{P}(o_{ti} | s_t) = (1 - \lambda) P(o_{ti} | s_t) + \lambda P(o_{ti}) \tag{9.17}$$

where $P(o_{ti})$ is the background probability of discrete feature o_{ti} in the training set τ, directly calculated as the frequency of o_{ti} in τ. λ is the parameter of this linear smoothing and tuned through optimizing the likelihood on a validation set created from a portion of the training sample. Note that we use one identical smoothing parameter λ for all the generative probabilities.

9.4.2. *Conditional Random Fields Framework*

A CRF[38] is defined as an undirected graphical model used to calculate the probability of a possible label sequence conditioned on the observation sequence. The structure of random fields is basically an arbitrary graph obeying the Markov property. Let $O = < o_1, o_2, \ldots, o_T >$ and

$S = < s_1, s_2, \ldots, s_T >$ denote the observation sequence and the label sequence respectively (In general CRFs, T need not be the same for O and S). A CRF formulates the conditional probability of S given O as:

$$P_\theta(S|O) = \frac{1}{Z_\theta(O)} \prod_q \left(\exp \left(\sum_k \lambda_k f_k(\mathbf{s}_q, \mathbf{o}_q) \right) \right) \qquad (9.18)$$

where feature functions $\{f_k\}$ are defined on any subset of the random variables in the sequences $\mathbf{s}_q \subset S$, $\mathbf{o}_q \subset O$, λ_k is a learned weight for each feature function, and Z is a normalization factor over all possible state sequences:

$$Z_\theta(O) = \sum_{S \in S^T} \prod_q \left(\exp \left(\sum_k \lambda_k f_k(\mathbf{s}_q, \mathbf{o}_q) \right) \right) \qquad (9.19)$$

In the simplest case, the graph is an undirected linear chain among output states, where CRFs make a first-order Markov independence assumption. Under this configuration, equation (9.18) is rewritten as:

$$P_\theta(S|O) = \frac{1}{Z_\theta(O)} \exp \left(\sum_{t=1}^T \sum_k \lambda_k f_k(s_t, s_{t-1}, O, t) \right) \qquad (9.20)$$

A feature function (as distinct from an image feature) is defined over the current state, the previous state and image features computed over the whole observation sequence. Usually feature functions are binary predicates. For example, assume that the only image feature used is the length of the current word image. Then, the feature function f_k is 1 if the current state corresponds to "Washington", the previous state to "Colonel" and the length of the current word is 8, else $k_k = 0$. Note that even in the simplest case the number of weights is $O(|S|^2 T)$, where T is the sequence length and $|S|$ is the size of the state space.

To reduce the number of parameters estimated, we further simplify the model into a conditionally-trained hidden Markov model, in which all the incoming transitions into a state will share the same weight and only at each separate step of the sequence we create weights for the current state and observation. In this case, the conditional probability becomes:

$$P_\theta(S|O) = \frac{1}{Z_\theta(O)} \exp \left(\sum_{t=1}^T \left(\sum_k (\lambda_k f_k(s_t, O, t)) + \sum_l (\mu_l g_l(s_t, s_{t-1})) \right) \right)$$
$$(9.21)$$

The number of parameters becomes $O(|S| T + |S|^2)$.

9.4.2.1. *Inference and Training in CRFs*

Inference in CRFs is done as follows: Given an observation sequence $\tilde{O}$, from all possible label (state) sequences find the one $\tilde{S}$ with the largest conditional probability over the distribution of $P(S|\tilde{O})$. This distribution is defined by the undirected graphic structure and the set of weights. Note the number of possible state sequences is exponential in the sequence length T. For an arbitrarily-structured CRF, it is intractable to calculate the normalization factor in equation (9.19). In HMM-Style CRFs, the normalization factor becomes:

$$Z_\theta(O) = \sum_{S \in S^T} \exp\left(\sum_{t=1}^{T}\left(\sum_k (\lambda_k f_k(s_t, O, t)) + \sum_l (\mu_l g_l(s_t, s_{t-1}))\right)\right) \quad (9.22)$$

A dynamic programming algorithm like Viterbi decoding can be used to efficiently calculate the normalization factor.

The parameters $\theta = \{\lambda_k, \mu_l\}$ are estimated by optimizing the model over a training set consisting of labeled sequences, $D = \{O^{(i)}, S^{(i)}\}_{i=1}^{N}$, i.e. by trying to find the set of weights that maximize the log-likelihood of the labeled sequences in the training set:

$$L = \sum_{i=1}^{N} \log(P(S^{(i)}|O^{(i)})) - \sum_k \frac{\lambda_k^2}{2\sigma^2} \quad (9.23)$$

where the second term is a Gaussian prior over parameters smoothing over the training data.[39]

Iterative scaling[38] is a general method to optimize parameters of CRFs and other exponential models. Sha and Pereira[40] use the limited memory quasi-Newton (L-BFGS)[41] method instead, which is shown to be several orders of magnitude faster than iterative scaling. Like iterative scaling, L-BFGS is also a gradient based optimization procedure but only requires the first-derivative of the objective function.

Here, every word is taken as a state so there could be thousands of states. We apply beam search for CRFs to significantly speed up the forward-backward procedure.

9.4.2.2. *Training and Inference with Beam Search*

The basic idea of beam search is simple. At each stage of the trellis for inference before passing any message to the next stage we first purge the states at this stage and keep only a small fraction of them. The number of states kept is usually called the width of beam. So when using beam search for forward-backward procedure, the number of outgoing transitions from the current stage to the next stage will dramatically drop. Our goal is to prune as many as possible states while minimize the loss of performance. To determine the states to eliminate, we need some criterion. Based on different criteria for purging states the beam search method works differently. Note that we talk about the probabilities of states here, but the actual implementations of inference and forward-backward algorithm uses costs which are equal to the negative logarithm of the probabilities. In the implementation of beam search these costs need to be converted into probabilities.

(1) **N-best Beam Search**
    The simplest way to do beam search is to sort all the states in the current stage according to their probabilities in descending order. Then only the top K states are kept and the other states are eliminated.

(2) **Ratio Threshold based Beam Search**
    At stage i, we first determine the maximal probability P_i^m of all the states:

$$P_i^m = \max_s P_i(s) \tag{9.24}$$

    Then a dynamic threshold is calculated based on the value P_i^m:

$$\tau_i = \frac{P_i^m}{K} \tag{9.25}$$

    where K is a empirically selected constant. Then all states s' at this stage whose $P_i(s') < \tau_i$ will be eliminated.

    This method doesn't have a fixed width of the beam at each stage and the criterion for purge is based on the individual probability of every state. This method is widely used with HMMs in speech recognition.[42]

(3) **K-L Divergence based Beam Search**
    Pal et al.[43] recently present a novel beam search method based on K-L Divergence. The basic idea is to approximate single variable potentials with a constrained adaptively sized sum of Kronecker delta functions and minimize the KL divergence between the approximated distribution and its original. At each stage of the trellis for Viterbi inference or forward-backward procedure, the probabilities of all the states form some arbitrary discrete probability distribution, say p. Any subset of these states, indexed with $I = \{1, \ldots, k\}$, forms some other distribution which could be approximated as a sum of weighted and normalized Kronecker deltas, say q. The goal is to find the subset of these

states which minimize the K-L divergence between p and q. Pal *et al.*[43] show this K-L divergence is equal to the negative logarithm of the sum of the probabilities of the subset states. More formally, suppose we want to find the minimal subset of states such that the K-L divergence $KL(q\|p) \leq \epsilon$, then that implies minimizing $|I|$ s.t.

$$KL(q\|p) = -\log \sum_{i \in I} p_i \leq \epsilon \qquad (9.26)$$

The solution involves sorting the states according to their probabilities in a descending order and then selecting the states from the top until the sum of their probabilities satisfies equation (9.26).

9.4.2.3. *Word Recognition with CRFs*

Using CRFs for word recognition is straightforward when the data are given as labeled handwritten documents. Handwritten documents are segmented into word images. Each word image is an observation and its corresponding label is the value of its state in CRFs.

The ideal case in each instance is a labeled sentence. However this is intractable for degraded handwritten documents because important clues for sentences such as punctuations are faded or connected with words resulting in a failure to detect them. In our case each sequence instance is a completely labeled page, with a length between 200 to 300 words. The drawback of using pages as training instances is that unreliable transitions between connections of two separate sentences will be involved and learned by the model.

Because both the size of the state space and the length of sequences in our project are large, we use the HMM-Style CRFs described by equation (9.21) in section 9.4.2.

Continuous image features are first extracted from each word image based on its scalar and shape. Each continuous feature is quantized into a fixed number of bins. The set of discretized features of each word image is its observation representation. Details on image features are given in section 9.5.

The model features are defined in a straightforward way. For example $f_k(s_t, O, t)$ is equal to 1 if the word image at position t is labeled as "Fredericksburgh" and its length is at level 10 (the highest level for our discretized image features), otherwise it is zero. The transition features $g_k(s_t, s_{t-1})$ are defined in a similar manner. For example $g_k(s_t, s_{t-1})$ is equal to 1 if the word image at position t is labeled as "Fredericksburgh" and the previous word is "defend", otherwise zero.

9.4.3. HMM with Gaussian Kernel Density Estimates

Both HMMs and CRFs discussed so far in this section use discrete word image features. Discrete features are easy to use, but could cause information loss when doing vector quantization. To utilize real-valued continuous features, we employs a Gaussian kernel density estimate for probabilities of generating features from a word state.

The HMM framework used here is just the same as in Section 9.4.1 except that now the observation sequence $O = < o_1, o_2, \ldots, o_T >$ is a sequence of real-valued feature vectors and the generative probability $P(o_i|w_i)$ is now estimated through a Gaussian kernel density function:

$$P(o_i|w_i) = \frac{1}{\|w_i\|} \sum_{i=1}^{\|w_i\|} \frac{\exp\{-(o_i - o_j)^T \Sigma^{-1}(o_i - o_j)\}}{\sqrt{2^k \pi^k |\Sigma|}} \qquad (9.27)$$

As in the equation 9.11, each kernel is parameterized by the feature covariance matrix Σ and assumed $\Sigma = \beta \cdot I$, where I is the identity matrix and β plays the role of kernel bandwidth, which determines the smoothness of $P(o_i|w_i)$ around the support points o_j. The value of β is selected empirically on a validation set.

9.5. Experimental Results

9.5.1. Experimental Setup

Our evaluation dataset consists of 20 pages from a collection of letters by George Washington. This is a publicly available standard dataset provided by[1]. Each page is accurately segmented into individual word images, each of which has been manually transcribed. We do not lowercase transcribed words, so "*region*" and "*Region*" are taken as two different words. There are 4865 words in the corpus in total and 1187 of them are unique. Figure 9.1 shows a part of a segmented page in our dataset.

For the purpose of fair comparisons between different models, we used the same features with those used by.[1] For a quick reference, the word images features are briefly described here. One can refer to[1] for more detailed information about the extracted features. Two kinds of features are extracted from each word image: scalar image features and profile-based image features. Scalar features consist of 6 different coarse measurements on each word image. Given a word image with a tight bounding box, the scalar features are respectively: the height h of the image in pixels, the width w of the image, the aspect ratio w/h, the area $w \cdot h$, the number of descenders in the word image, and the number of ascenders in the word. Profile-based features are computed from different profiles of the word image. This work use projection, upper word and lower word profiles, each of which has the same length as the image width. The project profile is computed by summing over the pixel values at each image column of the word. The upper/lower profile is calculated as the distance from the upper/lower boundary of the word image to the closest ink pixel at each image column. After these profiles are computed, the Discrete Fourier Transform (DFT) is applied to each of them and a fixed number of lower-order DFT coefficients are used to represent each profile. So given 3 profiles and 7 DFT coefficients for each of them, there are 21 profile-based features. Plus the 6 scalar features, 27 features are used for each word image.

We use word accuracy rate as our performance measure, i.e. the proportion of the words that are recovered exactly as they were in the manual transcript. 20-fold cross-validation is used to get a stable performance evaluation for each model. Each iteration leaves one page for test, and trains the model over the other 19 pages. We use the mean accuracy rate as the final evaluation measure. Since our dataset is relatively small, many words in the test set do not occur in any training pages - these are called out-of-vocabulary(OOV) terms as in[1] and cause errors of the recognition, we use two types of mean accuracy rate – mean accuracy rate with OOVs and mean accuracy rate without OOVs.

Since our data are from a collection of natural language documents(letters), the frequency of words can be approximated by a Zipf distribution. As Figure 9.2 shows, a few words have very high frequencies, however most words occur very infrequently. Over our whole dataset, 681 words have only one occurrence; 1008 words have less than 5 occurrences each but 30 words have 1856 occurrences in total. The unbalance and sparsity of training data for different words make the multi-classification problem intractable for some standard classifiers such as decision trees and neural networks as shown in.[44]

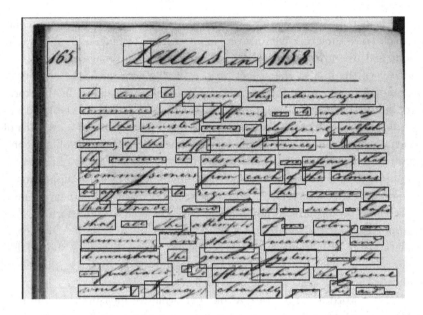

Fig. 9.1.   A part of one segmented page in our dataset.

9.5.2. *Results on Different Classification Models*

9.5.2.1. *SVMs*

We use the *MATLAB Support Vector Machine Toolbox* developed by Gavin Cawley to build the SVM model on the data. By using the 'max wins' algorithm, we tried linear kernels and polynomial kernels of degree 2 on the data.

Table 9.1.   Experimental results using SVMs.

Accuracy	with OOV	w/o OOV
Linear Kernel	0.3827	0.4642
Polynomial d-2	0.4463	0.5281

Table 9.1 shows the experimental results using support vector machines, from which we see that the polynomial kernel performs much better than the linear kernel. This is unsurprising since the kernel function plays a crucial role in SVMs. The kernel determines the mapping of instances to a high dimensional space and whether the space is separable or not. However, it is not generally easy to locate the proper kernel. In other words, deciding

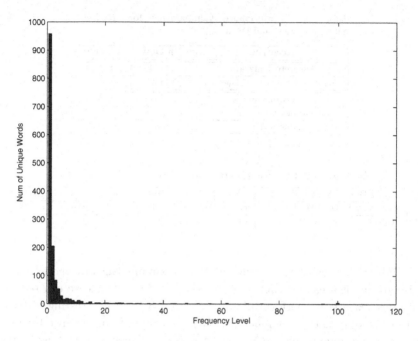

Fig. 9.2. The histogram of the word frequency in our dataset, which is subject to a Zipf distribution.

to which space the original data should be projected requires a deeper understanding of the data - usually background knowledge is needed. In our case, both the linear kernel and the polynomial kernel of degree 2 do not work very well on the data. Other kernels that project the data into higher dimension spaces might help in this case but there is no simple way to determine these short of trying all of them.

9.5.2.2. *Conditional Maximum Entropy Models*

We use the maximum entropy toolkit available at *http://homepages.inf.ed. ac.uk/s0450736/maxent-toolkit.html*, which was developed in C++ based on the java version at *http://maxent.sf.net*. To extract unigram and bigram discrete predicates in section 9.3.2, we linearly quantize each of the 27 continuous features into 19 bins. To test the influence of different numbers of bins into which the raw features is quantized, we also gradually changed the number of bins and re-ran the maximum entropy model. The performance varies only slightly with the change in the number of bins except at 100 bins the performance drops sharply.

Table 9.2. Performance Comparisons for maximum entropy models and features.

Accuracy	with OOV	w/o OOV
Discrete Unigram	0.4164	0.4939
Discrete Unigram + Bigram	0.4432	0.5234
Raw Continuous	0.4161	0.5259
Distance Continuous	0.4454*	0.5629*
Raw + Dist	0.4367	0.5515

Table 9.3. N-best Beam Search with different fixed beam widths.

Fixed Beam Width	10	80	105	106	107	132	264
Accuracy w/o OOV	0.001	0.001	0.001	0.645	0.645	0.645	0.645
Run Time (in Secs)	60	131	140	142	142	153	2944

Table 9.2 shows the results of the Maximum Entropy model using discrete predicates and continuous predicates, from which we can see the distance features outperform all other features. Significance testing with the t-test shows that the difference between the results from distance features and raw continuous feature are significant with P-value of 0.03, while the P-value for distance feature vs unigram + bigram is 0.003. These numbers also show that using both unigram and bigram information outperforms only using unigram information by a small margin. Note that the concept of bigram here is defined between label states and features unlike that in HMMs where it is depicted as the dependency between label spaces. Since our dataset is relatively small and the vocabulary is huge, it is more difficult to capture useful bigram information for maximum entropy.

9.5.2.3. *Naive Bayes with Gaussian Density Estimate*

The mean accuracies achieved using the Naive Bayes model with Gaussian kernel density estimates are 0.542 with OOVs and 0.640 without OOVs. It is not surprising that Naive Bayes achieves good results on our task for at least two reasons. One is that the model provides prior probabilities of the words - that is the frequency of the words. This corresponds to unigram language model information used in [1] where it was shown to improve performance. Another is that the Gaussian density emphasizes the local information provided by each instance, which has been shown to be very useful in multimedia data analysis.

Table 9.4. Ratio Threshold Beam Search with different K values.

K in Equation (9.25)	1.0001	1.001	1.01	1.1	1.2	1.5	2
Accuracy w/o OOV	0.505	0.518	0.645	0.645	0.645	0.645	0.645
Run Time (in Secs)	97	99	107	1127	1238	1340	1527

Table 9.5. KL Divergence Beam Search with different ϵ in $KL \leq \epsilon$.

ϵ in $KL \leq \epsilon$	0.9	0.8	0.79	0.77	0.75	0.5	0
Accuracy w/o OOV	0.001	0.001	0.475	0.584	0.645	0.645	0.645
Run Time (in Secs)	62	70	75	87	91	209	2944

9.5.3. *Tune and Compare Beam Search for Our CRF Model*

All the three kinds of Beam Search in section 9.4.2.2 require us to experimentally decide the parameters controlling the width of beam. For this purpose, we select two pages from our handwritten documents and use them as a training and a test example respectively. Even in this small dataset with 486 words in total, there are 264 states(unique words). On average there are less than 2 instances for each state, which means our model has been very starved for training data. But for this project, this is the largest unit we can use for tuning, including more pages results in a sharp increase in run time.

Tables 9.3, 9.4 and 9.5 show the results of using different values of tuning parameters for the N-best, ratio threshold and K-L divergence based beam search respectively. As the tables show the accuracy changes non-linearly with the tuning parameters. In certain regions it is relatively insensitive while in others it is very sensitive. The tables only show some values of the parameters - mostly those where very large changes occur.

Since with comparable accuracy N-best runs much slower than the other two methods, we did not do experiments using N-best over the whole dataset. We select $K = 1.01$ and $\epsilon = 0.75$ as the parameters of ratio threshold and KL-divergence respectively when testing over the whole dataset.

9.5.4. *Result Comparisons*

Table 9.6 compares the models we tested. To make the comparison fair, we report two set of results of the HMMs from a recent paper.[1] The first of the HMM models includes word bigrams obtained from the training set but not from the external corpora (the Naive Bayes model as well as the other models here do not use any bigrams). The second uses an external George Washington and Thomas Jefferson electronic text corpus for tran-

Table 9.6.   Results comparing different models. The external corpora used for transition estimates consists of a large electronic collection of writings by George Washington and Thomas Jefferson. CRFs cannot really be used with the continuous features described here and so are not directly comparable with HMMs using continuous features.

Accuracy Rate	with OOV	w/o OOV
SVM with polynomial d-2 kernel	0.446	0.528
ME with unigram (in[31])	0.416	0.494
ME with unigram and bigram	0.443	0.523
ME with distance predicates	0.445	0.563
Naive Bayes with Gaussian-KDE	0.542	0.640
CRFs with Ratio threshold beam search	0.417	0.503
CRFs with K-L divergence beam search	0.428	0.525
HMM with discrete features	0.336	0.404
HMM with discrete features after smoothing	0.504	0.595
HMM with continuous features (in[1])	0.497	0.586
HMM with Gaussian-KDE	0.583	0.688
HMM with continuous features + external corpora (in[1])	0.551	0.651
HMM with Gaussian-KDE + external corpora	0.611	0.723

sition estimation. We can see that, with external text corpus both HMMs from[1] and our HMMs improve the performance significantly. From this table, we see that HMMs with a Gaussian density estimate achieved the best performance on our task. The t-test shows that the HMM with a Gaussian density estimate outperforms other HMMs significantly by a P-value of 0.01. With a Gaussian kernel density estimate, even naive Bayes can achieve very good results. The good performance of naive Bayes in our experiments shows that the prior probabilities (unigram information) is important for analysis on natural language document corpus (especially heavily unbalanced datasets). In contrast, prior distribution information is difficult to utilize in other discriminative models such as maximum entropy and SVM. Gaussian density estimates also show that localized models and local information are preferable for handwriting recognition. Such local information is suitable for many multimedia data problem in which each category could be a mixture of different patterns.

Table 9.6 also shows the results using CRFs with ratio threshold based beam search and K-L divergence based beam search respectively and HMMs with discrete features. For the Maximum Entropy model with unigram predicates, the model features are defined as those in CRFs for observational-state pairs, only observation and state at the same position are considered (see[31] for details). From the results, CRFs with a K-L divergence based beam search outperforms that with a ratio threshold based beam search by a small margin. Both CRFs outperform the Maximum Entropy model with unigram predicates, showing the importance of transition information. The HMM with discrete features where the features are not smoothed does not perform that well (the words are smoothed for all HMMs). HMM performance can be improved substantially by also smoothing the features and as can be seen this makes them better than the CRF's. For reference, CRFs and Maximum Entropy use some kind of Gaussian prior for smoothing.[39] However, we believe that the poorer performance of CRFs is due to the substantially larger number of parameters that need to be estimated. In addition all the parameters are estimated at the same time while the probabilities for HMM's are estimated separately in this special case. More training data might improve the results but there are significant difficulties in using more training data. First, creating large amounts of training data is labor intensive and expensive. Second, CRFs are much slower and hence this would also require large amounts of computation. An alternative approach to increasing the amount of training data required would be to drastically reduce the state space. This would probably require dropping the whole word paradigm and moving to a character based approach with its attendant segmentation difficulties.

We have so far compared all techniques on the same features. Continuous features can substantially improve performance. However, directly using continuous features for CRFs is still problematical. CRFs require the continuous features to have a monotonic distribution. Most of the continuous features used in the paper here are not monotonic and in general it is non-trivial to find such features. Using the existing non-monotonic continuous features with CRFs leads to poor performance.

Acknowledgments

This work was supported in part by the Center for Intelligent Information Retrieval and in part by a grant from Google and in part by grant #NSF CNS-0619337. Any opinions, findings and conclusions or recommendations expressed in this material are the author(s) and do not necessarily reflect those of the sponsor.

References

1. V. Lavrenko, T. Rath, and R. Manmatha. Holistic word recognition for handwritten historical documents. In *the Proc. of DIAL'04*, pp. 278–287, (2004).

2. R. Plamondon and S. N. Srihari, On-line and off-line handwriting recognition: A comprehensive survey, *IEEE Trans. on Pattern Analysis and Machine Intelligence.* **22**, 63–84, (2000).

3. T. Steinherz, E. Rivlin, and N. Intrator, Offline cursive script word recognition - a survey., *Int'l Journal on Document Analysis and Recognition.* **2**, 90–110, (1999).

4. A. Vinciarelli, A survey on off-line cursive word recognition., *Pattern Recognition.* **35**, 1433–1446, (2002).

5. S. Madhvanath and V. Govindaraju, The role of holistic paradigms in handwritten word recognition, *IEEE Trans. on Pattern Analysis and Machine Intelligence.* **23**(2), 149–164, (2001).

6. N. Gorski, V. Anisimov, E. Augustin, O. Baret, D. Price, and J. Simmon. A2ia check reader: A family of bank check recognition system. In *Proc. of the 5th Int'l Conf. on Document Analysis and Recognition,* pp. 523–526, (1999).

7. A. Vinciarelli, S. Bengio, and H. Bunke. Offline recognition of large vocabulary cursive handwritten text. In *Proc. of ICDAR'03,* pp. 1101–1105, (2003).

8. U.-V. Marti and H. Bunke, Using a statistical language model to improve the performance of an hmm-based cursive handwriting recognition system, *the Jnl. of Pattern Recognition and Artifical Intelligence.* **15**, 65–90, (2001).

9. J. Edwards, Y. W. Teh, D. Forsyth, R. Bock, M. Maire, and G. Vesom. Making latin manuscripts searchable using gHMM's. In *Proc. of the 18th Annual Conf. on Neural Information Processing Systems,* Vancouver, Canada (December 14-16, 2004).

10. J. Edwards and D. Forsyth. Searching for character models. In *the Proc. of NIPS 2005,* (2005).

11. J. Chan, C. Ziftci, and D. Forsyth. Searching off-line arabic documents. In *CVPR 2006,* NYC, (2006).

12. T. Rath and R. Manmatha, Lower-bounding of dynamic time warping distances for multivariate time series., *Tech. rep., Center for Intelligent Information Retrieval, Univ. of Massachusetts Amherst, 2003.* (2003).

13. N. Howe, T. Rath, and R. Manmatha. Boosted decision trees for word recognition in handwritten document retrieval. In *the Proc. of ACM SIGIR'05,* pp. 377–383, (2005).

14. S. Madhvanath and V. Govindaraju. Using holistic features in handwritten word recognition. In *Proc. of the U.S. Postal Service Advanced Technology Conf.,* p. 183C199, Washington, DC (November 30 - December 2, 1992).

15. Y. Lu and M. Shridhar, Character segmentation in handwritten words - an overview., *Pattern Recognition.* **29**, 77–96, (1996).

16. R. Manmatha and W. B. Croft, Word spotting: Indexing handwritten manuscripts., *Intelligent Multimedia Information Retrieval.* pp. 43–64, (1997).

17. R. Manmatha, C. Han, and E. M. Riseman. Word spotting: A new approach to indexing handwriting. In *Proc. of the Conf. on Computer Vision and Pattern Recognition,* pp. 631–637, San Francisco, CA (June, 1996).

18. R. Manmatha, C. Han, E. M. Riseman, and W. B. Croft. Indexing handwriting using word matching. In *Digital Libraries 96: 1st ACM Intl Conf. on Digital Libraries,* pp. 151–159, Bethesda, MD (March, 1996).

19. T. Rath and R. Manmatha. Word image matching using dynamic time warping. In *Proceedings of CVPR'03*, vol. 2, pp. 521–527, (2003).
20. J. Rothfeder, S. Feng, and T. Rath. Using corner feature correspondences to rank word images by similarity. In *In Proc. of the Workshop on Document Image Analysis and Retrieval*, Madison, WI (June, 2003).
21. T. M. Rath, S. Kane, A. Lehman, E. Partridge, and R. Manmatha, Indexing for a digital library of george washingtons manuscripts: A study of word matching techniques., *Tech. rep., Center for Intelligent Information Retrieval Univ. of Massachusetts Amherst, 2000*. (2000).
22. T. M. Rath and R. Manmatha. Features for word spotting in historical manuscripts. In *Proc. of the 7th Intl Conf. on Document Analysis and Recognition*, pp. 218C–222, Edinburgh, Scotland, (August 3-6 2003).
23. S. Belongie, J. Malik, and J. Puzicha., Shape matching and object recognition using shape contexts., *IEEE Transactions on Pattern Analysis and Machine Intelligence*. **24:24**, 509–522, (2002).
24. T. M. Rath and R. Manmatha, Word spotting for historical documents, *International Journal on Document Analysis and Recognition*. **9**, 139–152, (2007).
25. C. L. Tan, R. Cao, and P. Shen, Restoration of archival documents using a wavelet technique., *IEEE Trans. on Pattern Analysis and Machine Intelligence*. **24**(10), 1399–1404, (2002).
26. B. Gatos, T. Konidaris, K. Ntzios, I. Pratikakis, and S. Perantonis. A segmentation-free approach for keyword search in historical typewritten documents. In *In Icdar05*, (2005).
27. M. Turk and A. Pentland. Eigenfaces for recognition. In *Journal of Cognitive Neuroscience*, vol. 3, pp. 71–86, (1991).
28. K. Terasawa, T. Nagasaki, and T. Kawashima. Eigenspace method for text retrieval in historical document images. In *Proceedings of the 2005 Eight International Conference on Document Analysis and Recognition (ICDAR05)*, (2005).
29. A. Balasubramanian, M. Meshesha and C. V. Jawahar. Retrieval from Document Image Collections. In *Proceedings of Seventh IAPR Workshop on Document Analysis Systems*, pp. 1–12, (2006).
30. T. Rath, R. Manmatha, and V. Lavrenko. A search engine for historical manuscript images. In *the Proceedings of SIGIR'04*, (2004).
31. S. Feng and R. Manmatha. Classification models for historical documents recognition. In *In the Proc. of ICDAR'05*, pp. 528–532, (2005).
32. S. Feng and R. Manmatha. Exploring the use of conditional random field models and hmms for historical handwritten document recognition. In *the Proceedings of the 2nd IEEE International Conference on Document Image Analysis for Libraries (DIAL 06)*, pp. 30–37, (2006).
33. http://www.clopinet.com/isabelle/Projects/SVM/applist.html.
34. A. Berger, S. D. Pietra, and V. D. Pietra. A maximum entropy approach to natural language processing. In *Computational Linguistics*, pp. 39–71 (March, 1996).
35. R. Rosenfeld. A maximum entropy approach to adaptive statistical language modelling. In *Computer, Speech and Language*, pp. 187–228, (1996).

36. E. C. Buehler and L. H.Ungar. Maximum entropy methods for biological sequence modeling. In *Workshop on Data Mining in Bioinformatics of KDD01*, (2001).
37. A. Ratnaparkhi. A simple introduction to maximum entropy models for natural language processing. Technical report, (1997).
38. J. Lafferty, A. McCallum, and F. Pereira. Conditional random fields: Probabilistic models for segmenting and labeling sequence data. In *Proc. ICML, 2001*, (2001).
39. S. Chen and R. Rosenfeld. A gaussian prior for smoothing maximum entropy models. Technical report, (2001).
40. F. Sha and F. Pereira. Shallow parsing with conditional random fields. In *Proceedings of Human Language Technology, NAACL, 2003*, (2003).
41. J.Norcedal and S. Wright., *Numerical Optimization*. (Springer, 1999).
42. F. Jelinek, *Statistical Methods for Speech Recognition*. (MIT Press, 2001).
43. C. Pal, C. Sutton, and A. McCallum. Constrained kronecker deltas for fast approximate inference and estimation. In *UAI 2005*, (2005).
44. N. Japkowicz and S. Stephen. The class imbalance problem: A systematic study. In *Intelligent Data Analysis*, (2002).

Chapter 10

Statistical Modeling of Document Appearance: A Survey

Prateek Sarkar

Palo Alto Research Center, California

psarkar@parc.com

The appearance of a document is complementary to its textual and symbolic content. Computational models of document appearance and geometric layout can be applied to compress, rectify, interpret, categorize, index and retrieve documents. Statistical models of appearance measure uncertainty and variability in the rendering, viewing and imaging process. Their parameters can be trained to learn the appearance characteristics of a document or a group of documents. Published statistical models of appearance target granularities ranging from subpixel imaging effects to broad characterization of document layout genre. Systematic constraints have to be included in appearance models for computational tractability of inference algorithms. Tables, diagrams, photographic images, charts, line drawings, informal documents and document genre are on the frontiers of the domain of statistical appearance models and inference algorithms.

Contents

10.1. Statistical appearance models

An appearance model is a collection of assumptions, abstractions, constraints, rules, or mathematical formulae that can help describe and distinguish the visual appearance of one or a group of document images. A model is statistical if it incorporates uncertainty, and variability of the document image due to rendering, viewing, and image acquisition conditions, and, more importantly, the parameters of the model are trainable from an ensemble of example images.

Figure 10.1 shows a few documents that we can categorize into content types or genres even without actually analyzing the symbolic content within them. Each row represents a different visual category. Some categories have rigid layout (such as fixed forms), some are fluid within the bounds of a layout "grammar" (such as technical articles), while others may be more freeform (such as memos or handwritten notes). Of course, the notion of visual similarity between documents can vary by application. A model of appearance may help us locate duplicates of the same image, images of the same template structure, images with similar local texture, or images with similar layout structure. In one context NIPS and PAMI articles may be deemed different, in others they may both be categorized as technical articles. Forms can be categorized by the form type, or by how they were received: mail or facsimile, or by the way they were filled: handwriting or machine print.

In this article, I survey models that are statistical, trainable from representative images, and that enable a computationally tractable inference algorithm for image interpretation — page categorization, layout analysis, functional role labeling, document recognition, and appearance based indexing and retrieval. Sophisticated models have been applied to compress, render, binarize, and rectify document images. But they are beyond the scope of this discussion.

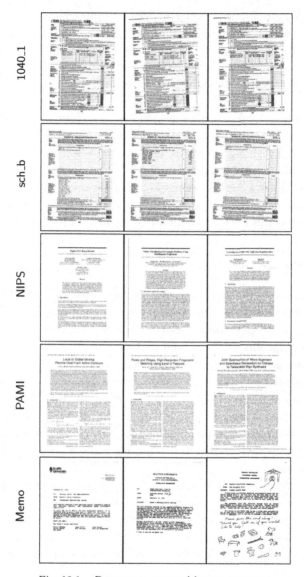

Fig. 10.1. Documents grouped by appearance.

I also restrict this survey to explicit models of appearance of a document page or a part. Assumptions about the document image characteristics such as dominantly textual content, Manhattan layout, black text on white background, blocky text (connected components) are often implicit in the algorithms for processing images. Compression algorithms make assumptions about local pixel redundancy.

Finally, document image appearance can be modeled at various levels of granularity: (a) sub-pixel level (b) stroke and character level (c) word and text-line layout level (d) multi-line structure level (e) page-layout level. There has been little work on statistical models of complex non-textual structure such as diagrams, photographic images, charts, and line-drawings. I mainly focus on major ideas in statistical modeling at the document page-layout level (e), although there are brief sections on interesting appearance models at more refined granularities (a)–(d).

Thus this is not a complete survey of statistical document image analysis (DIA). Even among published methods that propose or employ statistical models of appearance, the bibliography is representative but not complete.

10.2. Layout grammars and parsing

Layout analysis of document images is a prerequisite to OCR (Optical Character Recognition) transcription in proper reading order, but it has also been used for the document image classification, genre characterization, retrieval, and labeling of functional parts.

One approach to page layout modeling is to link visual appearance to semantic constructs through an intermediate grammar. Layout analysis is then achieved by parsing the page according to the grammar rules. In weighted grammars each production rule has a preference (or probability) and/or a measure of the applicability of the production rule in a parse. The best parse tree is then chosen to maximize a cumulative score derived from these numbers.

Most models of visual appearance, including layout grammars, specifically describe the appearance of the ink (usually black in binary images). Baird[2] suggested the idea of extracting meaning from analyzing the structure of background or whitespace in documents. This idea has mostly been employed for bottom up segmentation of the ink on a page (for example in Ref. 9).

10.2.1. Computational challenge

The primary challenge in parsing of images is the exponential number of alternate possibilities to be entertained. This is because of two different reasons.

10.2.1.1. *Exponential number of segmentations or groupings*

The mathematical concept of grammars and parsing developed in the field of computational linguistics and formal language theory. Because language is represented as a one-dimensional arrangement of non-overlapping symbols, there is a natural ordering of terminals. When the grammar assumes contiguous support for non-terminals, in a *sentence* of N terminals there are $O(N^2)$ possible supports for a non-terminal. If there are P non-terminals in a context free grammar, this leads to parsing in $O(PN^3)$ time.

Images, however, are two dimensional and there is no natural ordering of points or regions in two dimensions. The constraint of contiguous support still leaves an intractable number of possible partitions of any image region. Therefore more constraints have to be placed on the partitions to explore. One such constraint is that segmentation of a document image into its grammatical constituents always conforms to a X-Y tree representation.[39] This leads to the elegant formulation of a probabilistic context free grammar (PCFG) approach to document image parsing with polynomial time complexity. In particular, forcing alternate X and Y cuts can reduce image parsing to a one-dimensional string parsing problem. Siskind and collaborators present a precise mathematical formulation of X-Y tree based probabilistic context free grammars, generalizations to arbitrary shaped regions, and complexity analysis of training and parsing, although they dwell on the center-surround approach.[59,65]

Turbo recognition,[62] Document Image Decoding,[24] Shilman and Viola's non-generative grammars,[56] Hull's equation parser[23] all impose different constraints in their page appearance models to achieve computational tractability.

10.2.1.2. *Context sensitivity*

A second reason for computational complexity in image parsing is the context sensitivity in image generation. In a context free grammar, a production rule of the form $A \to BC$ can be applied regardless of the parse subtrees for B, C, the produced non-terminals. In a context sensitive grammar this no longer holds. An example of context sensitivity is that different text zones of a printed document page often share text-styles, text sizes, column widths, illumination contrast, and other factors. When context sensitivity can be modeled by shared parameters, attribute grammars[64] are a useful modeling and computational tool. There are other examples of context sensitivity in document layout such as table formatting, placement of floating figures and footnotes which cannot be easily modeled by a simple expansion of the set of non-terminals.

10.2.2. Generative context free and attribute grammars

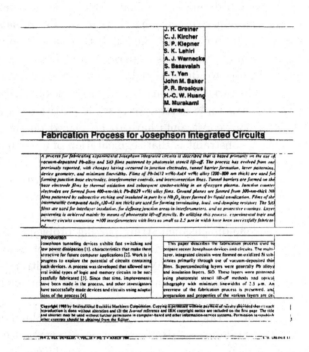

Fig. 10.2. Partition resulting from the X-Y decomposition of a technical article (from Ref. 31).

A hierarchical representation of document images by X-Y trees was first proposed by Nagy and Seth.[39] Each document image region (starting with the entire image) is recursively split in either the horizontal or vertical direction driven by the respective projection profile until some exit criterion halts further splitting. The result is a hierarchy of rectangular regions of the image. It turns out that in many document images logical chunks of images corresponding to nodes in such a tree.

Figure 10.2 shows the X-Y cut segmentation of a document image. Figure 10.3 shows two examples of layouts for which there are no X-Y tree decompositions corresponding to the logical structures.

Application of X-Y tree based grammars for layout analysis was introduced by Viswanathan et al.[31,63] The rectangular regions at the leaves of

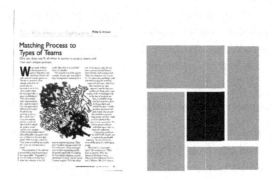

Fig. 10.3. *Left*: Non-Manhattan layout *Right*: Schematic of an axis-parallel layout. Neither document can be represented by X-Y decomposition without splitting zones that logically belong together.

an X-Y decomposition of an image become the observed terminals which are then parsed according to a context free grammar that describes the layout of a specific kind of document (for example the first page of a technical article in a specific journal.) Compiler tools such as `lex` and `yacc` are applied to deterministically parse the observations. The authors also propose a criterion and a branch and bound algorithm for selecting the "best" parse when the page grammar does not admit the X-Y tree segmentation of the image.

However, we can consider the "best" parse even when multiple valid parses exist for the X-Y tree. In weighted grammars each production in the parse tree can be also given a goodness and/or utility score (production rule probabilities in PCFG). Then an optimal parse tree can be computed by a parsing algorithm such as chart parsing[27] or A* parsing.[28] Most speedups over chart parsing exploit the sparsity of plausible parse trees.

The *context free* property of PCFG models of documents is severely limiting because document regions are generated with a shared stylistic context as described in Section 10.2.1.2. Attribute grammars offer one way of approaching this problem.[64] To enforce the constraint that all text-lines generated by a paragraph should have same line heights, justification, and text style, the `Paragraph` and `Textline` non-terminals can be augmented with attributes corresponding to line-height, justification, and text style. The grammar can then be expanded to enforce that an attributed `Paragraph` only generates `Textline` instances that share the same attributes. As long as the attribute values are discrete, this just represents an expansion in the set of non-terminals and production rules and the same polynomial time computing algorithms can still be applied in principle. In practice, even for modest grammars, the expansion into attribute space makes computation intractable. When attribute values can vary continuously, the same algorithms are no longer applicable.

10.2.3. Non-generative grammars

Shilman and Viola[56] propose an extension to the grammar approach in which they expand the scope of the functions that score individual productions. Their production scoring functions can now incorporate arbitrary measurements on the supports of all non-terminals in the respective production rules (such as justification and text size similarity of textlines), and even measurements that may be made on the document at large (such as the estimated dominant font size and line spacing). Thus they incorporate complex context sensitivity into their scoring of a parse tree. However, they carefully preserve computational tractability of parsing. The trick is to keep the scoring functions independent of the parse subtrees of the produced non-terminals, even though they can depend on the *supports* of the same non-terminals. The partitioning of supports is restricted by constraints on convex hulls of supports.[32,37]

The richly enhanced expressive power of the grammar and scoring functions comes at the expense of more complex training procedures and, perhaps, less intuitive parameters as compared to generative grammars – PCFG and attribute grammars. In the Shilman-Viola approach parameter training is made tractable by restricting scoring functions to linear combinations of features. Parameter values are computed to solve a two way classification problem – to tell correct parses from incorrect parses (correct entries on a parsing chart from all other entries.) The perceptron update rule and AdaBoost of decision stumps are applied to estimate the parameters.

The authors indicate the strength of their generic computational platform by applying it to parse technical journal pages, and mathematical equations, both with considerable success in their initial experiments.

10.3. Probabilistic Markov grammars

Markov grammars are more restrictive and inference is usually achieved through belief propagation, Viterbi algorithm or similar dynamic programming algorithms on a trellis.

10.3.1. *Separable layouts and Document Image Decoding*

Fig. 10.4. A part of a telephone book page that Kam and Kopec's separable source models targeted (from Ref. 24).

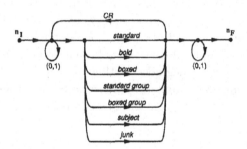

Fig. 10.5. An illustrative text column generator for the phone book example. This is a recursive Markov source, where each textline transition expands out to a full Markov source (not shown, see Ref. 29) for glyph layout along a textline (from Ref. 24).

Kam and Kopec[24] developed a notion of *separable source models* in which a text-column is generated by a Markov source that marks y locations as baseline or non-baseline. Text-lines are then generated by another kind of Markov source that lays out glyphs in a horizontal direction (see Section 10.7.2) over the marked baselines. Such a *recursive* Markov source is illustrated in Figure 10.5. Multiple kinds of text-lines are allowed, corresponding to different line-heights and font properties of glyphs. In this kind of Markov layout grammar all displacements are relative to the immediately preceding non-terminal. But Kam and Kopec also show how the Markov sources can be modified to incorporate range constraints on absolute locations of nodes such as column boundaries (text-line start/end nodes).

Locating and decoding text-lines is performed by maximum probability transition paths through an *expanded* trellis corresponding to the recursive source. But due to the separable nature of the source, the best paths for each horizontal text-line source can be computed and only their scores stored for the vertical Viterbi to consider. After the vertical pass picks some y locations as best bets for text-baselines, the appropriate horizontal sources are applied again to decode the content of those text-lines. The first pass of decoding every possible y location for the best text-line explanation can be computationally expensive. In[25] the authors show how the search can be made efficient on the average by computing cheap bounds on line-scores and using the Iterated Complete Path algorithm.

Kam and Kopec's models (and Kopec and Chou's Document Image Decoding, in general) were ambitious in that they endeavored to explain an entire text column (or even page of several columns) all the way to the generation of every black and white pixels with one elegant model. But inference with such models can be notoriously compute-intensive, and the use of hard constraints turn out to be both a boon and a bane for DID. Incorporating hard typographical constraints has enabled DID to provide high accuracy OCR of severely degraded textline images.[51,54] At the same time, the reliance on hard-constraints to narrow down the other wise explosive search space has made document or style specific training both extremely difficult and essential.

10.3.2. *Turbo recognition*

Turbo recognition for document layout analysis proposed by Tokuyasu and Chou[61,62] was inspired by the success of Turbo decoding in signal communication, and by the predominance of axis parallel layout in printed documents. In turbo decoding[6] two different representations (permutations) of a signal stream are sent through a lossy communication channel, and the signal stream is reconstructed by simultaneously heeding both degraded streams through iterative belief updates. Even though loopy belief propagation does not guarantee an optimal solution, turbo decoding became popular because of excellent empirical performance.

Tokuyasu and Chou's essential insight was that most rectangular layouts can be represented by intersecting two one-dimensional grammars for

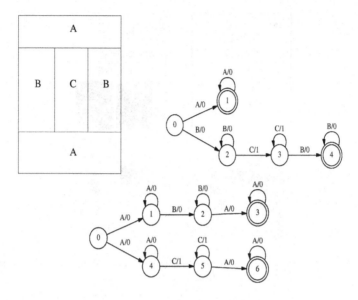

Fig. 10.6. An example of a simple layout and the corresponding horizontal (left) and vertical (right) grammars for turbo recognition (from Ref. 62).

pixel layout – one horizontal and one vertical (see example in Figure 10.6). The horizontal and vertical readout of images would correspond to the two permutations of the same image signal. The image is reconstructed by iterative (loopy) updates of pixel labels (text/left/right/top/bottom/gutter).

10.4. Local feature based models

There are a number of methods that characterize the appearance of document images much less precisely, and much less guided by the logical structure of the document. These methods rely completely on the visual characteristics. The goal of these methods is to make broad visual similarity/dissimilarity deductions. Image categorization, and retrieval by visual similarity are examples of applications.

10.4.1. *Features measured in subregions*

One approach is to divide an image into multiple zones, and represent the image by features measured in each zone. Hu *et al.* split a document image into fixed $m \times n$ grid blocks, and represent each block by a single binary feature: text or white, according to whether text or non-text dominates the

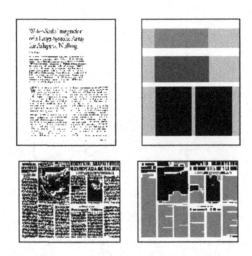

Fig. 10.7.   Examples of document thumbnails and layout segmentation and labeling (color coded) by turbo recognition (from Ref. 61).

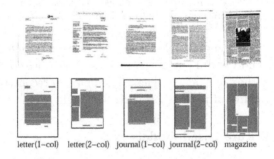

letter(1–col)   letter(2–col)   journal(1–col) journal(2–col)   magazine

Fig. 10.8.   Document appearance abstraction by labeling grid blocks as text/non-text (from Ref. 22).

block (Figure 10.8). A page image is then represented by the collection of contiguous runs of text blocks in the form of interval encoding. They define three different distance measures between interval encodings or representations derived from them, and demonstrate that they can classify images by layout and identify pages of similar layout structure.[22]

Shin et al.[57] represent document images by a variety of measurements designed to capture image properties at different levels. Each image is binarized and connected components are enumerated. Features include statistics of connected components (height, width, etc.) at window, projection, and page levels, proportion of content types (text/image/graphics), presence of tables, type of columnar structure, and type size estimates. Based on this multidimensional description an image is classified by a trained classifier tool. In[58] the same authors represent document image appearance by the zones resulting from layout analysis, and features such as content type, relative size, location, and aspect ratios of such zones. A matching algorithm is then used to recover visually similar documents from a database.

10.4.2. *Local descriptors*

The use of local descriptors has become extremely popular in computer vision. The idea is to characterize *interest* points in natural images, such as edges and corners, by computing features in small neighborhoods around them. Images are then represented by the characterizations of interest points they contain, and this can be used for matching, classification, and retrieval. The neighborhood features are usually designed to offer some robustness against minor variations in view angle, lightness, and scale. Especially if the neighborhood measurements can be effectively quantized, each local descriptor becomes a discrete *visual word*. An image can then be represented by the *bag* of visual words it contains, and indexing techniques inspired by text retrieval can be used for matching and retrieving images.

A few such techniques have been applied to document image appearance modeling.

10.4.3. *Locational distribution of intensity variations*

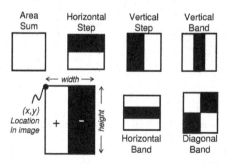

Fig. 10.9. Rectangular Haar filters used in DICE (from Ref. 53).

Sarkar[53] presents a system called the *Document Image Classification Engine (DICE)* for categorizing page images. Six different Haar filters are

1040_1 sample   sch_e_2 sample

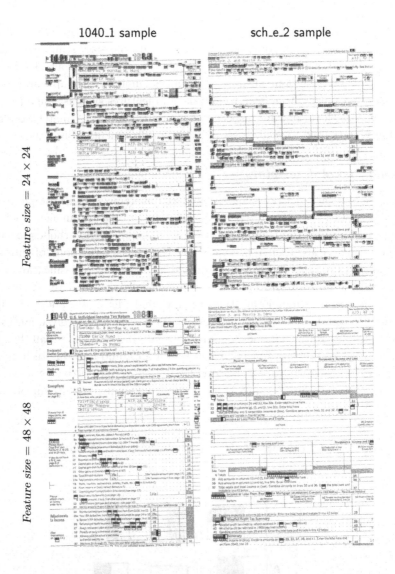

Feature size = 24 × 24

Feature size = 48 × 48

Fig. 10.10.   Illustrating the difference in locational distribution of Haar filter features (vertical and horizontal edge) that fired on two different images at two different scales.

applied to an image, each at multiple scales. Significant luminance variations in the image, as measured by high filter responses, are recorded as five dimensional features: (f, w, h, x, y). f represents the type of filter that produced a high response, (x, y) represent the location where the response was produced, (w, h) represent the width and height of the rectangular filter. Filter type, f, takes on discrete values such as AreaSum, VertEdge, HorizEdge, VertBand, HorizBand, DiagBand (see Figure 10.9). x, y, w, h are integer values in pixel coordinates but are treated as continuously varying values. The collection of five-dimensional features triggered by an image (typically in tens of thousands for a US letter sized page at 300 dpi) is a scatter in the five dimensional space and represents the visual appearance of the page.

The category of a page is represented by a probability distribution in the five-dimensional space that could generate such a scatter when sampled. Each category has a distribution associated with it. For classification, a new page (as characterized by its own feature scatter) is assigned to that category whose distribution maximizes the likelihood of the observed features. Each category is represented by a *latent conditionally independent (LCI)* model whose parameters are estimated by an Expectation Maximization (EM) algorithm.

DICE was shown to provide excellent classification accuracy on the NIST Tax forms datasets,[17] while requiring very little training data. However, its main advantages are in the use of simple, efficient, robust, local, and universal features for appearance signatures, and in the generative approach for modeling the distribution.

Unlike many connected component or layout based features, intensity variation measurements are *robust* to splitting and merging degradations that plague scanned high contrast documents. They are also *universal* because very little is assumed about the nature of the image. Images only need to demonstrate intensity variations to qualify, and need not be amenable to traditional connected component or layout analysis. This makes the system useful with gray scale images, as well as images of graphic art.

The generative model allows modular training in that one model is trained per category from only training samples of that category. This is useful in an application scenario where new categories can be added to the categorizer's library as and when needed without having to store all training data from all categories. The latter is usually the case in training discriminative classifiers. However, the benefits of modular training become even more apparent when we consider more detailed generative models for layout of document parts such as the ones described in.[19]

Notice that DICE actually builds a model of appearance for an image, and is not simply a device for category discrimination. Such an appearance model could be built for a part of a document image rather than the whole

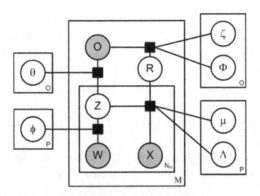

Fig. 10.11. A more detailed generative model for the distribution of local descriptors expressed as a factor graph (from Ref. 19).

image. So we could build models for document titles which are printed in larger fonts (so would respond to larger scale filters), for halftone images, for continuous shade photos, for line-drawing, for fine-print, line separators, and so on. These component models can then be used in a joint generative model for a complex page layout, as shown in Figure 10.11 and described in.[19] In that paper the document parts are trained in an unsupervized way. The feature extraction part is the same as in DICE, so is the general idea of inference through message-passing in a Bayesian network. But this model is now much more expressive. Each triggerred feature may come from any of the *document parts* indexed by Z, depending on the document category O. The feature location X combines an unknown absolute displacement R, and a part specific relative displacement. Unlike the parsing scenario this approach never attempts to extract crisp boundaries between document zones. But it does apply a simple compositional document model, even without having to create a grammar. By simply training on different sets of data, this generative model was applied to tell letters from technical article, as well as NIPS pages from PAMI pages.

For categorization or model matching DICE loops through the list of triggered features once, and is therefore $O(N)$. The shared parts model runs loopy belief propagation for inference of absolute location, part labels and category information. It loops through the feature list multiple times $- O(N)$.

10.4.4. *Feature descriptors without location*

The two local descriptor based approaches described above specifically model the locational distribution of the descriptors (or visual words) on a page. Other methods ignore the location of descriptors completely, deriving their mileage from more complex (high dimensional) and expressive local descriptors. If two images contain a local patch that match in the complex descriptor space, that contributes to the similarity between the two images. Most keypoint or patch descriptor based image categorization methods in computer vision literature adopt this approach. *Generic visual categorization (GVC)*[44,45,67] is one such method that has been successfully applied to document image categorization.

Local appearance descriptors have also been used for document image retrieval. Nakai *et al.* have developed a system that can retrieve copies or near copies of a query image from a database of several thousand images in real time.[40,41] Their algorithm is called *Locally Likely Arrangement Hashing (LLAH)*, and is targeted at the textual part of documents. Locations of text words are identified with a simple pre-processing step. The relative geometric layout of each word location with respect to its neigbors is encoded by a set of affine invariant measurements. Each of these encodings then becomes a signature of the document. These encodings are found to be very repeatable (will be found in other images of the same document) as well as discriminative (differentiate between different local arrangements of words). Each document image in the database is indexed by the measurements describing the neigborhood arrangement of every word. A query image is then matched to those documents by counting how many local word neighborhoods match. This method has been found to be highly accurate, and works on a database of 10,000 documents at video frame rates. The system can find a duplicate document in the database even if only part of the query is visible. The local affine invariance also allows the system to work even if the query image has global nonlinear distortions such as bending, folding or warping.

Liu and Doermann[33] present a similar system called *Mobile Retriever* for document image retrieval by query image. They apply a different set of local invariant measurements for word neighborhoods.

10.5. Graph representations of layout

The X-Y tree segmentation of an image itself has been used as a model to describe an image. Marinai and others measure similarity between images in terms of the a distance between respective X-Y trees for image retrieval.[35,36] The XY tree representation is also used to classify article pages into various functional categories, such as title page and index page, in order to aid metadata extraction.[12]

Bagdanov and Worring[1] characterize a document image by an attribute relational graph (ARG) representing the neighborhood relationship of various layout segmentation zones. Document genres are represented by first order random graphs (FORG) – an abstraction that can generate ARGs by instantiating vertex values. A FORG can be trained from example documents belonging to a genre. An observed ARG is classified by choosing the genre-specific FORG with maximum conditional probability.

10.5.1. *Hidden tree Markov model*

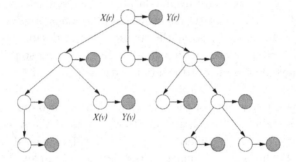

Fig. 10.12.   An example hidden tree Markov model. The tree branching is dictated by the recursive XY cuts process. Ys represent observation made on X-Y tree nodes. Xs represent the hidden "state" that generated those observations (from Ref. 16).

Diligenti *et al.* proposed the use of *Hidden Tree Markov Models (HTMM)* for document classification by appearance. Each document is represented by an X-Y tree, and features computed on the upright rectangular zone represented by each tree node. The generative model is a corresponding *hidden* tree of states (Figure 10.12) which represent an abstract characterization of zones. The Markov assumptions are (a) the features computed in a zone depend only on the corresponding hidden state, and (b) the (hidden) state label of any node only depends on the (hidden) state label of its parent node (see Figure 10.12). In variants of their algorithm the hidden state value is augmented by the tree-level of the node (level stationary), or whether the node is a left or right child (locally stationary).

The different kinds of stationarity induce different parameter sharing schemes. Parameters are estimated using an Expectation Maximization (EM) algorithm, and inference is driven by a junction tree algorithm. A set of HTMM parameters was learned from examples of each document category. At testing time a document image is assigned the category that maximizes the likelihood of the observed tree decomposition. This method was shown to be accurate in the classification of invoices from different sources.

Many of the X-Y tree based approaches to appearance modeling rely on the robustness or limited variability of the X-Y tree decomposition. They should work well, but may falter when the tree decomposition varies significantly due to noise, dynamic content, document warping or skew, or lighting variations (highlights, shadows, splitting and merging).

10.6. Models of multi-line structure

In the remainder of this article I review models that do not necessarily address appearance of full pages, but of smaller parts. Kam and Kopec's separable Markov sources (Section 10.3.1) model the appearance of text columns – and can be applied to multiline structures like lists and paragraphs. Two application domains that deserve special mention are tables and mathematical expressions. The latter are not necessarily multiline structures. We include them here because they are more localized structures than doucment pages. However, complex geometric layout and their implied meaning in mathematical expressions, together with small images, and strong syntactic structure make them an excellent test domain for grammar parsing techniques.

10.6.1. *Tables*

Table layout is an easy example for non context-free layout. From a grammar perpective, one may think of a table as a sequence of rows (or columns) where each row (column) generates a seuqence of table cells. However, such a definition does not work even for a simple grid table because cells are aligned within both rows and columns.

Model directed table analysis in document image analysis literature usually refers to a semantic rather than a visual appearance model for tables.[18] Table detection and table parsing are often driven bottom up by intra-cell text grouping or by finding whitepsace or line separators between rows and columns, with possibly a top down goodness model to choose from multiple hypothesis. Wang *et al.* describe such a system for finding tables in document images.[66] The system iteratively expands the boundaries of a table according to a complex goodness score that incorporates overlaps and alignment of text groups and the placement of separators. Cesarini *et al.* locate tables in a modified X-Y tree decomposition of a page.[13] Their model is implicit in an optimization algorithm that looks for parallel and perpendicular structure. There is a large body of literature on table analysis and recognition. Zanibbi *et al.*[69] offers a survey on published literature on tables recognition. Lopresti and Nagy,[34] and Hu *et al.*[21] provide insights into the domain of table recognition.

10.6.2. *Mathematical expressions*

Mathematical expression usually have nice syntactic structure, and it is natural to apply grammar driven analysis algorithms by augmenting the symbolic grammars with visual layout grammars. Chou,[15] Hull,[23] Miller *et al.*[37] are examples. Each system places different restrictions on layout and possible segmentations to achieve tractable parse time complexity. Shilman and Viola[56] apply their non-generative grammar approach to mathematical expression recognition.

This application domain has been a leading inspiration of visual grammar based approaches to recognition. Chan and Yeung[14] provide a survey of approaches.

10.7. Models of textline structure

Modeling of text-line structure in document images has been driven mainly by the need to inform segmentation or layout algorithms, or to perform *segmentation free* OCR.

10.7.1. *Baseline skew and warping*

Numerous algorithms have been published in literature for detection of skew angle in document images.[4] Breuel[8] developed a method for robust estimation of text baselines in document image. The baseline model included allowances for characters of different heights: x-height characters and those with ascenders and descenders. The system handles varying skew in the document by estimating the skew individually for each textline. Many methods have also been published for the modeling, measurement, and correction of page curl, warp and related distortions.[10,11,46,70]

10.7.2. *Glyph layout on baseline*

Kopec and Chou[29,30] introduced Markov source models for *Document Image Decoding (DID)* and music decoding, inspired by the successful use of Markov sources in speech recognition and signal processing. They cleverly encode the subtleties of a typographical layout process (called the sidebearing model) into a Markov model for rendering pixels black or white to generate a textline image from a string of text. This coupled with multi-level independent bit-flips provides a detailed visual model for the appearance of textlines. From a function that defines the baseline, multi-level glyph templates, and sidebearing model displacement parameters, a Viterbi algorithm is used to *decode* the textual content of the textline image.

A salient advantage of DID is that segmentation and recognition inform each other, and an *optimal* interpretation is picked from *all* possible segmentations of a textline into glyphs and corresponding interpretations. Since their seminal work, more efficient decoding algorithms have been developed,[7,38,48–50] and DID has been shown to be extremely robust in the face of heavy degradations.[48,51,54]

10.7.3. *HMMs for textlines*

Others have directly adapted the Hidden Markov Model (HMM) technology developed for speech recognition to recognize printed text lines.[5,42] These systems have been trained to recognize multifont machine print in multiple languages.

HMMs have been applied much more extensively to recognize handwriting – both online[20] and offline. Srihari and Plamondon[47] provides a detailed survey.

Nicolas *et al.* applied *Hidden Markov random fields* to find textlines in complex handwritten manuscript pages.[43] Zheng *et al.* applied Markov random field models of printed and handwritten textline continuity to smooth a raw segmentation of page content into handwriting, machine print and noise.[68]

10.8. Models of character and stroke appearance

The visual modeling of character appearance is the oldest, and most varied in document image analysis literature, contributing to its growth as a field. I will not attempt to survey six decades of research in this context. Many models of degraded character appearance have been proposed, of which Baird's model[3] is the most cited. It prescribes a model for bitmap generation (as in rendering) and does not prescribe an associated inference mechanism. The Baird model has been used primarily to simulate degraded data, which can then be used to train any classifier or visual model. Various methods have been developed to estimate parameters of the Baird model.[26,60]

Sarkar *et al.* explored the effects of random phase alignments between pattern and sampling grid in the digitization of binary images (such as character images).[52] Motion blur, lighting variations, color balance, highlights, low resolution and perspective distortions are the current challenges in the adoption of document image based applications to digital cameras and mobile devices.

10.9. Research frontiers

Although many document image appearance models have been proposed in literature — from the simple to the sophisticated, from sub-pixel granularity to layout genre — their domain of applicability still stands limited. Tables, charts, figures, drawings, equations, specialized visual languages such as engineering drawings and chemical structural formulae, document annotations, handwritten notes — all remain on the frontiers of appearance modeling capability. While OCR for commonly used European fonts has become sufficiently robust and commonplace to be considered commodity, software for processing images of forms, tables, charts and such is still not available in generic retargetable form with useable accuracy.

The goal of most of document image analysis research has been to convert a visual document (printed or handwritten) into a symbolic form that preserves its meaning. Of late, OCR and metadata extraction (author name, address, page numbering) for document indexing has been a major application. The role of appearance models is simply to aid symbol extraction, and the appearance characteristics are actually factored away.

However appearance characterization for its own sake is itself a major research goal. An example application is to group or organize documents by style — printed pages by publisher, or handwritten notes by handwriting style. For many documents, layout of parts is carefully designed to convey or amplify meaning in ways that are complementary to the symbolic content. Perceptual cues such as alignment, feature repetition, feature similarity, closure and proximity are immediately available to a human reader, and are loaded with implied meanings related to salience, grouping, hierarchy, and relations, that are not as readily available to a computer program.[55]

With the advent of camera phones, and perhaps a growth in handwriting capture devices (tablets, PDAs, smartphones) the nature and volume of communication through visual documents is expected to change. Appearance modeling for the sake of capturing the essence and salience in visual appearance can be extremely valuable in helping people to create, use and manage their communication artifacts.

References

1. Andrew Bagdanov and Marcel Worring. Fine-grained document genre classification using first order random graphs. In *Proceedings of the Sixth International Conference on Document Analysis and Recognition*, page 79, Washington, DC, USA, 2001.
2. Henry S. Baird. Background structure in document images. In *Proc., 1992 IAPR Workshop on SSPR*, Berne, Switzerland, 1992.
3. Henry S. Baird. Document image defect models. In H. S. Baird, H. Bunke, and K. Yamamoto, editors, *Structured Document Image Analysis*. Springer-Verlag, New York, 1992.
4. Henry S. Baird. *The skew angle of printed documents*, pages 204–208. IEEE Computer Society Press, Los Alamitos, CA, USA, 1995.
5. Issam Bazzi, Richard Schwartz, and John Makhoul. An omnifont open-vocabulary OCR system for English and Arabic. *IEEE Transactions on Pattern Analysis and Machine Intelligence*, 21(6):495–504, June 1999.
6. C. Berrou, A. Glavieux, and P. Thitimajshima. Near shannon limit error-correcting coding and decoding:turbo-codes. In *IEEE International Conference on Communications*, pages 1064–1070, Geneva, Switzerland, May 1993.
7. Dan S. Bloomberg, Thomas P. Minka, and Kris Popat. Document image decoding using iterated complete path search with subsampled heuristic scoring. In *Proceedings of the IAPR 2001 International Conference Document Analysis and Recognition (ICDAR 2001)*, September 2001.
8. Thomas M. Breuel. Robust least square baseline finding using a branch and bound algorithm. In *SPIE Electronic Imaging 2002: Document Recognition and Retrieval IX*, San Jose, CA, USA, January 2002.
9. Thomas M. Breuel. An algorithm for finding maximal whitespace rectangles at arbitrary orientations for document layout analysis. In *Seventh International Conference on Document Analysis and Recognition (ICDAR)*, Edinburgh, Scotland, August 2003.
10. M. S. Brown and W. B. Seales. Image restoration of arbitrarily warped documents. *IEEE Trans. on Pattern Analysis and Machine Intelligence*, 26(10):12951306, 2004.
11. H. Cao, X. Ding, and C. Liu. A cylindrical model to rectify the bound document image. In *International Conference on Computer Vision*, pages 228–233, 2003.

12. Francesca Cesarini, Marco Lastri, Simone Marinai, and Giovanni Soda. Page classification for meta-data extraction from digital collections. In *Proceedings of the 12th International Conference Database and Expert Systems Applications*, volume 2113/2001, page 82, Munich, Germany, September 2001.

13. Francesca Cesarini, Simone Marinai, L. Sarti, and Giovanni Soda. Trainable table location in document images. In *International Conference on Pattern Recognition*, pages 236–240, 2002.

14. K.-F. Chan and D.-Y. Yeung. Mathematical expression recognition: a survey. *International Journal on Document Analysis and Recognition*, 3:315, 2000.

15. Philip Chou. Recognition of equations using a two-dimensional stochastic context-free grammar. In *SPIE Conference on Visual Communications and Image Processing*, Philadelphia, PA, 1989.

16. Michelangelo Diligenti, Paolo Frasconi, and Marco Gori. Hidden Tree Markov Models for document image classification. *IEEE Transactions on Pattern Analysis and Machine Intelligence*, 25(4):519–523, 2003.

17. Darrin L. Dimmick, Michael D. Garris, and Charles L. Wilson. Structured Forms Database. Technical Report Technical Report Special Database 2, SFRS, National Institutte of Standards and Technology, December 1991.

18. E. Green and M. Krishnamoorthy. Model-based analysis of printed tables. In *ICDAR '95: Proceedings of the Third International Conference on Document Analysis and Recognition (Volume 1)*, page 214, Washington, DC, USA, 1995. IEEE Computer Society.

19. Mithun Das Gupta and Prateek Sarkar. A shared parts model for document image recognition. In *Proceedings of the Ninth ICDAR*, pages 1163–1167, Curitiba, Brazil, September 2007.

20. Jianying Hu, Michael K. Brown, and William Turin. HMM based on-line handwriting recognition. *IEEE Transactions on Pattern Analysis Machine Intelligence*, 18(10):1039–1045, 1996.

21. Jianying Hu, Ramanujan Kashi, Daniel Lopresti, George Nagy, and Gordon Wilfong. Why table ground-truthing is hard. In *Proceedings of the 6th International Conference on Document Analysis and Recognition*, pages 129–133, Seattle, WA, USA, September 2001.

22. Jianying Hu, Ramanujan Kashi, and Gordon Wilfong. Comparison and classification of documents based on layout similarity. *Information Retrieval*, 2(2/3):227–243, 2000.

23. J. F. Hull. Recognition of mathematics using a two-dimensional trainable context-free grammar. Master's thesis, Massachusetts Institute of Technology, June 1996.

24. Anthony C. Kam and Gary E. Kopec. Separable source models for document image decoding. In *Proceedings of the SPIE Document Recognition II Conference*, volume 2422, pages 84–97. SPIE–the International Society for Optical Engineering, SPIE, February 1995.

25. Anthony C. Kam and Gary E. Kopec. Document image decoding by heuristic search. *IEEE Transactions on Pattern Analysis and Machine Intelligence*, 18(9):945–950, September 1996.

26. Tapas Kanungo, Henry S. Baird, and Robert M. Haralick. Estimation and validation of document degradation models. In *Proceedings of Symposium on*

Document Analysis and Information Retrieval, pages 217–228, Las Vegas, NV, 1995.

27. Martin Kay. Algorithm schemata and data structures in syntactic processing. In Barbara J. Grosz, Karen Spark Jones, and Bonnie Lynn Webber, editors, *Readings in Natural Language Processing*. Morgan Kaufman, 1986.

28. Dan Klein and Christopher D. Manning. A* parsing: Fast exact Viterbi parse selection. Technical report, Stanford University, 2001.

29. Gary Kopec and Philip Chou. Document image decoding using Markov source models. *IEEE Trans. Pattern Analysis and Machine Intelligence*, 16(6):602–617, June 1994.

30. Gary E. Kopec and Phil A. Chou. Markov source model for printed music decoding. In *Proceedings of the SPIE Document Recognition II Conference*, volume 2422, pages 115–125. SPIE–the International Society for Optical Engineering, SPIE, February 1995.

31. M. Krishnamoorthy, G. Nagy, S. Seth, and M. Viswanathan. Syntactic segmentation and labeling of digitized pages from technical journals. *IEEE Transactions Pattern Analysis Machine Intelligence*, 15(7):737–747, 1993.

32. Percy Liang, Mukund Narasimhan, Michael Shilman, and Paul Viola. Efficient geometric algorithms for parsing in two dimensions. In *Proceedings of the International Conference on Document Analysis and Recognition*, pages 1172–1177, Washington, DC, USA, 2005. IEEE Computer Society.

33. Xu Liu and David Doermann. Mobile retriever - finding document with a snapshot. In *Proceedings of CBDAR07*, pages 29–34, September 2007.

34. Daniel P. Lopresti and George Nagy. A tabular survey of automated table processing. In *GREC '99: Selected Papers from the Third International Workshop on Graphics Recognition, Recent Advances*, pages 93–120, London, UK, 2000. Springer-Verlag.

35. Simone Marinai, Emanuele Marino, and Giovanni Soda. Layout based document image retrieval by means of xy tree reduction. In *International Conference on Document Analysis and Recognition*, pages 432–436, 2005.

36. Simone Marinai, Emanuele Marino, and Giovanni Soda. Tree clustering for layout-based document image retrieval. In *Document Image Analysis for Libraries*, pages 243–253, 2006.

37. Erik G. Miller and Paul A. Viola. Ambiguity and constraint in mathematical expression recognition. In *AAAI/IAAI*, pages 784–791, 1998.

38. Thomas P. Minka, Dan S. Bloomberg, and Kris Popat. Document image decoding using the iterated complete path heuristic. In *Proceedings of IS&T/SPIE Electronic Imaging 2001: Document Recognition and Retrieval VIII*, January 2001.

39. George Nagy and Sharad Seth. Hierarchical representation of optically scanned documents. In *Proceedings of the Seventh International Conference on Pattern Recognition*, pages 347–349, Montreal, Canada, 1984.

40. Tomohiro Nakai, Koichi Kise, and Masakazu Iwamura. Hashing with local combinations of feature points and its application to camera-based document image retrieval. In *Proceedings of CBDAR05*, page 8794, 2005.

41. Tomohiro Nakai, Koichi Kise, and Masakazu Iwamura. Use of affine invariants in locally likely arrangement hashing for camera-based document image retrieval. In *Document Analysis Systems*, pages 541–552, 2006.

42. Premkumar Natarajan, Zhidong Lu, Issam Bazzi, Richard Schwartz, and John Makhoul. Multilingual machine printed OCR. *International Journal of Pattern Recognition and Artificial Intelligence*, 15:43–63, 2001.

43. S. Nicolas, Y. Kessentini, T. Paquet, and L. Heutte. Handwritten document segmentation using hidden Markov random fields. In *8th International Conference on Document Analysis and Recognition (ICDAR05)*, pages 212–216, August 2005.

44. Florent Perronnin and Chris Dance. Fisher kernel on visual vocabularies for image categorization. In *Proceedings of Computer Vision and Pattern Recognition*, Minneapolis, Minnesota, USA, June 2007.

45. Florent Perronnin, Chris Dance, Gabriela Csurka, and Marco Bressan. Adapted vocabularies for generic visual categorization. In *9th European Conference on Computer Vision*, Graz, Austria, May 2006.

46. Maurizio Pilu. Undoing page curl distortion using applicable surfaces. In *IEEE International Conference on Computer Vision and Pattern Recognition*, page 6772, 2001.

47. Réjean Plamondon and Sargur N. Srihari. On-line and off-line handwriting recognition: A comprehensive survey. *IEEE Transactions on Pattern Analysis and Machine Intelligence*, 22(1):63–84, 2000.

48. Kris Popat. Decoding of text lines in grayscale document images. In *Proceedings of the International Conference on Acoustics, Speech, and Signal Processing*, Salt Lake City, Utah, May 2001.

49. Kris Popat, Dan Bloomberg, and Dan Greene. Adding linguistic constraints to document image decoding. In *Proceedings of the 4th IAPR Workshop on Document Analysis Systems (DAS 2000)*, December 2000.

50. Kris Popat, Daniel H. Greene, and Tze-Lei Poo. Adaptive stack algorithm in document image decoding. In *International Conference on Pattern Recognition*, pages 231–234, 2002.

51. P. Sarkar and H. S. Baird. Decoder banks: Versatility, automation, and high accuracy without supervised training. In *Proceedings of the 17th International Conference on Pattern Recognition*, pages 646–649, Cambridge, U.K., 2004.

52. P. Sarkar, G. Nagy, J. Zhou, and D. Lopresti. Spatial sampling of printed patterns. *IEEE Transactions on Pattern Analysis and Machine Intelligence*, 20(3):344–351, March 1998.

53. Prateek Sarkar. Image classification: Classifying distributions of visual features. In *Proceedings of the 18th International Conference on Pattern Recognition*, Hong Kong, 2006.

54. Prateek Sarkar, Henry S. Baird, and Xiaohu Zhang. Training on severely degraded text-line images. In *Proceedings of the International Conference on Document Analysis and Recognition*, pages 38–43, Edinburgh, Scotland, August 2003.

55. Prateek Sarkar and Eric Saund. Perceptual organization in semantic role labeling. In *Proceedings of 2005 Symposium on Document Image Understanding Technology*, College Park, Maryland, USA, November 2005.

56. Michael Shilman, Percy Liang, and Paul Viola. Learning non-generative grammatical models for document analysis. In *Proceedings of the International Conference on Computer Vision*, pages 962–969, Washington, DC, USA, 2005.

57. Christian Shin, David Doermann, and Azriel Rosenfeld. Classification of document pages using structure-based features. *International Journal of Document Analysis and Recognition*, 3(4):232–247, 2001.

58. Christian Shin, David Doermann, and Azriel Rosenfeld. Measuring Structural Similarity of Document Pages for Searching Document Image Databases. In *5th IASTED International Conference on Signal and Image Processing*, August 2003.

59. Jeffrey M. Siskind, Jr. James J. Sherman, Ilya Pollak, Mary P. Harper, and Charles A. Bouman. Spatial random tree grammars for modeling hierarchal structure in images with regions of arbitrary shape. *IEEE Transactions on Pattern Analysis and Machine Intelligence (PAMI)*, 29(9):1504–19, September 2007.

60. Elisa H. Barney Smith. Scanner parameter estimation using bilevel scans of star charts. In *Proceedings of International Conference on Document Analysis and Recognition*, pages 1164–1168, Seattle, WA, September 2001.

61. Taku A. Tokuyasu. Turbo recognition: decoding page layout. In *ACM/IEEE Joint Conference on Digital Libraries*, page 475, 2001.

62. Taku A. Tokuyasu and Philip A. Chou. Turbo recognition: a statistical approach to layout analysis. In *Proceedings of the Electronic Imaging Conference on Document Recognition and Retrieval*, San Jose, CA, January 2001. Document Recognition VIII, Proceedings of the SPIE.

63. Mahesh Viswanathan. *A syntactic approach to document segmentation and labeling*. PhD thesis, Rensselaer Polytechnic Institute, December 1990.

64. Mahesh Viswanathan, Ed Green, and Mukkai Krishnamoorthy. Document recognition: an attribute grammar approach. In Luc M. Vincent and Jonathan J. Hull, editors, *Proceedings of SPIE, Document Recognition III*, page 101111, March 1996.

65. W. Wang, Ilya Pollak, T.-S. Wong, Charles A. Bouman, Mary P. Harper, and Jeffrey M. Siskind. Hierarchal stochastic image grammars for classification and segmentation. *IEEE Transactions on Image Processing (TIP)*, 15(10):3033–52, October 2006.

66. Yalin Wang, Ihsin T. Phillips, and Robert M. Haralick. Table detection via probability optimization. In *DAS '02: Proceedings of the 5th International Workshop on Document Analysis Systems V*, pages 272–282, London, UK, 2002. Springer-Verlag.

67. Jutta Willamowski, Damian Arregui, Gabriela Csurka, Chris Dance, and Lixin Fan. Categorizing nine visual classes using local appearance descriptors. In *ICPR Workshop Learning for Adaptable Visual Systems*, Cambridge, United Kingdom, August 2004.

68. Yefeng Zheng, Huiping Li, and David Doermann. Machine Printed Text and Handwriting Identification in Noisy Document Images. *IEEE Transactions on Pattern Analysis and Machine Intelligence*, 26(3):337–353, March 2004.

69. Richard Zanibbi, Dorothea Blostein, and James R. Cordy. A survey of table recognition: Models, observations, transformations, and inferences. *International Journal of Document Analysis and Recognition*, 7(1):116, 2004.
70. Li Zhang, Zheng Zhang, Chew Lim Tan, and Tao Xia. 3D geometric and optical modeling of warped document images from scanners. In *Proceedings of the Conference on Computer Vision and Pattern Recognition*, pages 337–342, Washington, DC, USA, 2005.

Chapter 11

Reverse-Engineering of PDF Files

Rolf Ingold, Jean-Luc Bloechle and Maurizio Rigamonti

DIVA Group, Department of Informatics
University of Fribourg, Switzerland
rolf.ingold@unifr.ch

Physical and logical structure recovering from electronic documents is still an open issue. In this chapter, we propose a flexible and efficient approach for recovering document structures from PDF files. After a brief presentation of the PDF format and its major features, we report about our evaluation of different existing tools for PDF content extraction and analysis. To overcome the weaknesses of these systems, we propose a new analysis strategy, based on an intermediate representation, called XCDF, which enables representing physical structures in a canonical way. The chapter describes both stages of the transformation process leading further to logical structure recognition. Finally, the chapter concludes with potential future improvements and extensions.

Contents

11.1. Introduction

During the last decade, PDF has become a de facto standard for exchanging electronic documents over the Internet. More than 200 million PDF documents are currently available on the web. Furthermore, PDF has been widely adopted for long term storage and archiving documents in their electronic form. An ISO standard (ISO 19005-1:2005) has even been developed by the International Organization for Standardization, specifying how to use a subset of PDF (called PDF/A) for long-term preservation. Nowadays, PDF is recognized by industries and governments all around the world.

Several factors may explain such a success. In the article entitled "Why PDF is Everywhere",[1] McKinley emphasizes the strengths of the PDF file format for document management and information retrieval. Indeed, PDF can be considered as a universal document format, because it is able to represent any kind of printable information including text, drawings, business charts, 3D graphics, and photos. Regardless of the application used to create this information, PDF perfectly reproduces the appearance of original documents. The Adobe PDF file format is platform-independent. Therefore, it is very portable and can be viewed and printed on any commonly used computers. Since Adobe chose to publish the PDF specification, many companies worldwide developed their own PDF-based solutions and support tools to enhance PDF standard functionalities. Hence, an ever-growing list of creation, viewing, and manipulation tools is available. Recent versions of PDF include advanced security features such as password protection or digital signatures. Finally, in the last years, PDF has been extended with new high-level features, specialized for encapsulating human annotations, structural information, and other metadata.

Despite the fact that PDF makes possible to embed metadata and logical information about the content, most PDF documents do not make use of such features. Actually, most PDF producers focus only on the preservation of the physical rendering (i.e., the appearance) of documents. As a consequence, many interesting features based on logical structures are lost, although they were originally offered by document processing softwares. Document reusability, for instance, is limited to copy-paste operation of raw text data. In the case of complex multi-column layout, even copy-paste operation is not guaranteed to work correctly when the selected text spans over more than one column. Worse, for poorly encoded PDF files, simple character sequences within a text line may not be respected at all!

Such limited functionalities have several drawbacks for document processing. PDF documents cannot be reedited, restyled, or reflowed easily. For instance, it is not possible to change the general presentation of a document, to adapt another style, or to accommodate disabled people. Additionally, copy-paste operation does not preserve logical labeling of headers, titles, or figure captures. Thus, reusing text excerpts of existing PDF documents requires the restyling to be done manually.

To overcome these limitations, our group has developed two tools, called XED (eXploring Electronic Documents) and Dolores (Document Logical Restructuring), which aim at extracting the hidden physical layout and the logical structural information from PDF documents, respectively. The final goal is to convert a PDF file into a structured format that enables reapplying all kinds of editing operations offered by common text processing systems. We consider this task as a kind of reverse-engineering performance, in the sense that it opens the possibility of regaining the logical structure information from the physical rendering. To achieve this, we make use of our long experience on document analysis, obtained on scanned document images.

This chapter is organized as follows: in Section 11.2, we present some existing tools able to process the content of PDF files, and we summarize relevant researches about PDF analysis. In Section 11.3, we give an overview of the PDF format, by describing its overall structure and graphical primitives. Section 11.4 explains the principles of PDF documents reverse engineering. Section 11.5 is dedicated to XCDF, a canonical format we propose for representing analyzed PDF. In Section 11.6, we present XED, our tool for automatically recovering the layout of PDF documents.

Section 11.7 describes Dolores, our interactive system for supervised analysis of documents' logical structures. Finally, Section 11.8 concludes the chapter and announces future works.

11.2. Related Works

Today, almost 90% of the published or exchanged electronic documents uses the PDF format. Consequently, the need for reusing their content has incited the development of tools able to access, extract, and convert their data. In Subsection 11.2.1, the major tools are described and evaluated. The document analysis field has also been stimulated by the success of PDF: various fundamental researches have been accomplished, in order to recover the original layout and logical structures of electronic documents. These researches and their corresponding projects are described in Subsection 11.2.2.

11.2.1. Related Tools

A lot of tools have been designed and developed to manipulate PDF files. For instance, Adobe provides PDF producers, readers, and even an SDK, used by developers to create softwares and plug-ins able to interact and customize Adobe products. Furthermore, third party developers propose different softwares and API, either under license or as freeware. Consequently, a wide range of PDF tools are proposed in the market. Table 11.1 presents a possible classification of these tools (see Planet PDF[2]).

Table 11.1. Categorization used by Planet PDF in order to browse their PDF-related products database.

Creation & Conversion	Create and convert to PDF files from various file types.
Developer	Developer libraries for accessing, editing, and creating PDF files.
Editing & Management	Manage, edit, update, modify, and manipulate.
Extraction	Extract text, images, and data from PDFs to other file formats.
Forms & FDF	Create, edit, collect, and extract data from forms.
Imposition & Color	Check, separate, and correct colors. Order and re-order pages.
Links & Bookmarks	Add, edit, and manage navigational elements.
Prepress & Print	Prepress, preflighting, color management, trapping, and imposition.
Searching & Indexing	Meta data, document info, indexing, and searching.
Security & Copyright	Secure and protect PDF files. Restricted use and access control.
Server-side	Server-based software for conversion, manipulation, and delivery.
Split & Merge	Split, merge, append, and collate.
Stamp & Watermark	Add stamps, watermarks, and impressions.
Viewers	Open, view, access, and edit PDF files.

Planet PDF's database indexes more than 600 products, each of them might be classified into more than one category at the same time. In this plethora of PDF products, our concern mainly focuses on the extraction tools, able to extract and interpret either the entire content from PDF files, i.e., texts, graphics, and images, or a well-defined subset of their primitives. Most of these tools convert the result of the extraction into various formats, easier to manipulate than PDF. Such formats provide edition functionalities and allow the documents' content to be easily reused.

Able2Extract,[3] PDF Transformer,[4] PDF2Office,[5] and PDF-File Converter[6] are precisely extraction softwares allowing one to convert the content of PDF documents into Microsoft's Word format. This solution has certainly been chosen in order to enable the reedition of the converted documents with widespread applications. Furthermore, such an output format allows extraction tools to reproduce as accurately as possible the original layout of documents.

Tools such as Able2Extract, PDF Transformer, and PDF2Office also convert PDF files into HTML, whereas PDFTron[7] is specialized for producing SVG documents. Both formats have been developed for publishing on the Internet and allow documents with complex layouts to be reliably reproduced. Moreover, HTML and SVG are handy formats (XML-based), easy to read and manipulate for both users and computer applications.

Mimotek[8] and xtPDF Extractor[9] go a step further by making a deep analysis of PDF pages to determine their underlying logical structure. The inferred structure is then written back in the original PDF file or in an XML-based description.

Finally, applications such as PDFText[10] and TEXTfromPDF[11] only extract the PDF textual content into ASCII codes. The output document does not keep any information about the other primitives, i.e., graphics and images, as well as the original layout. Such applications can however be useful for indexing systems and applications working with raw text streams.

Table 11.2 shows the results of a comparison we did over a selection of well-known PDF extractors and converters. The rating of the PDF tools has been made thanks to four criteria, going from low- to high-level. At the lowest level stands *Text Extraction*, meaning that a tool is able to extract text primitives correctly and store them in a raw text file. Text, graphics, and image extractions are summarized by the term *Primitives Extraction*. Such PDF products have to be able to read various image formats, deal with vector graphics and font programs in order to convert the extracted primitives into new document formats (RTF, HTML, etc.). The *Physical Structure* criterion indicates that a phase of document analysis is performed to extract information about the document's layout. Finally, at the highest level stands *Logical Structure*, meaning that a tool is designed to recover the logical structure of predefined classes of documents, e.g., magazines, newspapers.

Table 11.2. Comparison of existing PDF tools. The "•" symbol indicates that a tool efficiently integrates the functionality. TE, PE, PS, and LS stand for Text Extraction, Primitives Extraction, Physical Structure, and Logical Structure, respectively.

PDF Tool	TE	PE	PS	LS
http://www.processtext.comABC Amber PDF Converter[12]	•			
http://www.investintech.comAble2Extract[3]	•	•	•	
http://www.adobe.comAcrobat Standard[13]	•	•	•	
http://www.docsmartz.comDocSmartz Pro[14]	•	•		
http://www.pdfdesk.comEasy PDF Creator[15]	•	•		
http://www.getpdf.comGetPDF[16]	•	•		
http://www.iceni.comINfix PDF Editor[17]	•	•	•	
http://www.jpedal.orgJPedal[18]	•	•		
http://www.mimotek.comMimotek Structuriser[8]	•	•	•	•
http://www.nitropdf.comNitro PDF[19]	•	•		
http://www.recosoft.comPDF2Office[5]	•	•	•	
http://www.cadkas.dePDF 2 Word[20]	•	•		
http://www.pdf-convert.comPDF-Convert[21]	•			
http://www.pdfkit.comPDF Export Kit[22]	•	•		
http://www.pdf-file.comPDF-File Converter[6]	•	•	•	
http://www.pixelplanet.comPDF Grabber[23]	•	•		
http://www.qoppa.comPDF Studio[24]	•	•		
http://www.pdf-analyzer.comPDFText[10]	•			
http://www.filehunter.comPDFText Converter[25]	•			
http://www.pdftransformer.comPDF Transformer[10]	•	•	•	
http://www.pdftron.comPDFTron[7]	•	•		
http://www.pdf2text.comPDF XML Converter[26]	•			
http://www.archisoftint.comSolidconverter PDF[27]	•	•		
http://www.pdftodocconverterpro.comSmart PDF Converter[28]	•	•		
http://www.textfrompdf.comTEXTfromPDF[11]	•			
http://www.mesadynamics.comTrapeze[29]	•	•	•	
http://www.verypdf.comVeryPDF Tools[30]	•	•		
http://www.glyphandcog.comXpdf[31]	•	•		
http://www.exti.comxtPDF Extractor[9]	•	•	•	•

Boundary lines are sometimes hard to determine, especially in the case of the physical structure extraction. Some tools pretend to extract this structure, whereas this extraction performs efficiently only on simple layout documents. Moreover, the chosen criteria do not reflect many integrated special features. For example, few PDF extractors are able to automatically remove inconsistencies from PDF files, such as non-sense blanks or odd text segmentation. Some PDF extractors also offer interactive windowed environment with WYSIWYG editors (cf. Table 11.2). A couple of them even provide application programming interfaces (APIs), allowing software engineers to create new applications accessing PDF files' content through the extractor.

11.2.2. *Related Researches*

In the recent past, several researches have been performed on PDF documents, in order to recover their physical and logical structures. Related researches belong to two main categories, the former analyzing raster images and the latter taking advantage of the extracted PDF primitives.

By rendering graphical primitives of a PDF document on a high-resolution raster context, high quality synthetic bitmap images, not affected by noise and skews, can be generated. Application of image analysis techniques over these synthetic images can then be done. In this sense, Doermann[32] was an avant-gardist; even before the advent of the PDF file format, he applied image analysis methods over DVI (device independent file format) files rendered as bitmap images, while profiting of precious information hold in the DVI description.

A key advantage of image analysis methods consists in being independent from the inner structure of PDF files: they can be applied to any kind of documents, either containing scanned pages (thus losing the interesting synthetic property) or composed of electronic primitives. But, above all, these methods benefit from the experience gained in the field of document image analysis (DIA) during the last decades. Classical techniques of document image analysis and recognition can be successfully applied on rendered images. Synthesis and reviews of such document analysis methods are presented and described in several major publications.[33–36] Complete DIA systems offering automatic document model generation for well defined subsets of document classes have recently appeared.[37,38] Altamura et al.[37] developed WISDOM++, a DIA system with real-time user interaction that is able to transform paper documents into high-level XML-based descriptions. More specific works have also been successfully done. For example, in a paper entitled "RASADE: Automatic Recognition of Structured Document Using Typography and Spatial Inference",[39] Lebourgeois and Souafi-Bensafi describe RASADE, an industrial project aiming at recovering the logical layout of content tables in order to automatically index books and magazines.

The second category of works takes benefit of the electronic primitives composing the document.[40] A straightforward scheme is to analyze PDF documents in order to recover their structures, and then to directly store them in the original electronic documents.[41-43] This method has the great advantage of preserving the information contained in the source PDF documents, but a plug-in is then necessary for accessing the inferred structures.

A different solution is proposed in various works[44-49] where instead of storing the analysis results in the original file, the inferred structures are expressed in an XML format. This solution is well suited for further analysis or for reusing documents, because both humans and automatic systems can easily manipulate XML data. Anjewierden and Kabel[44] propose to extract logical structures from PDF files, by detecting layout components and by classifying them using a set of rules. Logical structures are then associated to ontologies, in order to index the documents' content. Déjean and Meunier[47] try to recover the logical structure of PDF documents, by first recognizing their table of contents and then using it to reconstruct their logical hierarchy. Futrelle et al.[48] propose a technique for classifying bar-graphs and non-bar-graphs diagrams, extracted from PDF files, by analyzing the graphical primitives composing the documents. Classification is achieved thanks to a binary Support Vector Machine, processing statistics (forming feature vectors) extracted from PDF graphics.

The works of Chao aim at recovering the physical structures of PDF documents, in order to separate the information in the foreground from that in the background,[45] and to adapt the document's layout to the rendering constraints or printing device specificities.[46] Rahman[49] proposes a tool for recovering the physical structures of PDF files using geometrical properties. The processed PDF files and the layout analysis results are then converted into HTML documents.

The techniques developed for analyzing electronic content may give very good results, because they can take full benefit of the exact description of primitives. Unfortunately, they are completely inefficient for PDF files composed of scanned pages. Consequently, in previous works,[50,51] we proposed to mix electronic content analysis with image analysis, in order to overcome this problem.

To summarize, all the works presented in this Subsection target at extracting physical or logical information from PDF files. According to us, the conversion of the analyzed document into an XML format is an ideal solution, which allows further analysis to be performed and guarantees document's content reuse. Most of the works presented above store the extracted structures from PDFs into XML descriptions. Thus, an XML document containing extracted structures, must refer to a PDF document itself containing the content and its layout. Physical structures and PDF contents are sometimes stored as HTML files, thereby losing the exact document layout. As explained above, each of these works focuses on a specific task. Consequently, none of them provide a general solution.

Thus, our contribution consists of 1) providing a tool able to analyze all PDF documents composed of electronic primitives, 2) proposing a canonical XML format for representing them in a unique and structured manner, and 3) demonstrating how to efficiently build new analysis systems that use this format.

11.3. PDF File Format

The Portable Document Format (PDF) was developed by Adobe in the early 1990s as a successor of PostScript. Whereas Postscript is actually a programming language primarily used to drive laser printers, PDF has been designed specifically for exchanging documents to be rendered on screens. PDF is a descriptive format allowing each page to be rendered independently. On the contrary, PostScript needs a dedicated interpreter executing the program and containing a global state for the entire document. For instance, rendering a new page depends on previous page's state.

Since its beginning, the PDF format has greatly evolved, including progressively many new features. Annotation tools have been added, as well as interactive form fields which can be filled in by the user; new accessibility features have become available for disabled people; security features allowing document encryption and authentication were introduced and progressively improved. As of today, Adobe has released its version 1.7, a complete PDF Reference (more than 1300 pages) has been made available from Adobe via the Web.[52]

The PDF format is specialized for rendering on physical devices, i.e., screen, printer, etc., guaranteeing that text, graphics, and images will look exactly the same when the file is reproduced. It ensures high-quality print jobs with precise format layout and high resolution images. Furthermore, PDF integrates the Adobe imaging model, which gives a unified view of two-dimensional graphics, that is, vector graphics as well as raster graphics. Since this imaging model is meant to be device independent, positions and affine transformations are specified within an internal homogeneous coordinate space. Textual content is scattered into text chunks linked to spatial coordinates. Most of the time, text is represented as vector graphics and is rendered in the form of a set of character shapes mapping character codes. Font-embedding and replacement systems have been included to reduce the overall file size. Additionally, support for true graphic transparency has been added in version 1.4.

Due to its general scope, the PDF file format is rather complex and a given document can be represented in many different manners, even if each of these representations produces exactly the same result at rendering. Typically, the reading order of the text is not preserved, most of the time. No assumption can be made that the order in which character strings appear in the file does actually correspond to the reading order of the document. This is not only true for documents having a complex layout, but it may also appear on very simple documents with a single text flow. In fact, a PDF document can be thought as a canvas where text and graphics are placed without any structure information.

In several examples, we noticed that a few isolated words were missing in the natural text flow and were put at the end of the document. Our interpretation of such an artefact is that the file was probably generated from a document publishing tool using lazy deletion and putting latest modifications at the end of the file, thanks to the incremental update capacities of the PDF format.

11.3.1. *Internal File Structure*

Basically, the PDF file format can be thought as a flattened representation of a data structure, consisting of PDF objects identified by their unique references. The term object refers actually to eight different information types: boolean, number, string, name, array, dictionary, stream, and the null object. Composite objects such as arrays, dictionaries, and streams may refer to other objects directly, by embedding them, or indirectly by means of indirect references. An efficient mechanism enabling object random access is offered thanks to a cross-reference table containing byte offsets pointing to the root objects. These roots are the entry points for constructing document pages.

On a physical level, a PDF file consists of a sequence of bytes, grouped into syntactical tokens. PDF objects are precisely described by means of tokens, themselves composed of a subset of the printable ASCII set, whereas byte streams are used exclusively in stream objects. Thus, PDF file raw data can be viewed with any plain text editor. As a basic example,

Figure 11.1 presents the graphical output of an elementary PDF file. The corresponding ASCII/binary code is presented in Listing 11.1, whereas Listing 11.2 focuses on the decompressed content of the data stream object.

Fig. 11.1. Graphical output of an elementary PDF file.

11.3.2. *Content Streams*

Any graphical and textual information is embedded in dedicated PDF stream objects, named page content streams. Once decompressed, a content stream contains sequences of ASCII characters composing operators and operands, in the form of PDF objects. A variable amount of operands and a unique postfixed operator compose an instruction. Instructions allow drawing graphical primitives in the document or setting rendering properties. When drawing, the processing order of graphical primitives corresponds to their z-ordering.

Graphical primitives belong to three subclasses: text, graphic paths, and raster images. Each primitive, including character shapes, is drawn according to a current graphics state which consists basically of fill and draw colors, a clipping path, and a current transformation matrix (called CTM). This CTM allows the user space coordinates, in which the document is represented, to be mapped into output device coordinates. The current graphics state is updated by dedicated graphical instructions and can be saved and restored during the rendering of the content stream, using a stack-based mechanism.

11.3.2.1. *Text Representation*

In the content stream, text objects are defined by various attributes, including font, font size, character codes, and relative coordinates on a page. Formatting operators as line breaks, paragraphs, and indentations are non-existent. Moreover, text is broken down into fragments that have to be parsed and placed in their correct location in order to restore the final appearance of the page.

Since PDF considers character glyphs as graphical objects, many of the text operators are handled using the graphics state and painting operators. However, the data structures and mechanisms for dealing with glyphs and font descriptions are much more specialized. In fact, PDF provides high-level facilities that enables applications to describe, select, and render glyphs conveniently and efficiently.

```
%PDF-1.4
%
2 0 obj <</Length 3 0 R/Filter/FlateDecode>> stream
x ]N j#1   # #q% ,   P H 1# C    K     >8 Z {        ;#  4 0 '###>>   #
      q   0 ' h ## !gWtb# E @ '87   g M u#  # '  5 j #n          # ]
         V  g $    r d #c ]  # s q / 0     n " Z D P  ##  ##*  { 3 !
      C   S L E #   q , j 3 #U<N~
endstream endobj
3 0 obj 217 endobj
5 0 obj <</Type/Font/Subtype/Type1/BaseFont/Helvetica/Encoding/
    WinAnsiEncoding>> endobj
6 0 obj <</F1 5 0 R>> endobj
7 0 obj <</Font 6 0 R/ProcSet [/PDF/Text]>> endobj
1 0 obj <</Type/Page/Parent 4 0 R/Resources 7 0 R/MediaBox[0 0 595 842]/
    Group<</S/Transparency/CS/DeviceRGB/I true>>/Contents 2 0 R>> endobj
4 0 obj <</Type/Pages/Resources 7 0 R/MediaBox[ 0 0 595 842 ]/Kids[ 1 0
    R ]/Count 1>> endobj
8 0 obj <</Type/Catalog/Pages 4 0 R/OpenAction[1 0 R /XYZ null null 0]>>
    endobj
9 0 obj <</Creator<FE FF 00 57 00 72 00 69 00 74 00 65 00 72 > /Producer
    <FE FF 00 4F 00 70 00 65 00 6E 00 4F 00 66 00 66 00 69 00 63 00 65
    00 2E 00 6F 00 72 00 67 00 20 00 32 00 2E 00 33> /CreationDate(
    D:20071203141814+01'00')>> endobj
xref
0 10
0000000000 65535 f
0000000502 00000 n
0000000019 00000 n
0000000307 00000 n
0000000644 00000 n
0000000327 00000 n
0000000418 00000 n
0000000449 00000 n
0000000742 00000 n
0000000825 00000 n
trailer
<</Size 10/Root 8 0 R/Info 9 0 R/ID [ <35285DC804A94B9DCC0087798797448A
    ><35285DC804A94B9DCC0087798797448A> ]
/DocChecksum /27D50D004B7C9BEB26D80A52D8EA1303
>>
startxref
1011
%%EOF
```

Listing 11.1.   ASCII and binary codes (bold-faced) of the "tiny PDF drawing" PDF file.

The text rendering operators draw a string of characters according to a current text state. This state is a subset of the graphics state's parameters relevant to the text, coupled with additional functionalities for defining fonts, font sizes, and other parameters, e.g., for handling character spacing.

PDF is able to deal with many different font formats including the so-called *simple* and *composite* fonts. Simple fonts are limited to 256 glyphs, while composite fonts are unlimited in their glyph space. Since the file size is a key issue in PDF, fonts are frequently reduced to subsets, describing only used glyphs. Moreover, fonts are most of the time represented as compact descriptions, post-filtered by a compressing algorithm. This leads to very complicated solutions for representing font information. For instance, most of the fonts are defined by a specific font program, embedded in a PDF stream object.

```
2 0 obj <</Length 3 0 R/Filter/FlateDecode>> stream
0.1 w
q 0 0.1 595.3 841.9 re W* n
0.8 0.8 1 rg
108 733.4 m
88.1 733.4 72 741.6 72 751.7 c 72 761.8 88.1 770 108 770 c
127.9 770 144 761.8 144 751.7 c 144 741.6 127.9 733.4 108 733.4 c h
f*
q 0 0 0 rg
BT
83.3 754.6 Td /F1 12 Tf [<74>28<69>-28<6E>-11<7920>28<50>-16<44>-28<46>
    -14<20>]TJ
ET
Q
q 0 0 0 rg
BT
86.7 740.4 Td /F1 12 Tf [<64>-11<72>25<61>-11<77>-28<69>-28<6E>-2<67>]TJ
ET
Q
Q
endstream endobj
```

Listing 11.2. Decompressed content stream, corresponding to the previously bold-faced binary codes, containing graphical operands.

PDF provides fonts' encoding mechanisms which associate character codes obtained from text strings to glyph descriptions. In case of simple fonts, Latin-text is generally represented using a *Standard Encoding*. The *Expert Encoding* becomes necessary for fonts that contain additional characters useful for sophisticated typography. In PDF font dictionaries, the specified font encoding can be overridden or altered, by defining a different and custom encoding. Finally, a mapping from font codes to Unicode is frequently available in the font encoding description or in dedicated dictionary objects.

11.3.2.2. Graphics Representation

Graphics are built from a sequence of paths contained in a page content. Paths are themselves described as consecutive line segments and curves. Such paths can be used for painting strokes, filling areas, and even as clipping zones. Listing 11.3 shows a content stream for drawing a circle, which is composed of four Bezier curves. The operators m, c and h stand for *moveTo*, *cubicCurve* and *closePath*, respectively.

```
108 733.4 m
88.1 733.4 72 741.6 72 751.7 c 72 761.8 88.1 770 108 770 c
127.9 770 144 761.8 144 751.7 c 144 741.6 127.9 733.4 108 733.4 c h
f*
```

Listing 11.3. Decompressed content stream containing graphical operands.

11.3.2.3. Images Representation

Raster images are most of the time represented as embedded stream objects. They can as well be referenced as external resources. But this is not recommended since this would split the document's data into many files. Image byte streams are generally compressed using standard compression algorithms such as CCITT for binary images, LZW for synthetized images, or JPEG for digital images. Various color spaces may be defined to control the color rendering scheme. Alpha blending and image compositing are also supported as native PDF operators.

11.3.3. Structuring the Content

PDF provides various mechanisms for incorporating annotations, metadata and structural information about the document's content. A PDF document's logical structure is stored separately from its visible content, with pointers from each to the other. This separation allows the ordering and nesting of logical elements to be entirely independent of the order and location of graphics objects on the document's pages. Unfortunately, very few PDF producers take full benefit of these capabilities.

11.4. Reverse Engineering Approach

As explained in Section 11.1, our aim is to allow re-edition of a document, synthesized as a PDF file. This goal can only be accomplished by recovering both the content and logical structures of the original document.

In modern document engineering, documents are considered as structured information. In this approach, a document has an inherent logical structure, which is mapped to a physical structure by means of a formatting process and by using appropriate styling rules. Although the resulting document certainly reveals the underlying logical structure, the back-conversion from the physical to the logical structure is not easily feasible, because the formatting process is not reversible in a mathematical sense.

11.4.1. *Physical vs. Logical Structures*

According to the document engineering standards, we distinguish two levels of document structures. The lower level is called the *physical structure* and reveals the organization of the page in terms of hierarchy of regions delimited by images, graphics and text blocks, which can be further split into text lines, words and characters. Additionally, typographic attributes such as font, size, style and color information are assigned to these elements. However, at this level, no information is provided about the interpretation of such elements. This aspect is revealed by a second abstraction level which is called the *logical structure*. The latter is also organized as a hierarchy of nodes, where each node is associated with a logical label. Thus, the physical and logical structures of documents are generally represented by means of trees.

Whereas the physical structure can be defined universally, the logical structures depend on the targeted applications and are restricted to corresponding document classes. For example, the logical structure of a legal document is completely different from that of a business plan or a scientific paper. Therefore, a set of grammatical rules has to be provided to describe the structural constraints of specific document classes. These grammars are often referred to as *document models* (cf. Subsection 11.7.1).

The reverse engineering process can be seen as a way of transforming a physical tree into a logical one. Since trees are naturally expressed in the XML language, recovering the logical structure of a document may be formalized thanks to the XSLT language, in order to perform the transformation of an XML formalism into another XML formalism (defined by XML Schemas). Document models may thus be expressed by means of XSL transformations. In fact, this is not often the case, since transformation systems may be very complicated and cumbersome to express as XSL formalisms.

11.4.2. *Global Architecture*

At the University of Fribourg, our research group, called DIVA, has developed a set of tools to extract the physical and logical structures from PDF documents. For the reasons mentioned above, we consider that the document reverse engineering process requires two distinct steps, as shown in Figure 11.2:

- The first step converts the original PDF document into an intermediate representation called XCDF (standing for XML Canonical Document Format) describing the physical structure of the document. This initial step is supposed to be generic and applicable to any document class containing textual and graphical contents.
- The second step aims at analyzing the previously generated XCDF file, in order to recover the logical structure information. At this stage, the process needs to be customized to a specific document class. The transformations which are going to be performed must also be adapted to the targeted application. This is done by using contextual knowledge, such as the generic logical structure, language dependent keywords and statistical information.

The canonical document format used as an intermediate result is described in Section 11.5. The first step of our analysis system is realized by XED which is described in Section 11.6. Finally, our prototype implementing the second step is called *Dolores* and is described in Section 11.7.

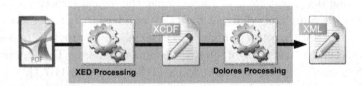

Fig. 11.2.   From PDF analysis to logical structures recognition.

11.5. XCDF Canonical Format

As introduced in Subsection 11.4.2, the XCDF document format has been developed to represent the physical structure and content extracted from

PDF documents. Over the years, a wide variety of OCR (optical character recognition) system output formats have been created such as DAFS and ALTO. Since XCDF aims at representing electronic extracted primitives and their physical structures in a reliably way, none of the existing OCR output formats were found to be suitable. Existing electronic format such as OpenDocument, RTF, SVG or VML have also been studied. But none of them was retained as a potential candidate since they do not address our defined requirements.

11.5.1. *Requirements*

The design of XCDF has been driven by the following considerations:

- Universality: XCDF must be able to represent any kind of static PDF document (i.e., documents without interactive elements or time-dependent media) containing either textual or graphical content.
- Completeness: although the set of operators is far more restrictive than in PDF, no loss of visual information should occur during the conversion from PDF to XCDF, i.e., bitmapped representations of a document should be the same when rendered from PDF and XCDF.
- Simplicity: XCDF must be as simple as possible in order to facilitate further manipulations, all information should be embedded in a single file. XCDF operators are kept to a minimum, there is only one way to represent a specific kind of data, e.g., font descriptions have to be expressed thanks to a single intuitive mechanism.
- Uniqueness: unlike PDF, we want text, graphics and images to be represented in a unique, non-ambiguous manner. This requirement must guarantee that two documents that are visually equivalent will produce the same canonical format.

11.5.2. *Format Description*

A formal specification of the XCDF format is given in form of the following DTD:

```
<!ELEMENT document (fonts, pages)>
<!ELEMENT fonts (font*)>
<!ELEMENT pages (page+)>
<!ELEMENT page (clips, images, graphics, texts)>
<!ELEMENT clips (clip*)>
<!ELEMENT images (imageblock*)>
```

```
<!ELEMENT imageblock (image+)>
<!ELEMENT graphics (graphicblock*)>
<!ELEMENT graphicblock (graphic+)>
<!ELEMENT texts (textblock*)>
<!ELEMENT textblock (textline+)>
<!ELEMENT textline (token+)>
```

An XCDF file consists of a preliminary section describing resources, such as font descriptions, and a main section holding the content of one or several pages. The content is represented thanks to four object types:

- Images, used to reproduce any kind of digital image and represented as raster graphics.
- Graphics, used to reproduce vector graphics and represented as geometrical primitives such as lines and curves composing paths.
- Text blocks, representing homogeneous chunks of text. Homogeneity criteria are close font sizes and text spanning over regularly spaced text lines. Text blocks are decomposed into text lines, tokens and characters.
- Clips, represented as vector paths, delimiting boundaries of regions in which painting operations can be applied. Images, graphics and text refer to clips by means of ID numbers.

Rendered objects, i.e., text, graphics and images, are all characterized by their bounding boxes expressed as absolute positions relative to the page's coordinate space.

11.5.3. *Representation of Text Blocks*

Because of the relevance of textual content for recovering the logical structures of documents, the representation of text blocks requires greatest attention. In complex documents, the text is usually organized as a hierarchy of text objects. However, in our canonical format we decided to represent text elements with a finer granularity, i.e., in blocks, lines and lexical units.

We also decided to restrict text units to be very homogeneous. With such a choice we expect our text splitting algorithm to produce over-segmentation rather than under-segmentation, a strategy that facilitates later logical structure recovering. Thus, in XCDF, a text block refers to homogeneous text spanning over one or several text lines. For this purpose, we restrict consecutive text lines to be regularly spaced and to have consistent margins regarding to the global text block layout.

Since paragraphs often contain isolated words or sequences of words written in another font (or font variant), we consider text blocks as homogeneous even if they include a limited number of font variations.

Listing 11.4 presents an extract of the canonical file corresponding to the previous PDF example "tiny PDF drawing", in order to demonstrate how XCDF represents text blocks, lines and lexical units.

```
<textblock id="1" bounds="83.3 78.8 46.3 25.3">
  <textline>
    <token clip-id="1" z-order="1" font-size="12.0" font-name="Helvetica
      " stroke="0 0 0 0" fill="0 0 0 255" type="text" coords="83.3
      87.4 86.3 87.4 89.3 87.4 96.1 87.4 102.1 87.4" content="116 105
      110 121"/>
    <token clip-id="1" z-order="1" font-size="12.0" font-name="Helvetica
      " stroke="0 0 0 0" fill="0 0 0 255" type="space" coords="102.1
      87.4 105.1 87.4" content="32"/>
    <token clip-id="1" z-order="5" font-size="12.0" font-name="Helvetica
      " stroke="0 0 0 0" fill="0 0 0 255" type="text" coords="105.1
      87.4 113.3 87.4 122.3 87.4 129.6 87.4" content="80 68 70"/>
  </textline>
  <textline>
    <token clip-id="1" z-order="9" font-size="12.0" font-name="Helvetica
      " stroke="0 0 0 0" fill="0 0 0 255" type="text" coords="86.7
      101.6 93.5 101.6 97.2 101.6 104.0 101.6 113.0 101.6 116.0 101.6
      122.7 101.6 129.4 101.6" content="100 114 97 119 105 110 103"/>
  </textline>
</textblock>
```

Listing 11.4. A text block containing the text "tiny PDF drawing" split into lines and represented in XCDF.

11.5.4. *Representation of Vector Graphics*

The XCDF format includes vector graphics support consisting strictly of line segments and Bézier curves (that is enough to represent any kind of path). These path primitives are grouped together within a unique graphic object, which is characterized by various attributes such as stroke and fill colors, stroke width, fill rule, a transformation matrix etc.

Graphic objects are often used for embellishing documents' background. Although XCDF does not include the concept of layers, the rendering order of foreground and background objects is revealed by a z-order parameter. Listing 11.5 presents an XCDF extract corresponding to the blue ellipse shown in the "tiny PDF drawing" example.

11.5.5. *Representation of Images*

Raster graphics support is also provided by the XCDF format. As a matter of fact, a digital image can be stored in an external file (which we do not recommend since we advocate XCDF documents to be represented as single files) or encapsulated in the main file. In the second case, a binhex representation of a PNG or JPG stream is used for the bitmap data, as shown in Listing 11.6. The image position and size are specified by an affine transformation matrix.

```
<graphicblock id="0" bounds="72.0 733.4 72.0 36.6">
  <graphic clip-id="1" z-order="0" stroke="0 0 0" fill="204 204 255
    255" stroke-width="0.1" cap-style="butt" join-style="round" dash-
    array="0.0" dash-phase="0.0" fill-rule="evenodd" transform="1.0
    0.0 0.0 -1.0 0.0 842.0" data="M 108.0 733.4 C 88.1 733.4 72.0
    741.6 72.0 751.7 C 72.0 761.8 88.1 770.0 108.0 770.0 C 127.9 770.0
    144.0 761.8 144.0 751.7 C 144.0 741.6 127.9 733.4 108.0 733.4 Z"/
    >
</graphicblock>
```

Listing 11.5. A blue ellipse graphic represented in XCDF.

11.5.6. *Space Coordinates and Device Independence*

XCDF represents graphics coordinates in a two-dimensional cartesian co-ordinate system. PDF defines a coordinate system whose origin is in the bottom left-hand corner of a page. On the other hand, the origin of the XCDF space is defined by the top left-hand corner of a page, as do most of the standard document representation systems. The x-coordinate increases from left to right, while the y-coordinate increases from top to bottom.

Device independence is ensured by defining a page resolution in dots per inch (dpi). Each coordinate is then expressed as a real number relative to this resolution: images, graphics, text positions and sizes. Every single page of an XCDF document contains a rotation attribute allowing a page orientation to be specified. Portrait and landscape page orientations are defined by rotation angles of 0 and 90 degrees, respectively. Listing 11.7 shows an XCDF extract describing an empty page with a resolution of 72 dpi, a null rotation angle (portrait orientation) and a bounding box corresponding to an A4 paper size.

```
<imageblock id="0" bounds="411.7 213.3 300.9 318.4">
  <image clip-id="3" z-order="1" transform="0.6 0.0 0.0 0.6 410.8 212.7"
    encoding="png" data="89504e470d0a1a0a0000000d494844[...]
    a083d70000000049454e44ae426082"/>
</imageblock>
```

Listing 11.6. An image represented in XCDF.

11.6. Document Analysis with XED

As introduced in Section 11.4, we have developed a very general tool, called XED, which is able to convert any PDF document composed of electronic primitives into our XCDF format. XED stands for eXploring Electronic Documents, since it has been initially designed to analyze the content of PDF documents. Being aware of the extreme complexity of PDF documents, we rapidly came to the conclusion that a normalization step was necessary. Therefore, we decided to store the intermediate result in a canonical form. The XCDF format was thus born.

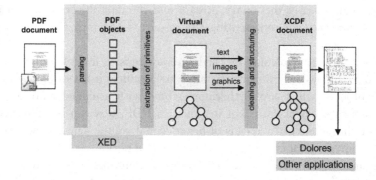

Fig. 11.3. Conversion of a PDF file into an XCDF one involves intermediate steps.

Figure 11.3 illustrates XED's architecture, with the sequential steps necessary to convert a PDF document into an XCDF one. First, XED parses the file containing the original document and generates a list of PDF objects. Second, these PDF objects are interpreted and combined together, in order to produce high-level objects representing the *virtual document*. The latter is composed of primitives, which are enriched by XED with their geometric and stylistic properties. At this stage, the document is represented as a poorly structured tree, with a limited depth. Third, the different primitives composing the document, i.e., text, graphics and images, are analyzed: the document's inconsistencies are removed, whereas the layout is extracted. Then XED reconstitutes a new tree, describing both document's structure and content. This resulting normalized tree is composed of XCDF objects and represents the XCDF document. It can eventually be stored into an XML-based file.

The following subsections describe in more detail the steps introduced above.

```
<page nb="1" dpi="72.0" rotation="0.0" bounds="0.0 0.0 595.0 842.0">
  <clips/>
  <images/>
  <graphics/>
  <texts/>
</page>
```

Listing 11.7. An empty A4 page represented in XCDF.

11.6.1. *Parsing PDF Objects*

Parsing consists in reading a PDF file, in order to convert its stream of bytes into a basic tree of uninterpreted PDF objects, i.e., boolean, number, string, name, array, dictionary, stream and the null object. These objects are further used for representing the resources and primitives composing the document.

More precisely, parsing proceeds in two steps: a lexical analysis of the raw data followed by a syntactic analysis produces a list of uninterpreted PDF objects, which are furthermore stored with a unique representation for each category of data. For instance, in PDF, text can be described by ASCII characters or by means of hexadecimal values. During the parsing, XED converts each type of strings into a list of normalized character codes.

Similarly, data streams can be encoded or compressed (for example, data for raster images). Thereby, various filters, such as LZW, DCT, CCITT Fax, etc., are used by PDF producers to reduce the size of documents. During the parsing, all PDF streams are decoded and their corresponding information is converted back to its original form. In a similar way, streams and strings can be encrypted, in order to protect the PDF contents from unauthorized access. Such filtered streams and strings are also decrypted during the PDF parsing phase.

11.6.2. *Creating the Virtual Document*

Once the parsing is done, the PDF objects are interpreted and combined together, in order to form new high-level *virtual objects* composing the document. This is a laborious task, since many different options are available for representing resources and graphical primitives. Furthermore, the format continuously evolves and new features and operators are introduced in each new release.

Thus, XED generates a PDF document as a tree of high-level virtual objects, called the *virtual document*. Composing this representation corresponds to rendering the document on the screen or printing it. This step is unavoidable, because virtual primitives' properties are not explicitly represented in the PDF objects, but they must be calculated during a rendering phase through an evolving graphics state. This graphics state contains detailed information such as transformation matrices, colors, strokes and fonts. it is updated after the rendering of each primitive, with the information required by the next primitive to create. Thus, creating the virtual document enriches all graphical primitives with their properties. Figure 11.4 illustrates this process: the textual part of the PDF stream of Figure 11.1 is interpreted in order to create the text primitives in the virtual document. PDF operators and operands, represented as PDF objects, are used in content streams in order to create new graphical primitives or update the current graphics state. When a graphical primitive is rendered in the virtual document, XED stores it with its contextual configuration, i.e., a snapshot of the current graphics state parameters relative to the current primitive. In our example, this process leads to the creation of a group of virtual text objects composing the string "tiny PDF drawing". The same mechanism is used for every category of graphical primitives, i.e., text, graphics and images.

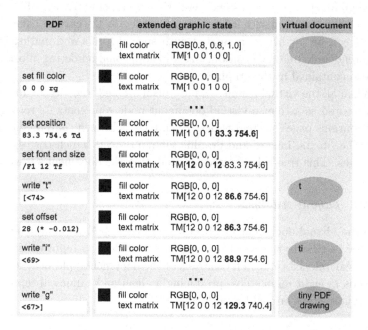

Fig. 11.4. Creation of the virtual document.

The complete virtual document generation is performed page by page. For each page, XED first prepares the corresponding resources, such as fonts, color spaces, masks, filters etc., and then, it renders all the primitives describing the document's page content.

The generation of the virtual text objects is accomplished by rendering the PDF strings, thanks to the virtual document context, with respect to the current font, colors, location and size specified in the graphics state. More precisely, text location and size are obtained by combining both the current transformation matrix, and the text transformation matrix which is updated after each text rendering step (see Figure 11.4).

The graphics' appearance is produced in a similar way. In fact, a graphical primitive contains a relative path description, its final position and size in the document are defined thanks to the graphics state. Colors, patterns and textures used for drawing or filling graphics are also described in the graphics state. When a graphical primitive has been rendered, it is stored in a virtual graphic object with its explicit properties such as location, size and color.

Finally, at this stage, images are also finalized for rendering and stored as virtual image objects. In some cases, the stream of bytes describing them needs to be completed with information provided by the current color space. Images can be further manipulated with special filters and masks, before being rendered. Images' position, size and additional rendering information are also contained in the graphics state.

When all the virtual primitives have been created, the virtual document is structured as a tree: a virtual document node represents its root which itself contains pages as child nodes. Each page is in turn composed of child nodes, i.e., texts, images and graphic virtual objects which correspond to the leaves. This tree is later used for analyzing the document's layout.

11.6.3. *Layout Analysis*

Once the virtual document has been reconstructed, XED analyzes its tree in order to recover the physical structure, and then to represent it in our XCDF canonical format. The analysis of the documents' physical structure proceeds in eight main steps, producing a clean and canonical representation. Those steps are explained below:

(1) Create a layer α for each different angle used for drawing the text primitives. Most documents only contain a unique zero degree layer. The following steps are further applied to each single layer.

(2) Apply a linear transformation performing a rotation of the current layer with an angle of minus α about the origin of the coordinate system. All the text primitives relative to the current layer have then a horizontal direction, their orientation being now equal to zero degree.

(3) Trim all the text primitives in order to remove superfluous stand alone white spaces, as well as to eliminate blanks from under-segmented textual primitives. This is a relevant step, since the layout is sometimes adjusted with blank spaces or, worse, blank characters may even be added between consecutive letters of a single word by PDF producers.

(4) Merge text primitives horizontally to correct under-segmented texts, according to a dynamic distance threshold. Thresholds are dynamically generated from the font size and occasionally from other relevant text features such as current word spacing or leading.

(5) Generate isolated tokens such as words, numbers, punctuation signs and special characters by tokenizing merged text according to a separators list. Label these tokens with one of the following syntactical attribute: *word, number, white space, punctuation* or *symbol*. These new-segmented and labeled entities correspond to the textual primitives in the XCDF canonical format.

(6) Merge horizontally canonical tokens into text lines given a dynamic distance threshold. Furthermore, add required nonexistent white spaces between consecutive tokens of a line. Indeed, all white spaces have been removed in a previous step. They need to be put back between each token of a line, if needed. The resolution of this problem is carried out by analyzing the horizontal distance between consecutive tokens (according to a dynamic threshold).

(7) Merge vertically text lines into blocks by applying a cluster component detection algorithm. Lines are clustered thanks to a bottom-up iterative algorithm (region growing). Each non-clustered line is tested with all the remaining lines, clustering takes place according to a dynamic vertical threshold. This technique allows the correct detection of overlapping text blocks, avoiding unwanted line merging (see Figure 11.5).

(8) Apply a retroactive merging over all text blocks in order to recompose over-segmented lines. This over-segmentation can be induced by too low thresholds, dynamically generated during Step 6. Indeed, in case of justified lines, the distance between strings increases and, consequently, text lines may not be correctly merged (see Figure 11.6). This step corrects all over-segmentation errors in text blocks.

Fig. 11.5.   Text blocks with overlapping bounding boxes are correctly merged.

Fig. 11.6.   Same text block as the previous one but without retroactive merging.

The height steps presented above have been especially developed and adapted for western newspapers, i.e., written in Latin or Anglo-Saxon languages. Thereby, datasets of Arabic and Asiatic newspapers have not yet been taken into account. A relevant feature of our algorithm consists in dealing with any text orientation, since the merging is applied to layers, in which text primitives have an identical angle. Furthermore, before each merging phase, textual elements are sorted according to their relative position, thus preserving their reading order.

XED processes PDF files without specific tuning, because all the thresholds are generated dynamically, using text properties ratios such as font size or line spacing. Moreover, used ratios and thresholds tend to be minimal. Indeed, over-segmentation is generally preferable to under-segmentation when dealing with textual content. Figure 11.7 precisely exposes the text segmentation produced by XED.

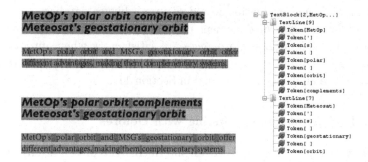

Fig. 11.7. At left, an example of PDF raw segmentation, followed by the corresponding XCDF segmentation. At right, the structure of the XCDF tree is illustrated.

11.6.4. *Evaluation of XED's Physical Structures Extraction*

XED's performances have been assessed through an evaluation campaign. Our tool has been run over an archive of 30 front pages, belonging to different western newspapers, i.e., *La Liberté*, *Le Monde* and the *International Herald Tribune*. Such newspapers are complex to analyse, and each of them has a specific layout, resulting in a totally different segmentation of their PDF textual primitives. Moreover, these three classes of newspapers are characterized by complex and variable layouts, difficult to automatically extract.

Table 11.3. The results of our preliminary experiment.

	La Liberté	Le Monde	IHT
% of correct words	99.90	99.94	99.94
% of correct lines	99.24	99.57	99.47
% of correct blocks	97.00	98.26	98.96

Each newspaper front page has been processed by XED and transformed into our XCDF canonical format. More precisely, the PDF content has been extracted, cleaned, unified and enriched with physical structures. These results have been further visualized in a graphical user interface, allowing three experts to appreciate the quality of reengineering, relative to the specification of the XCDF format. In particular, the experts investigated the percentage of correctly extracted words, lines and text blocks. Table 11.3 summarizes these results.

A more formal evaluation would require a bigger database containing many different types of document classes. However, this experiment already shows that XED performances are satisfactory when automatically producing XCDF documents. These documents are well suited for the logical structure analysis, as described in Section 11.7.

11.7. Document Understanding with Dolores

XCDF is our *pivot format* (i.e., an intermediate representation) used to store the physical structure, the content and layout of static documents. It has been especially designed for further high level processing such as logical structure reconstruction and document understanding. For this reason, reusing the XML canonical content is straightforward. Dolores (Document Logical Restructuring) aims precisely at recovering the underlying logical structures of documents such as newspapers, scientific papers, journals, magazines etc.

The following subsections focus on logical structures and the problems of their recovering. An overview of logical structures and their inferred document models is given in Subsection 11.7.1. In Subsection 11.7.2, we describe a basic experiment aiming at recovering logical structures from TV schedules. Its main purpose is to validate the XCDF format and its usability. The current learning environment integrated in Dolores is presented in Subsection 11.7.3. Since we advocate the idea that users must be involved in document understanding, Subsection 11.7.4 is dedicated to the interactive tools complementing Dolores' learning system and their future development.

11.7.1. *Logical Structures and Document Models*

Representing the physical structure of any document is achieved through the definition of a single document type. By contrast, each class of documents may have one or more generic logical structures associated with it. Distinct classes of documents and different application requirements may lead to totally different logical structures.

Prior to recovering the underlying logical structure of a document, a training phase including a manual logical labeling of the elements of the physical structure must be done. This infers the need for the description of a generic logical structure linked to a knowledge base (containing physical features, statistical information etc.) and corresponding to a given class of documents, i.e., a *document model* (cf. Figure 11.8).

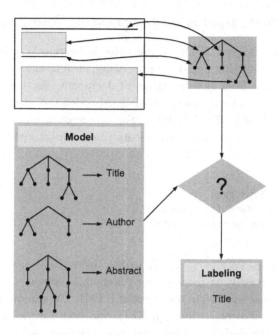

Fig. 11.8.   Document labeling thanks to a given model.

Various schemes can be used in order to produce document models: their representation may be implicit, explicit or inferred from examples. An implicit document model is directly hard-coded in the application and thus is difficult to modify, adapt or extend. This may be useful for very specific applications focusing on a particular class of documents. An explicit document model is written by hand, allowing the creation of new models by a human operator. Nevertheless, producing a new model is a complicated task and requires a high degree of expertise. Inferring document models from examples is certainly the most intuitive solution. But it needs the development of a complete learning system relying on representative ground-truthed training data.

In the recent past, tools for the automatic acquisition of document models have been developed in various ways. Unfortunately, they all share a common weakness: their flexibility is very poor. There is a need for more flexible tools: assisted environments with user-friendly interfaces, recognition improving with use, models being refined incrementally. For all these reasons, Dolores aims at producing document models thanks to user interfaces providing interactive and incremental learning functionalities.

11.7.2. A First Step Toward Document Reconstruction

One of the objectives of XCDF, as presented in Section 11.5, is to provide a pivot format permitting high-level processing, such as the recovering of the logical structures from various classes of document. As a first case study, we plugged Dolores with a simple basic hard-coded tool that generated the logical information of TV schedules. For this reason, we created a simple DTD corresponding to our requirements (for compactness, attributes are omitted):

```
<!ELEMENT tvprogram (tvdate+)>
<!ELEMENT tvdate (tvchannel+)>
<!ELEMENT tvchannel (tvshow+)>
```

TV schedules were extracted from the Swiss TV website (cf. Figure 11.9). More precisely, we focused on 6 different TV channels. 42 PDF documents were generated from one week of HTML TV schedules (6 channels during 7 days), processed through XED, and transformed into 42 XCDF files. Finally, our analyzing system processed the canonical files as follows:

- Removal of superfluous information, relative to the task, i.e., images, graphics and texts using small font sizes.
- Seeking of the most pertinent information, that is, TV show times. An easy way to achieve this step has been to apply a regular expression over all the remaining XCDF text blocks: \d{2}:\d{2}, in Perl style.
- Retrieving the text lines corresponding to the TV show times. This step has been accomplished by analyzing the relative positions of blocks: xy-coordinates, distance.
- Label text lines with *title* and *description* attributes. Font face has been used as the main criterion for labeling such information: in fact, a bold weight was used for titles and a plain style for descriptions.

As a result, we obtained the XML logical structure presented in Listing 11.8, corresponding to our previously defined DTD. The XML logical file generated from the 42 canonical files was free of errors. Our accurate results were, of course, trivial to extract since we dealt with basic layout and logical structures. This simplicity allowed us to implement an intuitive hard coded algorithm in a very short time.

```
<tvprogram descripiton="TSR schedule">
 <tvdate year="2005" month="09" day="25">
  <tvchannel channel="TSR1">
   <tvshow time="07:00" title="Quel temps fait-il ?" desc=""/>
   <tvshow time="09:10" title="Le doc expditions" desc="A la poursuite
     des pierres prcieuses"/>
   <tvshow time="10:00" title="Dieu sait quoi" desc="Le couple : b ni ou
     honni ?"/>
   <tvshow time="11:05" title="C'est tous les jours dimanche" d=""/>
   <tvshow time="12:20" title="Racines" desc="Le gospel du pasteur"/>
   <!--and so on-->
  </tvchannel>
 </tvprogram>
```

Listing 11.8. The resulting XML logical file containing the TV schedule.

However, this experiment proves the relevance of our canonical format and opens the field for more complex document logical restructuring. It appeared to us that XCDF was more than a pure pivot format. It was also an adequate representation for rapid prototyping of logical structure reconstruction algorithms.

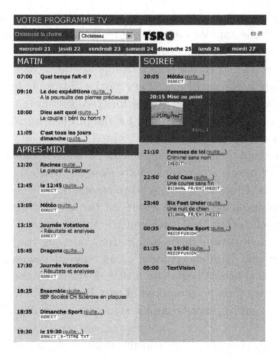

Fig. 11.9. A PDF file of the Swiss TV schedule (September 25, 2005).

11.7.3. Recovering the Logical Structure from Newspapers

Dolores focuses on the elaboration of restructuring processes which allow logical information to be recovered from our canonical format. Precisely, we currently focused our work on the newspaper class, because it offers various interesting and relevant features: a rich layout characterized by a lot of typographical and topological information, as well as deep logical hierarchies.

In the first stage, we elaborated a logical format which is able to represent logical structures of newspapers in an adequate way. This XML-based format does not embed any document content. In fact, the links to the physical representation, described by the canonical format, are established by means of unique identifiers. This logical representation is designed to handle topological intricacies such as an article distributed over different pages. It also enables to distinguish between various types of articles (e.g., news, interviews).

The method we applied to recover the logical structure from newspapers was inspired by the approach introduced by Souafi-Bensafi et al.[53] The authors focus on periodical magazines. Their system uses a nave Bayesian network that is trained on the basis of a representative dataset, in order to retrieve the labels of text blocks. They justify this probabilistic approach by the need to minimize the effect of errors resulting from the OCR phase. As we do not rely on an OCR system for the physical structure extraction phase, but on electronic documents, we opted for artificial neural networks (ANN). So, we kept their bottom-up scheme: first, the canonical text blocks were labeled by means of a trained ANN using topological and typographical information. Rules were then used to reconstruct the logical hierarchy, based, on the one hand, on the results of the labeling generated by the ANN, and, on the other hand, on geometric information. These rules were expressed as small deterministic automatons, keeping track of the article logical layout, and hard-coded for a given class of newspapers. For example, the typical article begins by a title, followed by the content of the article, which can then be composed of text blocks and images. Although this example is simple, more complex structures were described with this mechanism.

Even though these first experiments were promising, they underlined some severe limitations to overcome. Indeed, user interaction was totally absent of this learning system, requiring an experienced user to generate ground-truthed data and automatons. Thus, we decided to think again our general strategy in order to move on toward a more interactive and user-centered learning methodology.

11.7.4. *Dolores and its Future Interactive Learning Environment*

Using learning environments is one of the most restraining tasks when researchers and end-users want to recover structures from complex documents. Indeed, many plodding steps must be achieved in order to obtain satisfying results.

Dolores subscribes to the CIDRE philosophy,[54] which advocates the idea that an analysis system does not work in a fully automatic way, but cooperates with the user. This collaboration is achieved through interactive tools and has various advantages for both users and systems. On the one hand, interactions allow the efficiency of the system to be increased by incrementally learning from users' feedbacks, and dynamically adapting itself to the document characteristics. On the other hand, users take full benefit from graphical user interfaces, by rapidly retrieving and correcting analysis errors. Furthermore, interacting with the graphical representation of analysis results allows the system to be tuned at a high-level, without modifying thresholds and other numeric values.

The CIDRE philosophy has been successfully applied in 2(CREM),[55] where the users can supervise the analysis of documents logical structures, using the XMIllum graphical user interface.[56] Dolores is inspired by those works and connect together a learning system and an interactive tool. Our model generation and learning system will also benefit of recent works on document structure analysis based on perceptive cycles;[57] Rangoni used transparent neural networks instead of standard artificial neural networks, improving significantly the recognition rate.

Our main idea consists in analyzing the logical structures of documents converted from PDF into XCDF format, in order to create a generic model for each class of documents. More precisely, the user can define a logical model for a specific document (newspaper, magazine, etc.), by labeling physical blocks and by defining a logical hierarchy. Once a model has been correctly defined, and that it is stable, the user interactively applies it to other documents belonging to the same class and represented in XCDF. For each manipulated document, Dolores adapts itself to the information injected by the user (learning through user validation, correction, and feedback). This process is repeated iteratively, allowing the learning system to evolve, until the system's error rate is deemed to be significantly low.

At this stage, Dolores may be trained with documents belonging to new classes of documents, to which our current model may be applied. That is, suppose we work with the newspaper class; various newspaper editors may lead to various newspaper subclasses. Thus, a generic newspaper model may be produced, well suited for further describing each newspaper subclass. When researchers and end-users desire to focus on a specific class (i.e., subclass) of newspapers, or that they want to recognize an unknown class, they will have to specialize the existing generic model. This method has two main advantages: firstly, it produces a generic model that Dolores can apply to each class of newspapers. Secondly, the cost in time and resources for producing a specialized model is greatly reduced.

11.8. Conclusions

Document analysis methods have traditionally been developed for paper documents acquired by scanners or cameras. However, structural document analysis becomes more and more useful when dealing with documents that already exist in electronic form. In practice, there are tremendous needs for recovering the physical and logical structures of existing electronic documents. For instance, such structures allow documents to be reedited, restyled, or reflowed. In this context, structure recovering from PDF documents is of highest importance, since practically every printable document can be translated into PDF without much effort.

In this contribution, we propose a generic approach to recover physical and logical structures. Our strategy is applicable to nearly every kind of composite documents including text and graphics, it is built on a two-stages process. The first phase recovers the physical structure and generates an intermediate, XML-based, canonical format called XCDF. The second phase aims to extract logical structures from the physical structure by performing tree transformations. Whereas the first phase can be done universally, the second one must be tailored to the targeted application and the associated document class. Our experiments showed that this task is greatly facilitated by the use of the XCDF format.

Currently, the transformations from physical to logical structures have to be hard-coded in a programming language or a transformation language like XSLT. Such a situation is acceptable for small and midsize applications working with specific document classes whose layouts are close enough. However, in the case of loose document classes, i.e., the physical structure may have a great variability, more sophisticated analysis tools are required.

Our research group has a long experience with document modeling using incremental machine learning. We are currently investigating an architecture that allows document models to be setuped and refined according to user interactions. The idea of this solution is to infer document models iteratively, by progressively integrating user corrections thanks to an interactive environment. By combining these methods, we expect to improve drastically the usability and flexibility of our system in the near future.

Finally, we are also investigating technical issues for making XED available publicly on the web. At the present stage, a service allows the users to submit their PDF file and to get the corresponding restructured XCDF file back, i.e., an XML file containing the PDF data represented in our canonical document format. A future service will offer the possibility to directly inject XED's results in a new *purified* PDF document, thus preserving the original physical structure and reading order.

References

1. T. McKinley, Why pdf is everywhere, *Inform, the journal of AIIM.* **11**(8), (1997).
2. P. PDF. http://www.planetpdf.com.
3. Able2Extract. http://www.investintech.com.
4. P. Transformer. http://www.pdftransformer.com.
5. PDF2Office. http://www.recosoft.com.
6. P.-F. Converter. http://www.pdf-file.com.
7. PDFTron. http://www.pdftron.com.
8. M. Structuriser. http://www.mimotek.com.
9. xtPDF Extractor. http://www.exti.com.
10. PDFText. http://www.pdf-analyzer.com.
11. TEXTfromPDF. http://www.textfrompdf.com.
12. A. A. P. Converter. http://www.processtext.com/.
13. Adobe. Acrobat reader. http://www.adobe.com/fr/products/acrobat.
14. D. Pro. http://www.docsmartz.com.
15. E. P. Creator. http://www.pdfdesk.com.
16. GetPDF. http://www.getpdf.com.
17. I. P. Editor. http://www.iceni.com.
18. JPedal. http://www.jpedal.org.
19. N. PDF. http://www.nitropdf.com.
20. P. . Word. http://www.cadkas.de.
21. PDF-Convert. http://www.pdf-convert.com.
22. P. E. Kit. http://www.pdfkit.com.
23. P. Grabber. http://www.pixelplanet.com.
24. P. Studio. http://www.qoppa.com.
25. P. Converter. http://www.filehunter.com.

26. P. X. Converter. http://www.pdf2text.com.
27. S. PDF. http://www.archisoftint.com.
28. S. P. Converter. http://www.pdftodocconverterpro.com.
29. Trapeze. http://www.mesadynamics.com.
30. V. Tools. http://www.verypdf.com.
31. Xpdf. http://www.glyphandcog.com.
32. D. Doermann and R. Furuta. Image based typographic analysis of documents. In *Document Analysis and Recognition, 1993., Proceedings of the Second International Conference on*, pp. 769–773 (20-22 Oct., 1993). doi: 10.1109/ICDAR.1993.395624.
33. K. Y. Wong, R. G. Casey, and M. Wahl, Document analysis system, *IBM journal of Research and Development.* **26**(6), 647–656 (November, 1982).
34. L. O'Gorman and R. Kasturi, *Document image analysis.* (IEEE Computer Society Press, Los Alamitos, CA, USA, 1995). ISBN 0-8186-6547-5.
35. D. Dori, D. Doermann, C. Shin, R. Haralick, I. Philips, M. Buchman, and D. Ross, *Handbook on Optical Character Recognition and Document Image Analysis*, chapter The Representation of Document Structure: A Generic Object-Process Approach, pp. 421–456. World Scientific, (1997).
36. G. Nagy, Twenty years of document image analysis in pami, *IEEE Transactions on Pattern Analysis and Machine Intelligence.* **22**(1), 38–62, (2000).
37. O. Altamura, F. Esposito, and D. Malerba, Transforming paper documents into xml format with wisdom++, *International Journal of Document Analysis and Recognition (IJDAR).* **3**(2), 175–198, (2001).
38. K. Lee, Y. Choy, and S. Cho, Logical structure analysis and generation for structured documents: A syntactic approach, *IEEE Transactions on Knowledge and Data Engineering.* **15**(5), 1277–1294 (September/October, 2003).
39. F. LeBourgeois and S. Souafi-Bensafi. Rasade: Automatic recognition of structured document using typography and spatial inference. In *Document Layout Interpretation Analysis (DLIA'09)*, Bangalore, India, (1999). URL http://www.science.uva.nl/events/dlia99/.
40. M. D. Paknad and R. M. Ayers. Method and apparatus for identifying words described in a portable electronic document. U.S. Patent 5,832,530, (1998).
41. S. R. Bagley, D. F. Brailsford, and M. R. B. Hardy. Creating reusable well-structured pdf as a sequence of component object graphic (cog) elements. In *ACM Symposium on Document Engineering (DocEng'03)*, pp. 58–67, Grenoble (France), (2003).
42. M. R. B. Hardy, D. Brailsford, and P. L. Thomas. Creating structured pdf files using xml templates. In *ACM Symposium on Document Engineering (DocEng'04)*, pp. 99–108, Milwaukee (USA), (2004).
43. W. S. Lovegrove and D. F. Brailsford, Document analysis of pdf files: methods, results and implications, *Electronic Publishing - Origination, Dissemination and Design.* **8**(3), 207–220, (1995).
44. A. Anjewierden and S. Kabel. Automatic indexing of documents with ontologies. In *13th Belgian/Dutch Conference on Artificial Intelligence (BNAIC 2001)*, pp. 23–30, Amsterdam, Holland, (2001).

45. H. Chao and J. Fan. Layout and content extraction for pdf documents. In *IAPR International Workshop on Document Analysis Systems (DAS'04)*, pp. 213–224, Florence (Italy), (2004).
46. H. Chao and L. Xiaofan. Capturing the layout of electronic documents for reuse in variable data. In *Eighth International Conference on Document Analysis and Recognition (ICDAR'05)*, pp. 940–944, Seoul (Korea), (2005).
47. H. Déjean and J.-L. Meunier. A system for converting pdf documents into structured xml format. In *IAPR International Workshop on Document Analysis Systems (DAS06)*, pp. 129–140, Nelson, New Zealand, (2006).
48. R. P. Futrelle, M. Shao, C. Cieslik, and A. E. Grimes. Extraction, layout analysis and classification of diagrams in pdf documents. In *Seventh International Conference on Document Analysis and Recognition (ICDAR'03)*, pp. 1007–1012, Edinburgh (Scotland), (2003).
49. F. Rahman and H. Alam. Conversion of pdf documents into html: a case study of document image analysis. In *Conference Record of the Thirty-Seventh Asilomar Conference on Signals, Systems and Computers 2003*, pp. 87–91, USA, (2003).
50. K. Hadjar, M. Rigamonti, D. Lalanne, and R. Ingold. Xed: A new tool for extracting hidden structures from electronic documents. In *DIAL'04: Proceedings of the First International Workshop on Document Image Analysis for Libraries (DIAL'04)*, p. 212, Washington, DC, USA, (2004). IEEE Computer Society. ISBN 0-7695-2088-X.
51. J.-L. Bloechle, M. Rigamonti, K. Hadjar, D. Lalanne, and R. Ingold. Xcdf: A canonical and structured document format. In *7th International Workshop, DAS'06*, number 3872 in LNCS, pp. 141–152, Nelson (New Zealand) (February, 2006). Springer-Verlag.
52. Adobe. Pdf reference, sixth edition: Adobe portable document format version 1.7, November. 2006.
53. S. Souafi-Bensafi, M. Parizeau, F. Lebourgeois, and H. Emptoz. Logical labeling using bayesian networks. In *Document Analysis and Recognition, 2001. Proceedings. Sixth International Conference on*, pp. 832–836 (September, 2001). doi: 10.1109/ICDAR.2001.953904.
54. F. Bapst. *Reconnaissance de documents assiste : architecture logicielle et intgration de savoir-faire*. PhD thesis, University of Fribourg, Switzerland, (1998). thesis Nr. 1228.
55. L. Robadey. *2(CREM) : Une mthode de reconnaissance structurelle de documents complexes base sur des patterns bidimensionnels*. PhD thesis, University of Fribourg, Switzerland, (2001).
56. O. Hitz. *A Framework for Interactive Document Recognition*. PhD thesis, University of Fribourg, Switzerland, (2005). thesis Nr. 1488.
57. Y. Rangoni and A. Belad. Document logical structure analysis based on perceptive cycles. In *IAPR International Workshop on Document Analysis Systems (DAS06)*, pp. 117–128, Nelson, New Zealand, (2006).

Chapter 12

Recognition of Bangla Handwriting: Current Status and Future Directions

U. Bhattacharya*, S. K. Parui[†] and B. B. Chaudhuri[‡]

Computer Vision and Pattern Recognition Unit, Indian Statistical Institute, Kolkata-700108, India
ujjwal@isical.ac.in, [†]swapan@isical.ac.in, [‡]bbc@isical.ac.in

India is a country of multiple scripts. Bangla is its second most popular script. It is also the Official language of Bangladesh, a neighbouring country of India. There exist a few studies on Bangla handwriting recognition in the literature. However, these are far from exhaustive or effective in view of its various real-life applications. One of the early bottlenecks of some effective recognition studies for Bangla handwriting was the non-availability of benchmark databases of samples of Bangla handwriting. Recently, the situation has changed. A few databases of on-line and off-line samples of Bangla handwriting have been developed. These databases have been used in some recent recognition studies. More such studies are expected to appear in the near future.

Contents

12.1. Introduction

Digitally available handwritten data can be either online or offline. Online handwritten data consists mainly of the (x, y) coordinates along the trajectory of the pen on a tablet stored in the order of time while an offline handwritten sample is an image. Efficient recognition approaches for both types of handwritten data do exist[4,25,33,62] and real-life systems providing good performance are commercially available. Higher recognition accuracies are obtained in case of online handwritten data. Most of these studies deal with Latin-based scripts[24,48,70] and a few of them can also handle Arabic,[1,2,8,50] Chinese,[36,43,44] Japanese,[39] and Korean[37,40,72] scripts. Although India has a large market of prospective users, handwriting recognition studies on its scripts have not progressed much.

Reports on character recognition of Indian scripts available in the literature are only a few and most of them deal with printed documents. A recent review of the methodologies for OCR of Indian language scripts is found in.[53] On the other hand, majority of the handwritten character recognition experiments on Indian scripts available in the literature are based on small databases collected in laboratory environments. Possibly this is one of the crucial reasons that the impact of such works could not be realized through the development of real-life applications. In other words, the desired progress in research on handwriting recognition of Indian scripts has not been significant due to non-availability of standard databases of samples of handwritten characters and words. Fortunately the situation has started to change in recent years and a collection of databases have already been reported.[12,22,59]

Bangla is the second most popular among Indian scripts. Also, it is the fifth most popular script in the world. This script is used by about 230 million people of Eastern India and Bangladesh. Systematic recognition studies on Bangla handwriting has been started only recently. The aim of this chapter is to provide a detailed account of current status of Bangla handwriting recognition and discuss its future directions.

12.2. Background

The earliest recognition study of handwritten characters of an Indian script[65] reported the use of stroke-based feature and a tree classifier for off-line handwritten numerals of Devanagari, the most popular Indian script. Bhattacharya et al[15] proposed a scheme for recognition of off-line handwritten Devanagari numerals on the basis of MLP and HMM. A few recognition studies[26,35] on online handwritten Devanagari character recognition have also been reported. Joshi et al[35] used a three stage system involving structural recognition, feature based recognition and output mapping for recognition of online handwritten Devanagari characters. Connell et al[26] designed an HMM-based method for recognition of 40 major Devanagari characters. Structural properties of these characters were used to improve the recognition performance. Shaw and Parui[59] have proposed a limited lexicon recognition scheme for offline handwritten Devanagari words.

There exist a few recognition studies of online handwritten characters of Tamil,[3,34,67] a major script of Southern India. Sundaresan and Keerthi[67] studied four sets of features along with a neural network classifier. Joshi et al[34] presented a comparison of various elastic matching algorithms for online handwritten Tamil character recognition. Aparna et al[3] used a string matching approach along with a shape feature vector for recognition of these characters.

Telugu is another major script of Southern India. Automatic recognition of online handwritten Telugu characters has also been studied[5] in the literature. In this report, Babu et al[5] used both time and frequency domain features along with an HMM-based classifier for this online handwritten character recognition problem.

Swethalakshmi et al[69] presented a study of recognition of Devanagari and Tamil characters. Swethalakshmi et al[68] also presented another study for recognition of online handwritten Devanagari and Telugu characters. Garain and Chaudhuri[30] studied recognition of online handwritten characters of Devanagari and Bangla, the two most popular Indian scripts.

Parui et al[55] proposed a syntactic recognition scheme for handwritten Bangla numerals while Dutta and Chaudhuri[29] used a neural net classifier to recognize isolated handwritten alphanumeric characters of Bangla. Among other studies, Bhattacharya et al[9,10] used a self-organizing neural net while Bhattacharya and Chaudhuri[12] used a classifier combination approach for recognition of handwritten Bangla numerals. Development of benchmark databases for handwritten numerals of Devanagari and Bangla scripts has also been reported recently.[20]

For recognition of offline handwritten Bangla characters Rahman et al[63] proposed a multistage scheme while Bhowmick et al[21] used a neural network based approach and Parui et al[57] used an HMM-based approach. Basu et al[7] presented a segmentation-based hierarchical approach for recognition of Bangla characters from their off-line handwritten word images.

In a few recent studies,[17,19,49,56,61] recognition results of Bangla on-line handwriting have been presented. Parui et al[56] studied an HMM-based scheme for recognition of Bangla online handwritten numerals. Bhattacharya et al[17] used direction code histogram feature along with a neural network classifier for recognition of online handwritten Bangla basic characters. Also, a hidden Markov model based recognition scheme[61] was proposed for recognition of these online handwritten characters. Recently, a database of online handwritten Bangla basic characters and their recognition based on sub-stroke features was reported.[49] A segmentation scheme[19] of online Bangla handwritten cursive words was proposed recently.

In the remaining portion of this chapter we shall concentrate on the state of the art of Bangla handwriting recognition research. In fact, majority of the available handwriting recognition studies of Indian scripts deal with the Bangla script. Also, Bangla is the second most popular language of India and it is the official language of Bangladesh and West Bengal, a state of the Indian Union.

12.3. Bangla Character Set

Printed Bangla texts have three distinct horizontal zones, namely, upper, middle and lower zones as it is shown in Fig. 12.1. Majority of the Bangla characters have a head line which is also the upper boundary of the middle zone. The part of a Bangla text below an imaginary line, called the base line, is the lower zone. The alphabet of Bangla has 11 basic vowels and 39 basic consonant characters. These are shown in Fig. 12.2.

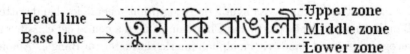

Fig. 12.1.   Three zones of Bangla text.

Fig. 12.2. Shapes of Bangla basic characters; the first 11 shapes are vowels and the remaining ones are consonants.

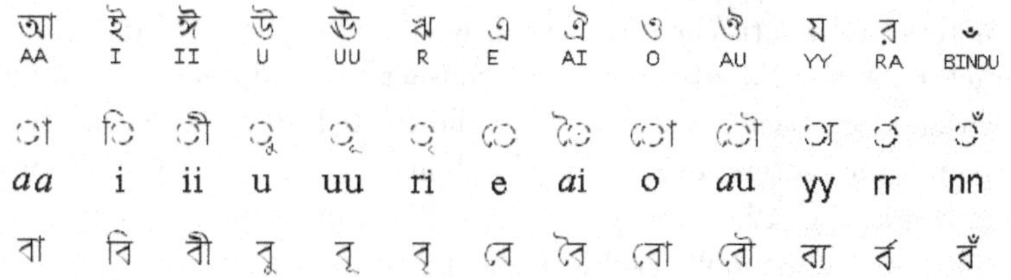

Fig. 12.3. Shapes of modifiers of Bangla basic characters; basic character shapes for which there exist modified shapes are shown in the first row while respective modified shapes of them are shown in the 2nd row; circular region shown adjacent to each of these character modifiers show the position of associated consonant; character modifiers when attached to the consonant 'BA' are shown in the 3rd row.

Often the basic shape of a Bangla vowel (except the first vowel 'অ') while occurring with a consonant gets modified. Similarly, shapes of two consonants 'য' and 'র' respectively following and preceding a consonant take modified shapes. These are respectively called vowel and consonant modifiers and their occurrences do not alter the shape of the consonant to

which they are attached. Ten vowel modifiers are shown in Fig. 12.3 and
two consonant modifiers are shown in Fig. 12.4.

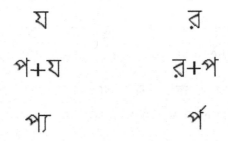

Fig. 12.4. Shapes of Bangla consonant modifiers; shapes of two basic consonants are
shown in the first row, the rules of their association with the basic character 'PA' are
shown in the second row while the shapes of corresponding modifiers along with the
attached consonant are shown in the third row.

A few exceptions include the following. When the vowels 'উ' or 'ঊ'
gets attached to the consonant 'র', shapes different from those in Fig. 12.3
are formed in the middle zone. When 'র' gets attached to a consonant
from the right, it creates a new shape in the middle zone (as in 'প্র'). These
cases are not considered as modifiers. The characters in such situations are
considered to form compound characters. In fact, when two or more basic
characters are so attached forming a new shape, it is called a compound
character. A few Bangla compound characters produced by combinations
of two or more basic consonants are shown in Fig. 12.5. Similarly, a few
compound characters formed by combination of a vowel and a consonant
are shown in Fig. 12.6. There are about 250 compound characters and the
total number of symbols used in Bangla writing is more than 300 and this
number includes basic characters, vowel modifiers, consonant modifiers and
compound characters.

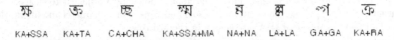

KA+SSA   KA+TA   CA+CHA   KA+SSA+MA   NA+NA   LA+LA   GA+GA   KA+RA

Fig. 12.5. Some of the compound characters formed by combinations of two or more
consonants; a few such compound characters are shown in the 1st row and their constituent basic characters are shown in the 2nd row.

In view of the existence of different types of symbols used in Bangla
texts, the existing or future studies of Bangla handwriting recognition con-

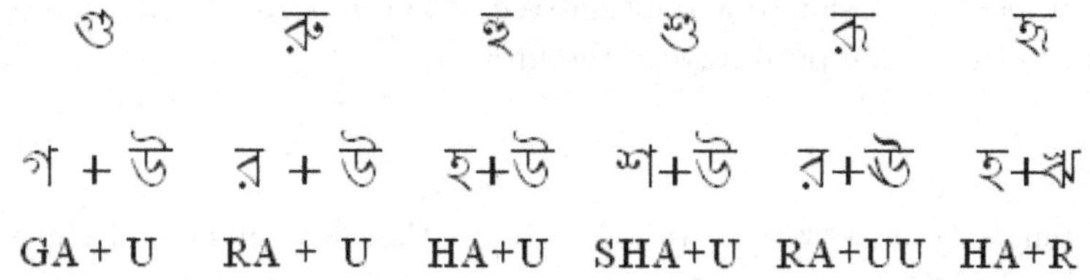

ও   রু   হ   ঙ   ক্র   হ

গ + ঊ   র + ঊ   হ+ঊ   শ+ঊ   র+ঊ   হ+ঋ

GA + U   RA + U   HA+U   SHA+U   RA+UU   HA+R

Fig. 12.6. In several cases vowels combine with consonants forming compound characters; a few such compound characters are shown in the 1st row and their constituent basic characters are shown in the 2nd row.

sider or should consider one or more of the following sets of symbols: (1) numerals; (2) basic (both vowel and consonant) characters without modifier; (3) basic characters with one or more modifiers; (4) compound characters without modifier; (5) compound characters with one or more modifiers.

To the best of our knowledge, there does not exist any Bangla handwriting recognition study in the literature which has considered the combined set of graphemes covered by all the five sets defined above. Possible reasons of this : (i) non-availability of a database of sufficiently large number of handwritten samples of such a large number of symbols which necessarily requires enormous efforts and (ii) complexities in designing an effective recognition scheme to handle such a large number of character classes.

12.4. Initiatives for Creation of Standard Databases

However, there have been a few attempts to develop standard databases[66] of Bangla handwriting samples although with limited scopes only. These databases are developed at the Computer Vision and Pattern Recognition Unit of the Indian Statistical Institute (ISI), Kolkata and they include: (1) a database of offline handwritten Bangla numerals, (2) a database of offline handwritten Bangla basic characters, (3) a database of offline handwritten Bangla character modifiers, (4) a database of offline handwritten Bangla words, (5) a database of online handwritten Bangla alphanumeric (numerals and basic characters) characters and (6) a database of online handwritten Bangla cursive words.

12.4.1. *Offline databases*

At present there are four databases of offline handwritten numerals / characters / words of Bangla ready for use in academic research. Some of these have already been shared with other research groups and recognition results on them have been published in the literature.[7,45]

12.4.1.1. *Sample collection*

Different sets of writers were selected for the development of the above databases. A writer provided his/her handwriting samples on a varying number (maximum 4) of occasions. The writers consisted of people from various strata of the society like employed and unemployed persons, entrepreneurs, retired personnel, housewives and students from different age groups.

Samples of these databases are composed of both primary and secondary data. The secondary data are obtained from real-life postal mails. The primary data had been collected using a few documents *viz.*, Indian Railway reservation forms (Fig. 12.7(a)), job application forms (Fig. 12.7(b)), school admission forms (Fig. 12.7(c)) and a tabular form (Fig. 12.7(d)) that was designed in the laboratory for collection of these samples.

These form documents were printed on three types of papers of 56, 70 and 80 gsm (grams per square meter) quality. A wide variety of pens were used to fill these forms and the list of pens includes roller ball pens and gel pens both with 0.7 mm and 0.5 mm tips, fine liner pens with 0.8 mm polyacetal tip and ball point pen with medium sized tip. For color of the ink, only blue and black were used.

Each form document consists of several rectangular boxes and the writers were instructed to write a single numeral/character/word per box. These documents were scanned using an HP flatbed scanner at 300 dpi. A software was developed for automatic extraction of a sample of an individual numeral or character or word from each box of the scanned images of the form documents. These extracted samples were manually checked and individual samples were stored as grayscale TIFF images with 1 byte per pixel.

12.4.1.2. *Database statistics*

The numeral[20] database consists of 23,392 samples written by 1106 persons. A few samples from this database are shown in Fig. 12.8. This database is randomly partitioned into a training set of 19,392 samples and a test set of 4000 samples. The test set has equal number of samples in each of the 10 classes. But the number of training samples differ slightly from one class to another.

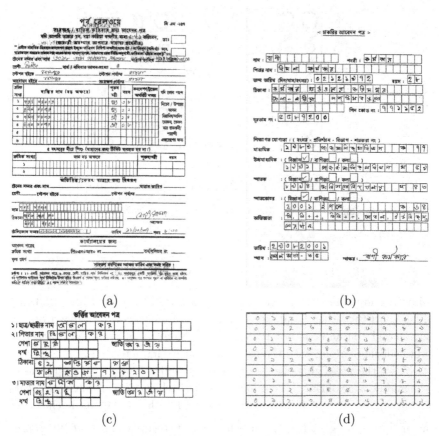

(a) (b)

(c) (d)

Fig. 12.7. Different forms used for data collection (a) Indian railway reservation form; (b) a job application form; (c) a school admission form; (d) a tailormade form used for data collection.

The character database consists of 35,270 samples of Bangla basic characters written by 216 persons. A few samples from this database are shown in Fig. 12.9. This database is randomly partitioned into a training set of 25,000 samples and a test set of 12,270 samples. The training set contains equal number of samples from each of the 50 underlying classes. As in the case of the numeral database, no validation set of character samples was formed.

As described in Section 12.3, there are 10 vowel modifiers and 2 consonant modifiers in Bangla alphabet. Such a modified character appears

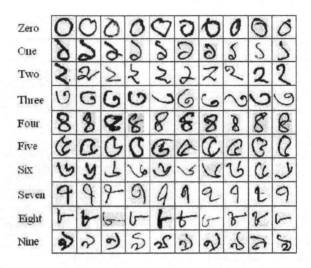

Fig. 12.8.   Samples from the numeral database.

only in conjunction with another character (as shown in Figs. 12.3 and 12.4). On the other hand, segmentation of a character modifier from its associated character is not trivial. Thus, samples of modified characters were collected along with the associated basic character.[58]

Also, the nasalizing sign ' ৺ ' (called 'chandra bindu' never appears in the middle zone of Bangla text like other basic characters. It always appears in the upper zone of Bangla text associated with another basic character as in ট̐ or ২̐ or ২̐ or ট̐. Such a behaviour of the appearance of ' ৺ ' causes its segmentation from the associated character a non-trivial problem. We have placed it in the class of modifiers, though traditionally it is considered as a basic consonant.

There are 40,290 handwritten samples in this database of modified characters. These are non-uniformly distributed over 13 classes. Some examples from this database is shown in Fig. 12.10. Of these, 1600 samples from each of the 13 classes are randomly selected to form the training set. The remaining samples belong to the test set.

The handwriting word database[22] has been developed using a lexicon of 119 town names of West Bengal. This database consists of 35,700 offline handwritten image samples. In each word class, there are 300 samples, of which 250 are randomly selected as training samples. The remaining samples form the test set. A few samples from this word database are shown in Fig. 12.11.

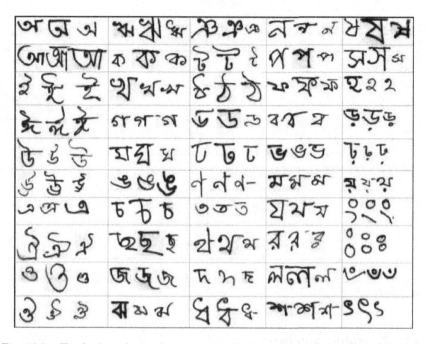

Fig. 12.9. Handwritten basic character samples from the basic character database (Three samples per class are shown).

12.4.1.3. *Salient features of the databases*

Each of the databases described above includes samples taken from real life documents. It also includes samples collected from a wide variety of native Bengalis. These samples are available as the original gray-level images which are not size-normalized. An interesting aspect of handwritten documents in Indian scripts is that they often have one or more entries written in English. Some of the possible reasons of this phenomenon are (i) India is a multilingual country with a colonial past, (ii) English is one of its official languages, (iii) at the school level, about 2 or 3 languages are taught one of which is usually English, (iv) school level text books written in Indian scripts have entries in English, especially the numerals, (v) Indian currencies are often printed in English script. We observed that while writing a numeric information (such as pin code, phone number, age etc.), the writer may casually enter one or more English numerals, causing a mixed-script situation as shown in Fig. 12.12.

Fig. 12.10.   A few samples from the present database of handwritten character modifiers of Bangla.

12.4.2. *Online databases*

Recently, three databases of Bangla online handwriting samples have been developed. These include a database for each of (i) isolated numerals, (ii) isolated basic characters and (iii) cursive words.

Samples of these databases have been collected using devices like WA-COM Intuous2 tablet, Genius G-note 7000, and HP tc4400 Tablet PC. The maximum sampling rate is 200 points per second. Samples of isolated numerals or basic characters are individually stored as separate files in UNIPEN format consisting of (x, y) coordinates along the pen trajectory, pen pressure and the writer information such as age, sex, profession, writing skill, writing habit etc. Ground truths are encoded into respective filenames. Some samples of isolated numeral and character databases are shown in Fig. 12.13.

Online numeral database[56] consists of 6000 samples of handwritten Bangla numerals. In each numeral class, there are 600 samples. The whole set of samples is divided into training and test sets consisting of 4000 and 2000 samples, respectively. Online character database[49] consists of 25,948 samples of online handwritten Bangla basic characters. Since each writer was asked to write a selected set of Bangla words covering all basic characters, there are different number of samples in different classes. Samples in

Fig. 12.11.   A few samples of offline handwritten Bangla words.

each class are randomly divided into 17,332 training and 8,616 test samples (approximately in the ratio 2:1). This database is a part of the LipiToolkit[41] resource.

Online cursive word database has 1,02,060 handwritten cursive Bangla words. The lexicon of this database consists of 682 words. These samples were written by 77 writers coming from different groups of native Bengali population. Each writer wrote each of the lexicon words twice. Each word in a page is first segmented by a tool developed at the Indian Statistical Institute. This data was manually checked to discard samples for which the signal was not captured properly. Finally, an XML file was created for each writer to store all of its samples, their ground truth and other relevant information. Some samples from this cursive word database are shown in Fig. 12.14.

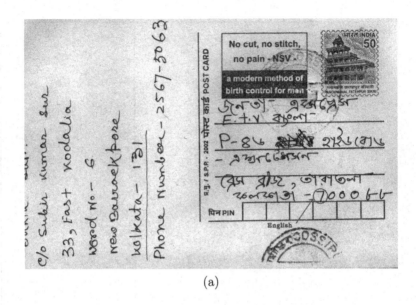

(a)

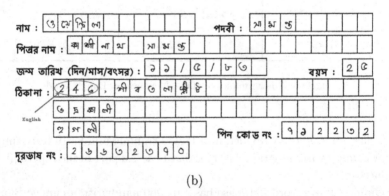

(b)

Fig. 12.12. Examples of handwritten documents where mixed numerals (English numerals are encircled) have been used: (a) a postcard and (b) a job application form.

12.5. Recognition Schemes for Offline Handwriting

12.5.1. *Feature Extraction*

In the studies made so far on recognition of Bangla offline handwriting, fewer features have been used in comparison to those used for English

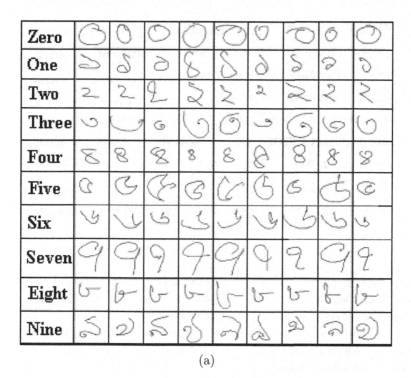

(a)

(b)

Fig. 12.13. (a) Samples of online handwritten Bangla numerals (b) Samples of online handwritten Bangla basic characters.

handwriting recognition. A short description of features used in Bangla experiments is provided below.

Certain topological and structural features were used by Bhattacharya et al[10] for recognition of handwritten Bangla numerals. An existing topol-

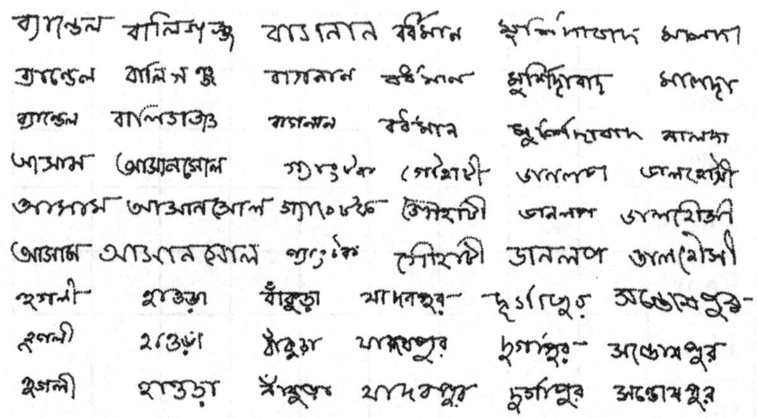

Fig. 12.14.　Samples of online handwritten Bangla cursive words.

ogy adaptive self-organizing neural network (TASONN)[27] model was modified to extract a graph representation of the shape of input numeral image. Several topological and structural features like loops, junctions, positions of terminal nodes etc. (a few are shown in Fig. 12.15) were obtained for some coarse classification of input numeral into smaller groups with the help of a hierarchical tree classifier.

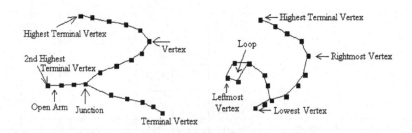

Fig. 12.15.　Topological and structural features of Bangla numeral shapes 2 and 9.

View based features were used for recognition of handwritten Bangla characters/words by Bhowmik et al,[21] Bhattacharya et al[18] and Bhowmik.[22] The aim here is to determine the vertical and horizontal strokes that constitute the shape of a handwritten Bangla character/word image. Let E be a binary image consisting of pixels in a character/word image A that are visible from the right side. Then the pixels of A whose right neighbour is in the background, form the object pixels of the image E. Similarly, suppose S is the binary image consisting of object pixels in A that are visible from below. E and S images are cleaned by removing smaller connected components from them. The remaining connected components of E and S respectively indicate the vertical and horizontal strokes present in a word image and each stroke is a one-pixel wide digital curve (Fig. 12.16). For each stroke, 6 equidistant points $(P_i, i = 0, 1, \ldots, 5)$ are found on a stroke with P_0 and P_5 being the end points. Let θ_i be the angle that the i-th segment makes with the x-axis. The feature vector of the stroke is defined as $\Theta_1 = (\theta_1, \theta_2, \theta_3, \theta_4, \theta_5, L_1, L_2, X, Y)$ where L_1, L_2, X, Y represent respectively the degree of linearity, normalized length and coordinates of the centroid of the stroke. This feature was used for recognition of handwritten Bangla characters. The feature vector $\Theta_2 = (\theta_1, \theta_2, \theta_3, \theta_4, \theta_5)$ representing only the shape of a stroke was used for recognition of handwritten Bangla words, assuming a mixture of multivariate Gaussian distributions for Θ_2. The feature vectors Θ_2 obtained from the training word images are grouped into several clusters using Expectation Maximization (EM) algorithm. This grouping is done separately for vertical and horizontal strokes, in order to avoid the difficulties due to the circular nature of the features. The number of clusters was 9 for the vertical strokes and 10 for the horizontal strokes on the basis of the minimum mutual description length (MMDL) criterion. The shapes corresponding to the mean vectors of these clusters are shown in Fig. 12.17 for vertical strokes and in Fig. 12.18 for horizontal strokes. The sequence of feature vectors Θ_2 in a word image was fed to a hidden Markov model (HMM) based classifier for word recognition.

Direction code histogram features have been used for recognition of handwritten Bangla basic characters by Bhattacharya et al.[14,16] For this, both the skeleton and the contour of a character image are studied. Both the skeleton and contour images of a character are divided into 5×5 and 7×7 equal blocks, and the components of histogram feature based on 4 direction codes are computed for each such block. The feature vector sizes of a character image are 100 and 196 for 5×5 and 7×7 block sizes respectively.

Wavelet transform based features have been used for recognition of handwritten Bangla numerals by Bhattacharya and Chaudhuri.[11,13,20] Similar features have been studied for recognition of handwritten Bangla characters by Bhattacharya et al[18] and Bhowmik et al.[22,23] The wavelet transform[28,47] is a well-known tool that finds application in many areas including image processing. Due to the multi-resolution property, it decomposes the

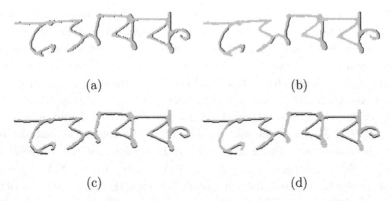

Fig. 12.16.   A Bangla word image with gray pixels indicating A image and dark pixels indicating E and S images, (a) A and E images, (b) E image after cleaning, (c) A and S images, (d) S image after cleaning.

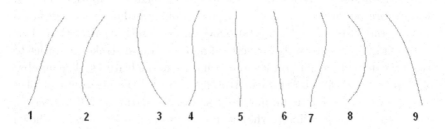

Fig. 12.17.   Average shapes of vertical strokes.

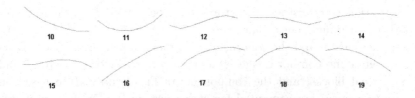

Fig. 12.18.   Average shapes of horizontal strokes.

signal at different scales. For a given image, the wavelet transform produces one low frequency subband image reflecting an approximation of the original image and three high frequency components of the image, reflecting the detail. The approximation component was used to generate the feature vector in the recognition problem. The authors considered Daubechies wavelet transform with four coefficients (l_0, l_1, l_2, l_3) forming the lowpass or smoothing filter and another four coefficients (h_0, h_1, h_2, h_3) forming the highpass filter where

$$l_0 = \frac{1+\sqrt{3}}{4\sqrt{2}}, l_1 = \frac{3+\sqrt{3}}{4\sqrt{2}}, l_2 = \frac{3-\sqrt{3}}{4\sqrt{2}}, l_3 = \frac{1-\sqrt{3}}{4\sqrt{2}},$$

and $h_0 = l_3, h_1 = -l_2, h_2 = l_1, h_3 = -l_0$.

First, the bounding box of an input image is found and then the box is normalized to a square image of size, say $N \times N$, with an interpolation technique. Wavelet decomposition algorithm with the above lowpass and highpass filters is applied to this normalized image twice (row-wise and column-wise) to get four $\frac{N}{2} \times \frac{N}{2}$ images. The approximation image that is obtained by using the lowpass filter twice is either considered as the feature vector or is filtered again in a similar fashion until an approximation image of a desirable size is obtained as the feature vector.

Boundary change point features have been used for recognition of handwritten Bangla words by Bhowmik.[22] These features are based on pixel positions where there is a change in direction and the type of change. A word image is described as a sequence of such features to be fed to a hidden Markov model (HMM) based classifier.

Gradient direction histogram features have been successfully used for handwritten character recognition in several scripts. The gradient value can be computed based on different operators. For recognition of handwritten Bangla numerals, the Kirsh and Roberts operators have been used by Wen et al[71] and Pal et al.[54] Liu and Suen[45] have recently used gradient direction histogram features on the ISI handwritten Bangla numeral database to show that the Sobel operator outperforms the Roberts operator.

Basu et al[7] used a 76-element feature vector for recognizing segments belonging to each of the three individual zones (as shown in Fig. 12.1) of Bangla text. Their feature components include 36 longest-run features, 24 modified shadow features and 16 octant-centroid feature.

12.5.2. *Classification*

Only a few works on recognition of offline handwritten Bangla numerals/characters/words have so far been reported. Different classification strategies studied for recognition of handwritten numerals/characters/words of Bangla script include schemes that are primarily based on neural network models,[9] hidden Markov models,[57] support vector machines,[23] quadratic discriminant functions,[54] classifier combination,[10,11,13] multi-stage classification[20,63] and hierarchical classification.[7]

Bhattacharya et al[10] used a hierarchical tree classifier along with topological and structural features to classify shapes of handwritten Bangla numerals into smaller subgroups. MLP neural networks were employed to uniquely classify Bangla numerals belonging to each subgroup. Different sets of distinguishing features were fed to MLPs corresponding to different subgroups. The system was trained using a sample set of 1800 numerals. This scheme provided 93.26% correct recognition and 1.71% rejection on a separate test set of 7760 samples of handwritten Bangla numerals.

Basu et al[6] studied Dempster-Shafer technique towards combination of two MLP classifiers with different feature sets for handwritten Bangla numeral recognition. Wen et al[71] presented a handwritten Bangla numeral recognition system towards postal automation based on a support vector machine classifier. Pal et al[54] studied a modified quadratic discriminant function classifier[38] for recognition of handwritten Bangla numerals. Bhattacharya and Chaudhuri[20] have developed a multistage recognition scheme based on MLP classifiers. Liu and Suen[45] made a comparative study of the performance by a number of classifiers for recognition of handwritten Bangla numerals. These authors observed that the performances by discriminative learning quadratic discriminant function (DLQDF), polynomial network classifier (PNC), class-specific feature polynomial classifier (CFPC) and one-versus-all support vector machine (SVM) based classifier are comparable and better than those obtained by MLP networks and modified quadratic discriminant function. Similar results were also obtained by Liu et al[43] in the case of recognizing handwritten Latin numerals.

Several two-stage classification approaches to the recognition of handwritten Bangla basic characters have been reported.[14,16,23] The idea here is to partition the 50 basic character classes into several groups such that the character classes within each such group have similar shapes. The similarity of shapes is measured on the basis of the 50×50 confusion matrix computed from the training set using a single stage classification scheme. For example, a larger value of $n_{ij} = a_{ij} + a_{ji}$ will indicate that classes i and j are more similar where the confusion matrix is given by a_{ij}, the number of training samples belonging to class i that are classified as class j. After grouping of classes is done, the first stage classification involves these groups of classes. In other words, an unknown sample is to be classified in one of these groups. In the second stage classification, there is a classifier for each group where an unknown sample placed in a group, is further classified in one of the character classes that constitute the group. The classification scheme in the first stage need not be the same as that in the second stage. Similarly, the feature set in the the first stage may be different from that in the second stage. In fact, in the second stage, the feature set may differ from one group to another.

In a recent work on recognition of handwritten Bangla basic characters,[23] grouping of classes is done in a more objective way. It is based on the confusion matrix obtained using a single stage classifier on the basis of a validation set. The grouping scheme is iterative where initially there are as many groups as the number of classes. In each step two groups are merged into one. In the first step, classes i and j are merged for which n_{ij} is the maximum. For merging of two groups of classes, the minimum among all the pairwise n_{ij} values between the two groups, is found. The pair of groups for which this minimum value is the largest, are merged. The process bears a resemblance to complete linkage clustering algorithm. The resulting groups of classes are compact in the sense that each pair of character classes within a group has a certain degree of similarity.

Another grouping scheme based on a similarity matrix obtained by the neural gas (NG) method is also studied in the same work.[23] The NG method is a vector quantization technique and is applied here to the training set of samples to output a set of neurons. For each neuron, its Voronoi region is considered. If such a region contains training samples from only one class, it is called pure. It is impure, otherwise. Only impure Voronoi regions are considered for constructing the confusion matrix. If an impure region contains p_i samples from class i, then let q_{ij} $(i < j)$ be the minimum value of p_i and p_j. The upper triangular similarity matrix is computed as $((m_{ij}))$ where m_{ij} is the sum of q_{ij} over all the impure Voronoi regions. Grouping of classes on the basis of the similarity matrix is done in the same way as is done on the basis of the confusion matrix above.

Support vector machine (SVM) classifiers based on wavelet features were used in both stages of the above classification scheme. SVM classifier was shown to outperform classifiers based on both multilayer perceptron (MLP) and radial basis function (RBF) networks.

12.5.3. *Recognition of Modifiers*

A major problem encountered in Bangla handwriting recognition is the presence of modifiers occurring with a basic or compound character. There are 10 vowel modifiers that may occur with a consonant or a compound character. Among the 3 consonant modifiers, two may accompany a consonant or a vowel or a compound character and the other one may occur with a consonant or a compound character. A basic consonant or a compound character do not get attached with more than one vowel modifiers at the same time. However, a consonant modifier and a vowel modifier or two vowel modifiers may simultaneously get attached with a basic or compound character.

Among these modified characters (shown in the 2nd row of Fig. 12.3), three vowel modifiers 'u', 'uu' and 'ri' appear only in the lower zone, another three vowel modifiers 'aa', 'e', 'o' and one consonant modifier 'yy' appear only in the middle zone, two consonant modifiers 'rr' and 'nn' (nasalizer) appear only in the upper zone and four vowel modifiers 'i', 'ii', 'ai' and 'ou' appear in both upper and middle zones of a basic or compound character, in their printed forms. In the last row of Fig. 12.3, all of these 13 character modifiers are shown occurring with the basic consonant character ব('BA').

It is to be noted that the large variations in the handwritten forms of these modifiers pose a challenging problem towards their automatic detection. A few samples of handwritten modifiers including the nasalizer had been shown in Fig. 12.10.

Detection and recognition of three modifiers appearing in the lower zone was studied by Parui et al.[58] Shape and positional features were used in this study. Bayes classifiers based on mixtures of multivariate Gaussian distributions and also on mixtures of multivariate Gaussian-Beta distributions were used for classification purpose.

Another study by Parui et al[60] has dealt with detection and recognition of the 3 vowel modifiers appearing only in the middle zone and parts of the other 4 vowel modifiers that reside in the middle zone. Features based on shape, size and position were used and recognition was made using Bayes classifier on the basis of mixtures of multivariate Gaussian and Dirichlet distributions.

In both of the above studies, features were extracted from the skeleton of a character image. The recognition rates were not very satisfactory. Moreover, there are problems in recognizing the original basic/compound character after removing the identified vowel modifier part from the input image. This is because in many cases, after removal of the vowel modifier from the input image, either a part of the original basic/compound character image gets removed along with the vowel modifier or a part of the vowel modifier does not get removed but remains attached to the original basic/compound character image, making recognition of the original basic/compound character more difficult.

No work has been reported in the literature on detection and recognition of the 3 consonant modifiers and parts of the 4 vowel modifiers that appear in the upper zone. The problem becomes more complex when a part of a vowel modifier and a consonant modifier simultaneously appear in the upper zone. The situation becomes even more complex when this phenomenon occurs with a basic/compound character that itself has a part in the upper zone.

Let us consider the eight modifiers occurring in the middle zone, partly or completely, in Fig. 12.3. From this figure, it can be seen that parts of these modifiers that appear in the middle zone have only three distinct patterns, namely, ۱, ſ and ʃ. The first of these three patterns can appear both on the left and on the right sides of a basic/consonant character while the second occurs only on the left and the third occurs only on the right.

The shapes of the above three patterns occurring in the middle zone vary widely in the handwritten form. Skeletal shapes of several handwritten samples consisting of major varieties are shown in Fig. 12.19. The skeletal representation of the first pattern may have an end pixel in the lower half (Figs. 12.19(a), (c), (e), (k), (l), (m) and (n)) or it may contain a loop that is vertically elongated (Figs. 12.19 (b), (d), (f), (o), (p), (q) and (r)). The skeleton of the second pattern also may have an end pixel in the lower half (Figs. 12.19 (i), (j), (k), (l), (o) and (p)) or it may have a loop that is not vertically elongated (Figs. 12.19. (g), (h), (m), (n), (q), (r)). However, the shape of the third pattern does not vary so much.

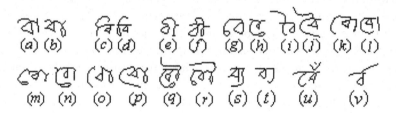

Fig. 12.19. Variations in handwritten forms of 8 modifiers of Bangla whole or part of which occur in the middle zone.

12.5.4. *Word Recognition*

There are two major classes of approaches to recognize a handwritten word: analytical approach[31,51] and holistic approach.[46] In the analytical approach, a word image is first segmented into a series of sub-images and the input word image is then recognized after recognition of individual sub-images. These sub-images are normally either individual characters or parts of a character. A common problem encountered in this process is that of under and over segmentation. The holistic approach, on the other hand, considers the word image as a single, indivisible entity, and recognizes the word from its overall shape. Both the approaches have some advantages and disadvantages. The error found in the segmentation based analytical approach originates from both the segmentation technique and the recognition procedure. The errors of these two procedures are propagated in the final recognition and the recognition performance degrades. But the advantage of the segmentation based recognition approach is that it can cope with a large lexicon size of handwritten words.[32] On the other hand, for a smaller lexicon size, the holistic approach produces a better recognition accuracy. Usually in the holistic approach, the hidden markov model (HMM) is used as the recognition engine. Here, one HMM is constructed for each distinct word in the lexicon. Because of this, it is not efficiently applicable to large lexicons of words. If we look into the real-life problem, say, reading amounts on bank checks,[52] we see that the lexicon size is rather small. Even if the lexicon size appears large for some practical problem, we cope it by reducing the lexicon size or reorganizing the search space, or using heuristics to limit the search efforts.[22]

Studies on recognition of handwritten words in Bangla are few. In a recent work,[22] both analytical and holistic approaches have been proposed for recognizing handwritten Bangla words using a lexicon set of 119 town names. These town names cover all but eight rare basic characters and all 10 vowel modifiers except a rare vowel modifier 'ri'. In the analytical approach, a robust segmentation technique has been proposed that segments a word image into several characters/sub-characters in such a way that the possibility of under segmentation is minimized. There are certain Bangla characters which may remain unsegmented or may get segmented into two sub-characters, depending on the handwriting style. Thus, such a character will generate three different entities. A few examples of these characters/sub-characters they could generate are shown in Fig. 12.20. These entities obtained after segmentation are called *pseudo-characters*.

On the basis of the lexicon set, it has been observed that the segmentation algorithm generates 76 pseudo-characters. Using the database of the handwritten word samples, a database of pseudo-character samples for each pseudo-characters class is generated. For recognition of individual pseudo-characters a support vector machine (SVM) based hierarchical classifier has been built with this database.

Fig. 12.20. After segmentation a handwritten sample of the character in column 1 may remain unaffected (column 2) or may be segmented into two sub-characters (columns 3 and 4).

For final word recognition, the concept of an *atomic pattern* is defined as follows. If a pseudo-character is not segmented further in any sample, it is called an atomic pattern. For example, in Fig. 12.20, in the first four rows, the first pseudo-characters (in column 2) are not atomic patterns, but the last two (in columns 3,4) are. In the last row, there is only one pseudo-character which is not segmentable and hence is an atomic pattern. Now, each word in the lexicon set is transformed into a sequence of such atomic patterns and the new lexicon set is used for word recognition. For an unknown handwritten Bangla word, after segmentation, each pseudo-character is recognized and the resultant string of pseudo-characters is converted into a string of atomic patterns. For the final word recognition, this string of atomic patterns is matched against the new lexicon set based on the edit distance.

A weakness of this approach is that due to the small size of the lexicon set, the set of pseudo-characters and the set of atomic patterns reported above do not truly reflect the Bangla script in general. It is believed that both these sets will be a little larger if a sufficiently large lexicon set is used.

12.6. Online Handwriting Recognition

Reports on online Bangla handwriting recognition available in the literature are relatively rare compared to its offline counterpart. In an early study,[30] Garain and Chaudhuri developed a recognition algorithm based on the human motor functionality while writing characters and simulated the same on a database of 2840 alphanumeric Bangla characters. However, since this database is not available to the academic community, a benchmark database[41] was developed later and recognition studies based on this database have been reported.

12.6.1. *Numerals*

Parui et al[56] proposed a hidden Markov model (HMM) based scheme for recognition of online handwritten Bangla numerals. One HMM is constructed for each numeral class. A numeral sample is decomposed into several sub-strokes based on the changes in directions along the pen trajectory. For each sub-stroke, 6 feature values are computed representing its shape and size. Thus, a numeral sample is represented by a string of these feature vectors corresponding to its sequence of sub-strokes. This representation of a handwritten numeral is used by the HMM. Here, the states of the HMM are automatically determined based on the training database, using EM (Expectation Maximization) algorithm in the feature space. A database[41] of 4000 training samples and 2000 test samples were developed for this work. This recognition scheme provided 98.05% classification accuracy on the test set.

12.6.2. *Basic characters*

Recently, Tanmay et al[49] presented a moderately large database[41] consisting of 25,948 samples of online handwritten Bangla basic characters. The purpose of generation of this database is to encourage systematic research on Bangla handwriting recognition. The report also described a scheme for extraction of sub-strokes of simpler shapes from the online samples of handwritten Bangla characters.

Parui et al[61] described an HMM-based two-stage recognition scheme for online handwritten basic characters of Bangla. In the first stage, collection of all the strokes obtained from the training samples are manually grouped into 54 classes based on the shape similarity of the graphemes that constitute the ideal character shapes. HMM is employed to classify these strokes. One HMM is constructed for each stroke class. In the second stage, 50 lookup-tables corresponding to 50 character classes are used for recognition of characters using stroke classification results.

12.6.3. *Cursive words*

Recently, the Department of Information Technology (DIT), Govt. of India provided funding to the Indian Statistical Institute for the development of Bangla online handwriting recognizer. With the help of this funding, a large database of handwritten cursive Bangla words has been developed. This database consists of little more than one hundred thousand word samples written by 77 writers. The lexicon of this database consists of 681 words. Selection of the lexicon was primarily based on a large corpus. This database will be made available by the TDIL (Technology Development in Indian Languages) group of the DIT, Govt. of India for academic research purposes.

On the other hand, to the best of our knowledge, till date no significant work on recognition of cursive Bangla handwriting has been reported. In the only available work, Bhattacharya et al[19] presented a scheme for segmentation of online handwritten Bangla cursive words into psuedo-characters. This segmentation approach consists of estimation of the headline in a handwritten Bangla word sample. Here, it is important to note that obtaining the position of this headline from a handwritten Bangla word sample is a tricky job. The algorithm for the same described in the report by Bhattacharya et al[19] involves computation of the frequency distribution of the y-values of all points that lie in the upper 75% portion of the word. Suppose that M is the modal value of this frequency distribution. The estimated headline is $y = Y$, where $Y = \min\{y|\text{frequency}(y) > 0.5M\}$.

A stroke is segmented into sub-strokes of smaller lengths at the middle point(s) of two successive crossings between the stroke and the headline. A few such segmentation points are shown in Fig. 12.21 on the basis of two sample words.

12.7. Future Directions

12.7.1. *A Potential Application*

In view of the work done so far for Bangla handwriting recognition, we feel automatic processing of tabular form documents in Bangla script, is now possible. However, in order to achieve this, it is necessary to rationalize several aspects of handwriting style of Bangla script. For this, the following aspects of Bangla basic (vowel/consonant) characters may be noted.

(i) Four basic vowels (ই, ঈ, উ, ঊ) and one basic consonant (ট, ঢ) have a portion that occurs in the upper zone and has the same shape and size.
(ii) One basic consonant (ট, ঢ) has a portion that occurs in the upper zone and has shape and size different from the portion mentioned above.

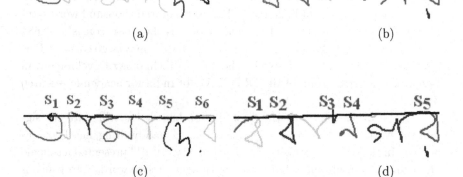

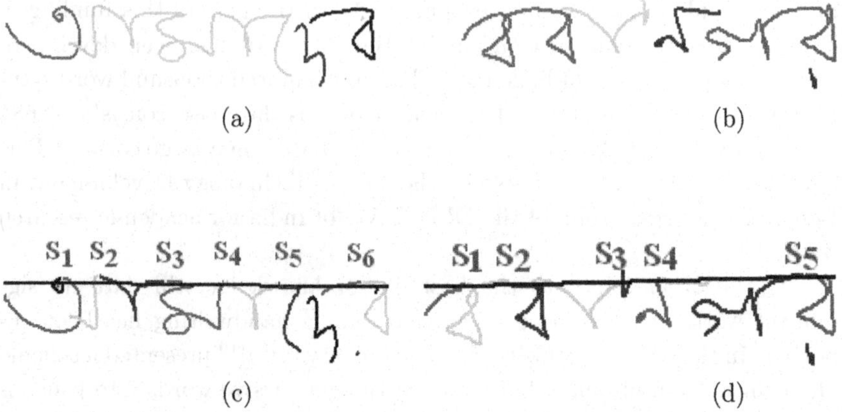

(a)   (b)

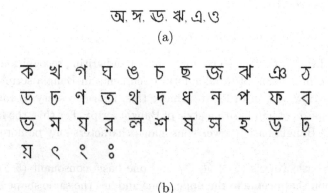

(c)   (d)

Fig. 12.21. (a) & (b) Two word samples of online cursive Bangla handwriting; (c) & (d) estimated headlines and five segmentation points of the two samples in (a) & (b) are shown by the points $S_1, S_2, \ldots, S_5, S_6$.

(iii) Two basic vowels (অ, ও) have a portion that occurs in both the middle and upper zones and has the same shape and size.

Let us term the three possible patterns occurring above the middle zone as *pseudo-modifiers*. If these pseudo-modifiers are segmented, the total number of distinct basic vowel shapes reduces from 11 to 6 and the total number of distinct basic consonant shapes reduces from 39 to 37. This reduced set of basic characters is shown in Fig. 12.22.

অ. �. ড. ঋ, এ.ও

(a)

ক খ গ ঘ ঙ চ ছ জ ঝ ঞ ঠ
ড ঢ ণ ত থ দ ধ ন প ফ ব
ভ ম য র ল শ ষ স হ ড় ঢ়
য় ৎ ং ঃ

(b)

Fig. 12.22.   (a) 6 Basic vowel shapes; (b) 37 Basic consonant shapes.

For efficient segmentation of the portion in the upper part of Bangla text (as described above), we propose the design of a tabular form where each box has a smaller box within it located centrally (Fig. 12.23). The inner box should make room for one of the 6 basic vowel shapes or 37 basic consonant shapes (Fig. 12.22) or a compound character. The upper part of the outer box should be used for parts of 4 vowel modifiers (ি, ী, ে, ো in Fig. 12.3), one consonant modifier, the nasalizer (ঁ, ঁ in Fig. 12.3) and the three pseudo-modifiers discussed above. As far as the lower part of the outer box is concerned, only 3 vowel modifiers (ু, ূ, ৃ in Fig. 12.3) will be written in it. The left part of the outer box will contain (partly or completely) 5 vowel modifiers (ি, ে, ৈ, ো, ৌ in Fig. 12.3) leading to only 2 distinct shapes, namely, ⎸ and ⌈. The right part of the outer box will contain (partly or completely) 4 vowel modifiers (া, ী, ো, ৌ in Fig. 12.3) leading to only one distinct shape, namely, ⎹, one consonant modifier (ঁ in Fig. 12.3) and part of the third pseudo-modifier. All these will have 3 distinct shapes. In addition, only one combination of these 3 may also occur in the right part.

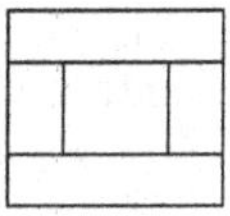

Fig. 12.23. Design of a form for writing a Bangla *akshara* to make segmentation and classification of modifiers easier.

An example of form filling in Bangla is shown in Fig. 12.24. The common style of form filling in Bangla or any other script has been shown in the left-hand side of this figure while the style as discussed above is shown in the right-hand side of the same figure. In this proposed style, extraction of vowel or consonant modifiers will be easier and more robust.

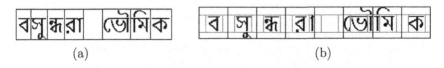

(a)   (b)

Fig. 12.24. (a) Existing and (b) proposed styles of form filling in Bangla.

12.8. Conclusion

In the present chapter, we have discussed the progress that has been made so far in recognition of Bangla handwriting. The work done in this context has been is sporadic which was primarily due to the lack of proper databases of handwritten samples. However, some large databases of handwritten numerals/basic characters/words have recently been created. It is expected that concerted attempts will be made for recognition of Bangla handwriting. In fact, the Govt. of India has through its TDIL project started promoting research in the area of handwriting recognition of Indian scripts. Potential application areas include census data collection, railway reservation process, postal automation etc.

References

1. Y. Al-Ohali, M. Cheriet, and C. Suen, "Databases for recognition of handwritten Arabic cheques," *Pattern Recognition*, vol. 36, pp. 111–121, 2003.
2. A. Amin and H. B. Al-Sadoun, "Hand printed Arabic character recognition system," *Proc. of the 12th. Int. Conf. on Pattern Recognition*, pp. 536–539, 1994.
3. K. H. Aparna, V. Subramanian, M. Kasirajan, G. V. Prakash, V. S. Chakravarthy, and S. Madhvanath, "Online handwriting recognition for Tamil", *Proc. of the 9th Int. Workshop on Frontiers in Handwriting Recognition*, pp. 438–443, 2004.
4. N. Arica and F. Yarman-Vural, "An overview of character recognition focused on off-line handwriting," *IEEE Trans. on Systems, Man, and Cybernetics, Part C: Applications and Reviews*, vol. 31, pp. 216–233, 2001.
5. V. J. Babu, L. Prashanth, R. R. Sharma, G. V. P. Rao, A. Bharath, HMM-based online handwriting recognition system for Telugu symbols, *Proc. of 9th Int. Conf. on Document Analysis and Recognition* (ICDAR 2007), Brazil, pp. 63-67, 2007.
6. S. Basu, R. Sarkar, N. Das, M. Kundu, M. Nasipuri and D. K. Basu, "Handwritten Bangla digit recognition using classifier combination through DS technique," *Proc. Int. Conf. On Pattern Recognition and Machine Intelligence (PReMI'05), LNCS 3776, Springer-Verlag*, pp. 236-241, 2005.
7. S. Basu, N. Das, R. Sarkar, M. Kundu, M. Nasipuri and D. K. Basu, "A hierarchical approach to recognition of handwritten *Bangla* characters,", *Pattern Recognition*, vol.42, pp.1467-1484, 2009.
8. A. Benouareth, A. Ennaji, M. Sellami, "Semi-continuous HMMs with explicit state duration for unconstrained Arabic word modeling and recognition", *Pattern Recognition Letters*, vol. 29, pp. 1742-1752, 2008.
9. U. Bhattacharya, T. K. Das, and B. B. Chaudhuri, "A cascaded scheme for recognition of handprinted numerals," *Proc. of the 3rd Indian Conf. on Comp. Vis., Graph. and Image Proc.*, pp. 137–142, 2002.
10. U. Bhattacharya, T. K. Das, A. Datta, S. K. Parui, and B. B. Chaudhuri, "A hybrid scheme for handprinted numeral recognition based on a self-

organizing network and MLP classifiers," *Int. Journ. Patt. Recog. and Arti. Intell.*, vol. 16(7), pp. 845–864, 2002.

11. U. Bhattacharya and B. B. Chaudhuri, "A majority voting scheme for multiresolution recognition of handprinted numerals", *Proc. of the 7th Int. Conf. on Document Analysis and Recognition (ICDAR)*, pp. 16-20, 2003.

12. U. Bhattacharya and B. B. Chaudhuri, "Databases for research on recognition of handwritten characters of Indian scripts," *Proc. of the 8th Int. Conf. on Document Analysis and Recognition*, vol. II, pp. 789–793, 2005.

13. U. Bhattacharya and B. B. Chaudhuri, "Fusion of combination rules of MLP classifiers for improved recognition accuracy of handprinted Bangla numerals", *Proc. of the 8th Int. Conf. on Doc. Anal. and Recog. (ICDAR)*, pp. 322-326, 2005.

14. U. Bhattacharya, S. K. Parui, M. Sridhar and F. Kimura, "Two-stage recognition of handwritten Bangla alphanumeric characters using neural classifiers", *Proc. of IICAI-05*, Pune, India, pp.1357-1376, 2005.

15. U. Bhattacharya, S. K. Parui, B. Shaw, and K. Bhattacharya, "Neural combination of ANN and HMM for handwritten Devanagari numeral recognition," *Proc. of the Int'l Workshop Frontiers in Handwriting Recognition*, pp. 613-618, 2006.

16. U. Bhattacharya, M. Shridhar and S. K. Parui, "On recognition of handwritten Bangla characters", *Proc. Indian Conf. on Computer Vision, Graphics and Image Processing*, LNCS 4338(eds.) P. Kalra and S. Peleg, Springer-Verlag, pp. 817-828, 2006.

17. U. Bhattacharya, B. K. Gupta and S. K. Parui, "Direction code based features for recognition of online handwritten characters of Bangla", *Proc. of the 9th Int. Conf Doc. Anal. Recog. (ICDAR)*, vol. 1, pp. 58-62, 2007.

18. U. Bhattacharya, S. K. Parui, and B. Shaw, "A hybrid scheme fo recognition of handwritten Bangla basic characters based on HMM and MLP classifiers", *Proc. 6th Int. Conf. on Advances in Pattern Recognition, (ICAPR) 2007*, (ed.) P. Pal, World Scientific, pp. 101-106, 2007.

19. U. Bhattacharya, A. Nigam, Y. S. Rawat and S. K. Parui, "An analytic scheme for online handwritten Bangla cursive word recognition", *Proc. of the 11th Int'l Conf. on Frontiers in Handwriting Recognition*, pp. 320-325, 2008.

20. U. Bhattacharya and B. B. Chaudhuri. "Handwritten numeral databases of Indian scripts and multistage recognition of mixed numerals", *IEEE Trans. Pattern Analysis and Machine Intelligence*, vol. 31(3), pp. 444–457, 2009.

21. T. K. Bhowmik, U. Bhattacharya and S. K. Parui, "Recognition of Bangla Handwritten Characters Using an MLP Classifier Based on Stroke Features", *Int. Conf. on Neural Information Processing (ICONIP)*, LNCS 3316, (Eds. N. R. Pal et al.), pp. 814-819, 2004.

22. T. K. Bhowmik, "An Efficient Scheme for Recognition of Handwritten Bangla Words", Ph. D. Thesis, Visva-Bharati, West Bengal, India, 2008.

23. T. K. Bhowmik, P. Ghanty, A. Roy and S. K. Parui, "SVM-based hierarchical architectures for handwritten Bangla character recognition", *Int. Journ. of Document Analysis and Recognition*, vol. 12, pp. 87-108, 2009.

24. F. Camastra, "A SVM-based cursive character recognizer", *Pattern Recognition*, vol. 40, pp. 3721-3727, 2007.
25. M. Cheriet, N. Kharma, C. -L. Liu, C. Y. Suen, *Character Recognition Systems: A Guide for Students and Practitioners*, Wiley, NewYork, 2007.
26. S. D. Connell, R. M. K. Sinha and A. K. Jain, "Recognition of unconstrained on-line Devanagari characters", *Proc. of the 15th Int. Conf. on Pattern Recognition (ICPR)*, Bercelona, Spain, 2000.
27. A. Datta, S. K. Parui and B. B. Chaudhuri, "Skeletonization by a topology adaptive self-organizing neural network," *Pattern Recognition*, vol. 34, pp. 617-629, 2001.
28. I. Daubechies, *Ten Lectures in Wavelets*, Society for Industrial and Applied Math., Philadelphia, 1992.
29. A. K. Dutta and S. Chaudhury, "Bengali alpha-numeric character recognition using curvature features" *Pattern Recognition*, vol. 26, pp.1757-1770, 1993.
30. U. Garain, B. B. Chaudhuri, T. Pal. "Online handwritten Indian script recognition: a human motor function based framework", *Proc. of the 16th Int. Conf. on Pattern Recognition*, pp. 164-167, 2002.
31. V. Govindaraju, G. Kim, "A lexicon driven approach to handwritten word recognition for real-time applications", *IEEE Trans. Pattern Analysis and Machine Intelligence*, vol. 19(4), pp. 366-379, 1997.
32. L. Huette, A. Nosary, T. Paquet, "A muliple agent architecture for handwritten text recognition," *Pattern Recognition*, vol. 37(4), pp. 665-674, 2004.
33. S. Jaeger, C. L. Liu, and M. Nakagawa, "The state of art in Japanese online handwriting recognition compared to techniques in Western handwriting recognition", *Int. Journ. on Document Analysis and Recognition*, vol. 6, pp. 75–88, 2003.
34. N. Joshi, G. Sita, A. G. Ramakrishnan, and M. Sriganesh, "Comparison of elastic matching algorithms for online Tamil handwritten character recognition", *Proc. of 9th Intl. Workshop on Frontiers in Handwriting Recognition (IWFHR)*, Tokyo, pp. 444–449, 2004.
35. N. Joshi, G. Sita, A. G. Ramakrishnan, V. Deepu, and S. Madhvanath, "Machine recognition of online handwritten Devanagari characters," *Proc. of 7th Int. Conf. on Document Analysis and Recognition (ICDAR 2005)*, 2005.
36. H. J. Kim, K. H. Kim, S. K. Kim, and F. T. -P. Lee, "On- Line Recognition of Handwritten Chinese Characters Based on Hidden Markov Models," *Pattern Recognition*, Vol. 30(9), pp. 1489–1499, 1997.
37. S. H. Kim, S. Jeong, G. S. Lee and C. Y. Suen, "Gap metrics for handwritten Korean word segmentation", *Electronics Letters*, vol. 37, pp. 892–893, 2001.
38. F. Kimura, K. Takashina, S. Tsuruoka, and Y. Miyake, "Modified quadratic discriminant functions and the application to Chinese character recognition," *IEEE Trans. Pattern Anal. Mach. Intell.*, vol. 9(1), pp. 149-153, 1987.
39. A. Kitadai, M. Nakagawa, "Prototype learning for structured pattern representation applied to on-line recognition of handwritten Japanese char-

acters", *Int. Journ. of Document Analysis and Recognition*, vol. 10, pp. 101-112, 2007.

40. S. W. Lee and J. S. Park, "Nonlinear shape normalization methods for the recognition of large-set handwritten characters," *Pattern Recognition*, vol. 27, pp. 895–902, 1994.

41. http://lipitk.sourceforge.net/resources.htm

42. R. P. Lippmann, "An introduction to computing with neural nets," *IEEE ASSP Mag.*, vol. 4, pp. 4-22, 1987.

43. C.-L. Liu, K. Nakashima, H. Sako, and H. Fujisawa, "Handwritten digit recognition: benchmarking of state-of-the-art techniques," *Pattern Recognition*, vol. 36, pp. 2271-2285, 2003.

44. C.-L. Liu, S. Jaeger, and M. Nakagawa, "Online Recognition of Chinese Characters: The State-of-the-Art," *IEEE Trans. on Pattern Analysis and Machine Intelligence*, pp. 198-213, vol. 26(2), 2004.

45. C.-L. Liu and C. Y. Suen, "A new benchmark on the recognition of handwritten Bangla and Farsi numeral characters", *Pattern Recognition*, vol. 42, pp. 3287-3295, 2009.

46. S. Madhvanath, V. Govindaraju, "The role of holistic paradigms in handwritten word recognition", *IEEE Trans. Pattern Analysis and Machine Intelligence*, vol. 23(2), pp. 149-164, 2001.

47. S. G. Mallat, "A theory for multiresolution signal decomposition : The wavelet representation," *IEEE Trans. on Patt. Anal. and Mach. Int.*, vol. 11(7), pp. 674-693, 1989.

48. U.-V. Marti, H. Bunke, "The IAM-database: an English sentence database for offline handwriting recognition", *Int. Journ. on Document Analysis and Recognition*, vol. 5, pp. 39-46, 2002.

49. T. Mondal, U. Bhattacharya, S. K. Parui, K. Das and V. Roy, "Database generation and recognition of online handwritten Bangla characters", *Proc. of the Int. Workshop on Multilingual OCR (MOCR)*, Article No. 9, ACM Int. Conf. Proceeding Series, Barcelona, Spain, 2009.

50. S. Mozaffari, K. Faez, V. Märgner, H. El-Abed, "Lexicon reduction using dots for off-line Farsi/Arabic handwritten word recognition", *Pattern Recognition Letters*, vol. 29, pp. 724-734, 2008.

51. C. Olivier, T. Paquet, M. Avila, Y. Lecourtier "Recognition of handwritten word using stochastic models," *Proc. Int. Conf. Document Analysis and Recognition*, vol. I, pp. 19-23, 1995.

52. C. Olivier, T. Paquet, M. Avila, Y. Lecourtier, "Optimal order of Markov models applied to bank cheks," *Int. Journ. Patt. Recog. and Arti. Intell.*, vol. 11, pp. 789-800, 1997.

53. U. Pal, and B. B. Chaudhuri, "Indian script character recognition: a survey", *Pattern Recognition*, vol. 37, 1887-1899, 2004.

54. U. Pal, T. Wakabayashi, N. Sharma and F. Kimura, "Handwritten numeral recognition of six popular Indian scripts", *Proc. of the 8th Intl. Conf. on Document Analysis and Recognition*, pp. 789-793, 2007.

55. S. K. Parui, B. B. Chaudhuri, D. Dutta Majumder, "A procedure for recognition of connected hand written numerals", *Int. J. Systems Sci.*, vol. 13, pp. 1019–1029, 1982.

56. S. K. Parui, U. Bhattacharya, B. Shaw, K. Guin, "A hidden Markov model for recognition of online handwritten Bangla numerals", *Proc. of the 41st National Annual Convention of CSI*, pp. 27-31, 2006, Tata McGraw Hill Pub. Comp. Ltd.

57. S. K. Parui, U. Bhattacharya, B. Shaw, D. Poddar, "A novel Hidden Markov Model for recognition of handwritten Bangla characters", *Proc. of the 3rd Workshop on Computer Vision, Graphics and Image Processing (WCVGIP)*, pp. 174-179, 2006.

58. S. K. Parui, U. Bhattacharya, A. K. Datta, B. Shaw, "A database of handwritten Bangla vowel modifiers and a scheme for their detection and recognition", *Proc. of the 3rd Workshop on Computer Vision, Graphics and Image Processing (WCVGIP)*, pp. 204-209, 2006.

59. S. K. Parui and B. Shaw, "Offine Handwritten Devanagari Word Recognition: An HMM Based Approach", *Proc. Int. Conf. Pattern Recognition and Machine Intelligence*, LNCS4815 (eds.) A. Ghosh, R. K. De and S. K. Pal, Springer-Verlag, pp. 528-535, 2007.

60. S. K. Parui, U. Bhattacharya and S. K. Ghosh, "Recognition of handwritten Bangla vowel modifiers", *Proc. 6th Int. Conf. on Advances in Pattern Recognition, ICAPR 2007*, (ed.) P. Pal, World Scientific, pp. 129-134, 2007.

61. S. K. Parui, K. Guin, U. Bhattacharya, and B. B. Chaudhuri, "Online handwritten Bangla character recognition using HMM", *Proc. of 19th Int. Conf. on Pattern Recognition*, 2008.

62. R. Plamondon and S. N. Srihari, "On-line and off-line handwriting recognition: A comprehensive survey," *IEEE Trans. Patt. Anal. and Mach. Intell.*, vol. 22, pp. 63-84, 2000.

63. A. F. R. Rahman, R. Rahman and M. C. Fairhurst, "Recognition of handwritten Bengali characters : a novel multistage approach", *Pattern Recognition*, vol. 35, pp. 997-1006, 2002.

64. A. W. Senior and T. Robinson, "An off-line cursive handwriting recognition system," *IEEE Trans. on Patt. Anal. and Mach. Intell.*, vol. 20, pp. 309-321, 1998.

65. I. K. Sethi and B. Chatterjee, "Machine recognition of constrained handprinted Devanagari," *Pattern Recognition*, vol. 9, pp. 69-75, 1977.

66. T. Su, T. Zhang, and D. Guan, "Corpus-based HIT-MW database for offline recognition of general-purpose Chinese handwritten text," *Int. Journal of Document Analysis and Recognition*, vol. 10, pp. 27-38, 2007.

67. C. S. Sundaresan and S. S. Keerthi, "A study of representations for pen based handwriting recognition of Tamil characters", *5th Int. Conf. on Doc. Anal. Recog. (ICDAR)*, pp. 422-425, 1999.

68. H. Swethalakshmi, A. Jayaraman, V. S. Chakravarthy and C. C. Sekhar, "Online handwritten character recognition of Devanagari and Telugu Characters using support vector machines", *Proc. of the 10th Int. Workshop on Frontiers in Handwriting Recognition*, October 2006.

69. H. Swethalakshmi, C. C. Sekhar, and V. S. Chakravarthy, "Spatiostructural features for recognition of online handwritten characters in Devanagari and

Tamil scripts", *Proc. of Int. Conf. on Artificial Neural Networks (ICANN)*, vol. 2, pp. 230-239, 2007.

70. A. Vinciarelli, S. Bengio, "Writer adaptation techniques in HMM based off-line cursive script recognition", *Pattern Recognition Letters*, vol. 23, pp. 905-916, 2002.

71. Y. Wen, Y. Lu and P. Shi, "Handwritten Bangla numeral recognition system and its application to postal automation", *Pattern Recognition*, vol. 40, pp. 99-107, 2007.

72. D. You, G. Kim, "An efficient approach for slant correction of handwritten Korean strings based on structural properties", *Pattern Recognition Letters*, vol. 24(12), pp. 2093-2101, 2003.

Author Index